Transcending Fictionalism

Also available from Bloomsbury:

Classical Theism and Buddhism, by Tyler Dalton McNabb and Erik Baldwin
God's Action in the World, by Marek Slomka
Four Views on the Axiology of Theism, edited by Kirk Lougheed
Philosophical Hermeneutics and the Priority of Questions in Religions, by Nathan Eric Dickman
Philosophical Perspectives on Existential Gratitude, edited by Joshua Lee Harris, Kirk Lougheed and Neal DeRoo

Transcending Fictionalism

God, Minimalism and Realism

Jessica Eastwood

BLOOMSBURY ACADEMIC
LONDON • NEW YORK • OXFORD • NEW DELHI • SYDNEY

BLOOMSBURY ACADEMIC
Bloomsbury Publishing Plc, 50 Bedford Square, London, WC1B 3DP, UK
Bloomsbury Publishing Inc, 1359 Broadway, 12th Floor, New York, NY 10018, USA
Bloomsbury Publishing Ireland, 29 Earlsfort Terrace, Dublin 2, D02 AY28, Ireland

BLOOMSBURY, BLOOMSBURY ACADEMIC and the Diana logo are
trademarks of Bloomsbury Publishing Plc

First published in Great Britain 2024
This paperback edition published 2026

Copyright © Jessica Eastwood, 2024

Jessica Eastwood has asserted her right under the Copyright,
Designs and Patents Act, 1988, to be identified as Author of this work.

For legal purposes the Acknowledgements on p. vii constitute
an extension of this copyright page.

Cover image: Pobytov/Getty Images

All rights reserved. No part of this publication may be: i) reproduced or transmitted in any form, electronic or mechanical, including photocopying, recording or by means of any information storage or retrieval system without prior permission in writing from the publishers; or ii) used or reproduced in any way for the training, development or operation of artificial intelligence (AI) technologies, including generative AI technologies. The rights holders expressly reserve this publication from the text and data mining exception as per Article 4(3) of the Digital Single Market Directive (EU) 2019/790.

Bloomsbury Publishing Inc does not have any control over, or responsibility for, any third-party websites referred to or in this book. All internet addresses given in this book were correct at the time of going to press. The author and publisher regret any inconvenience caused if addresses have changed or sites have ceased to exist, but can accept no responsibility for any such changes.

A catalogue record for this book is available from the British Library.

Library of Congress Cataloging-in-Publication Data
Names: Eastwood, Jessica (Jessica Grace), author.
Title: Transcending fictionalism : God, minimalism and realism / Jessica Eastwood.
Description: 1. | London : Bloomsbury Academic, 2024. | Revision of the author's thesis (Ph.D.)–University of Durham, United Kingdom, 2021. |
Includes bibliographical references and index. | Summary: "Exploring alternative conceptions of the divine, Jessica Eastwood considers the ways of believing in God that are authentic and sincere, moving beyond traditional metaphysical structures that many find difficult to accept. She examines a unique branch of religious anti-realism known as religious fictionalism, making the case for its ability to resonate on an intellectual and emotional level. Considering the extent to which fictionalism allows us to make sense of the role of religion in our spiritual lives, she also presents its limitations on adhering to what might be an attractive contemporary model for philosophy of religion called 'the humane turn'"– Provided by publisher.
Identifiers: LCCN 2023048283 (print) | LCCN 2023048284 (ebook) | ISBN 9781350327627 (hardback) | ISBN 9781350327665 (paperback) | ISBN 9781350327641 (epub) | ISBN 9781350327634 (ebook)
Subjects: LCSH: God. | Religion–Philosophy. | Realism. | Fictions, Theory of.
Classification: LCC BL473 .E33 2024 (print) | LCC BL473 (ebook) | DDC 211–dc23/eng/20240524
LC record available at https://lccn.loc.gov/2023048283
LC ebook record available at https://lccn.loc.gov/2023048284

ISBN: HB: 978-1-3503-2762-7
PB: 978-1-3503-2766-5
ePDF: 978-1-3503-2763-4
eBook: 978-1-3503-2764-1

Typeset by Deanta Global Publishing Services, Chennai, India

For product safety related questions contact productsafety@bloomsbury.com.

To find out more about our authors and books visit www.bloomsbury.com
and sign up for our newsletters.

Contents

List of Illustrations	vi
Acknowledgements	vii
Introduction: Religious seriousness and the realism/non-realism debate	1
1 What does it mean to have belief? Conceptions of belief and faith	25
2 Standard non-realism and the nature of 'God' à la Don Cupitt	59
3 Can faith without belief be meaningful?	77
4 Are our emotions toward fiction real?	107
5 Fictionalism and 'the humane turn'	141
6 God and numbers: A minimal realism	165
Conclusion: Post-traditional realism and a distinctive 'minimalist' conception of God	201
Notes	205
Bibliography	238
Index	250

Illustrations

Figures

1	Axis one: A spectrum of conceptions of God	3
2	Axis two: A spectrum of commitments to God	10
3	Axis one and two combined	16
4	Axis one and two combined and Cupitt's position emphasized	75
5	Axis one and two combined	78
6	Axis two: A spectrum of commitments to God	97

Table

1	Characteristics Typically Assigned to the Right Hemisphere and Left Hemisphere	151

Acknowledgements

I would like to, first, thank my family: my mother and father, my brother and my grandfather – without their support, I would not have been able to pursue a career in academia. To them I am forever grateful. To Chris Deacy, the first lecturer to truly inspire me, who helped me to channel and pursue my passion for the philosophical study of religion – a pursuit that led me to Don Cupitt. I want to thank you, Don, for responding to my letter in 2017 which initially sparked intelligent conversation and has led to friendship. Without your off-the-beaten-track philosophy I would not have been able to confidently explore different textures of divine reality. To Robin Le Poidevin, who also inspires me with his investigation into alternative ways in which to meaningfully live out a religious life. I want to thank you for your continued support and willingness to hear me tease out my own ideas. And, last but by no means least, to Chris Insole: my supervisor and mentor. From our very first conversation I immediately felt confident in the knowledge that you understood what it is I was looking to do; you would go on to strike the perfect balance between allowing me time and space to grow my thoughts and giving me guidance and insight. I want to thank you for always believing in me, in my thesis and in my ability to teach as a TA throughout my research years and now as a lecturer. I am grateful to you for giving me the opportunity to enquire into that which weighs on my heart, and perhaps many other people's hearts too.

Introduction

Religious seriousness and the realism/non-realism debate

There are two questions that I want to address in this book, the first is: 'Can you have a "genuine" religious position if it is not rooted in classical philosophical theism (CPT)?' My answer will be, yes. The second question is: 'If it is possible, can it only be a non-realist position?' My answer to this question will be, no. What constitutes a 'genuine' religious position is contested, as both realists and non-realists have accused each other of a lack of 'religious seriousness'. But in both cases the targets have been a rather extreme form of each position: on the one hand, a realism which commits to a detailed theism as an explanation of the universe (and so is quasi-scientific), and on the other a non-realism which seeks to reduce theological/religious language to something else. One way that non-realism frames the debate is to put forward the following impasse: 'theological realism or religious seriousness?'[1] This way of framing the debate will be used; however, the argument of this book is that there is a more moderate position between these extremes, which avoids some of the criticism from each side, and is an appropriately serious religious response to the world. It is a subtle and enigmatic position reflective of Friedrich Hölderlin's exquisite dictum: 'Was ist Gott? unbekannt, dennoch ...' ('What is God? Unknown, and yet ...').[2]

Moreover, this book will suggest that if we can widen the parameters of what might be considered 'religious realism' and re-evaluate what it means to be 'religiously serious', then we can avoid this impasse. In regard to the former, I posit that there exists a latent texture of reality in the realism/non-realism debate, and that the theological realism/religious seriousness impasse reveals this 'gap'. This 'gap' is not simply a certain possible state of mind, but rather a genuinely coherent (and hitherto unacknowledged) position in conceptual space. Thus, I will argue for a reality that is both non-traditionally realist by nature and serious by disposition. In terms of the latter, it will be suggested that because we seem to be working only with the God of CPT and questioning whether *this* God exists 'out there' (realism) or not (non-realism), the 'seriousness' of any religious position rests on this particular perfect being conception of God.

The purpose of the book, then, is twofold. The primary purpose is to defend the possibility of a distinct minimalist account of realism which exists somewhere 'between' 'traditional realism' which is ascribed to the God of CPT and 'standard non-realism' based on a Cupittian style of non-realism which claims that religious discourse cannot be cashed out in terms of an ontological commitment to a supernatural being. The secondary purpose is to ascribe this sui generis reality to a theologically rooted but a non-CPT conception of God. What is meant by this sui generis space is a conceptual texture known about in other branches of philosophy, which has not been explicitly applied in philosophy of religion, although some minimalist theologians might recognize the space.

Furthermore, this book hopes to broaden the horizon by challenging the scope of the current realist/non-realist distinction and offer one way to avoid the impasse as it is presented by the non-realist. The best way to map this distinctive conceptual space might be to set out two axes. Therefore, in this chapter I will set out each of these axes in turn and, in doing so, demarcate the conceptual space being argued for. In the course of doing this, I will refine and nuance the philosophical terms used throughout the book, and locate myself in relation to the wider current literature, as well as gesturing, briefly, to the wider and deeper historical tradition of philosophical theology.

It is worth inserting a caveat here before we continue, to clarify what I mean when I say, 'a religious position rooted in classical philosophical theism' and 'the God of CPT'. In this book I will be 'using' the classical philosophical theistic tradition as *a* representation of theological realism. This is *not* to say that CPT is *the only* route to Christianity or indeed the only or the best way to interpret what it means for a Christian to be Christian. That is to say, when I 'use' the phrase 'the God of CPT' and 'traditional realism' throughout this book, I do so on the basis that this conception of God and this particular type of religious commitment illustrate one way in which to interpret faith. That is, through philosophical investigation. Thus, any dis/agreements presented in this book can only be made in relation to this specific interpretation of the tradition. I will not, for example, talk about Scripture, the incarnation, life or resurrection of Jesus Christ, nor will I talk about revelation. Instead, I will focus on a broad philosophical approach which defends religious realism through the works of thinkers such as Richard Swinburne and Alvin Plantinga.

Axis one: From CPT to minimalism

The realist/non-realist distinction might have two main parts to it. We will focus on the first here, which will be different conceptions of God. As a quick caveat, this graph and its two axes should not be read literally as one would read a mathematical model, this is because these axes are connected, whereas proper mathematical axes are independent. The first axis is: *a spectrum of conceptions of God* from a classical philosophical theistic conception, to a distinctive 'minimalist' conception. I plot what might be three conceptions of God on this axis. On one end of the spectrum is the classical conception of God, otherwise known as *the perfect God of CPT*. Further along the spectrum is what I interpret to be *Don Cupitt's conception of God*, and at the other end of the spectrum is *a distinctive 'minimalist' conception of God* – the position that will be defended in this book. This first axis helps give shape to one part of the distinctive conceptual space that might exist somewhere 'between' traditional realism and standard non-realism. Thus, this first axis demonstrates an increasing openness to the omni-God of CPT. An illustration of what the axis might look like is shown in Figure 1.

In this section we will briefly answer the following questions on each conception of God: How do we define this conception of God? Who holds this conception of God? What are the important differences between this conception and the other conceptions? These *how, who and what* questions will help us to work through the issue of 'religious seriousness' by offering an alternative conception of God and, thus, opening up the conversation as to whether *this* conception of God ought to/can represent a 'religiously serious' position. At the same time, I will demarcate the conceptual space that I am interested in *and* locate myself in the literature.

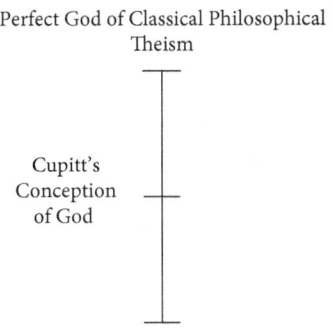

Figure 1 Axis one: A spectrum of conceptions of God. © Jessica Eastwood.

The perfect God of Classical Philosophical Theism

In Western Christianity, a 'traditional' conception of God can be described as *the perfect God of classical philosophical theism*. The perfect God of CPT is omnipresent, omniscient, omnibenevolent and, thus, Creator, Sustainer and moral Judge. This is the God that is described and defended in the philosophical theological works of Swinburne and Plantinga.[3] Swinburne gives the following description:

> God is a necessarily existing person without a body who necessarily is eternal, perfectly free, omnipotent, omniscient, [perfectly rational], perfectly good, and the creator of all things.[4]

Naturally, those who we have identified as 'traditional realists' hold this conception of God, but who else recognizes the God of CPT? If we can, for the moment, put aside any questions surrounding 'ontology' and instead focus solely on 'semantics', then we can say that there is a particular branch of non-realism that recognizes the God of CPT, namely *religious fictionalism*[5] (hereafter, 'fictionalism' unless stated otherwise).[6] Fictionalism is the view that language about God (and related religious language) is best understood as concerning a fictional world, and that engaging in such language involves engaging in a (rather complex) game of make-believe. Like the traditional realist, the fictionalist takes 'God-talk' to be true (or false), which means that religious statements are propositional insofar as they are fact-stating, but they are only *fictional fact-stating*. Thus, they are true within a fiction – the Christian fiction, the Buddhist fiction and so on. Moreover, they are not answerable to a reality which is independent of our beliefs, attitudes or conventions.[7] For instance, the statement 'God is eternally omnipotent' is true, but by virtue of the content of the relevant fiction.

In other words, the general schema that the fictionalist adheres to is this: 'any given theological statement p is true if and only if it is true in the theological fiction that p'.[8] That is to say, God could have the same (non-realist) ontological status as a fictional character in a novel or a film. Moreover, although the fictionalist would not place God (of CPT) in any kind of supernatural reality, that is a reality that transcends human language, concepts and social forms, they do, however, recognize the God of CPT insofar as they engage with this God in what they deem to be 'theological fiction'. What about other non-fictionalist non-realists?

There are a number of non-fictionalist non-realist positions, including 'expressivism', which takes theological statements to be non-propositional and expressive of either an emotional attitude or a moral commitment. There is what one might call 'theological positivism', which takes theological statements to be encoded moral statements. What these two positions have in common is that they are forms of 'reductionism'. Reductionism is the view that theological statements can be reduced, without loss of meaning, to other kinds of (non-theological) statements. Fictionalism denies this. The term 'standard' will be used in this book as it represents a 'basic' (or 'standard') ontological approach to apprehending religious truths from non-realism *without* appealing to a whole, rich, albeit fictional, context in which to situate religious discourse.

Moreover, the standard non-realist does not share the fictionalist attitude that in order to participate in God-talk one must enter into a game of 'make-believe'. Nor do they interpret religious texts as truth or knowledge-apt (albeit fictionally true). Rather, the standard non-realist offers an alternative, more nuanced conception of God. It is important to note this distinction because, for the fictionalist, within the fiction, that is, the religious text, 'God is creator, and is also perfectly good. The fiction of a less-than-perfect God would simply have no useful role to play in [the fictionalist's] religious outlook'.[9] That is to say, the standard non-realist 'reconceptualizes' the classical conception of God, whereas the fictionalist 'reframes' the God of CPT from a reality 'out there' (realism) to a fictional reality (fictionalism).[10] We will now briefly explore Cupitt's conception of God to demonstrate how his standard non-realist conception of God differs from the CPT conception held by the traditional realist and the fictionalist. We will explore it further in Chapter 2.

Cupitt's conception of God

Cupitt is a self-proclaimed religious non-realist, who has published over fifty books since the 1960s insisting (nay, demanding) that we abandon religious realism and the idea that God exists objectively 'out there'. In other words, Cupitt promotes the 'theological realism or religious seriousness' impasse found in the realist/non-realist debate, and he urges us to make a decision.[11] Of course, Cupitt believes that there is only one right answer: 'religious seriousness' and, for him, you cannot claim to take religion seriously if you identify as a religious realist (of any kind).[12] Instead, we must accept that God is, and has always been, purely and wholly *ideal* with no external reality.

What largely separates Cupitt's *conception* of God from the God of CPT is this: although Cupitt's God 'is still the *deus absconditus*, the hidden God who is found at last to hide himself in the depths of the heart',[13] God will always be subject to change. 'With historical change, people change, and so the idea of God is in continual change', Cupitt tells us.[14] We will go through the evolution of Cupitt's conception of God more thoroughly in the next chapter.

A distinctive 'minimalist' conception of God

Now we will turn our attention to the third conception of God on this axis, which is a distinctive 'minimalist' conception of God. Before I offer this particular conception, I will first say something about the current landscape of 'minimalist theology' and what might be considered 'minimalist' conceptions of God. As a brief caveat, it will be worth mentioning that the thinkers we will look at now do not (always) explicitly refer to 'God' in their search for a meaningful conception of the divine in light of ethical concerns. Instead, they talk about 'transcendence'. I follow Hent de Vries's interpretation that what is being spoken about here can have direct theological implications for how we ought to interpret or approach our understanding of God (as a legitimate, specific theological interpretation of talk about 'transcendence').

A good place to start might be with a series of questions asked by twentieth-century philosophers, Theodor Adorno and Emmanuel Levinas. Those being: Are theology, metaphysics and ethics outdated modes of rigorous philosophical inquiry? Is faith possible 'after Auschwitz'? How are we to understand the nature of God in the aftermath of the twentieth century? In their writings, Adorno and Levinas suggest that one can no longer assume the presence of a God in accordance with the classical philosophical conception, that is, as originating or directing the course of the world. However, they refuse to submit to what might be the obvious alternative: nihilism and lax relativism.[15] Instead, in their own way, Adorno and Levinas argue for an alternative approach to what they believe remains: *a trace of a transcendent Other*, whatever its nature. Or, in other words, transcendence in a minimal sense. What might this mean?

Both Adorno and Levinas sought to re-envision an adequate mode of ethical thinking post-Auschwitz, which allowed them to keep hold of their notion of transcendence 'with all its theological inflections' as they believed it to be 'indispensable for any attempt to develop an ethically mature response to the event of the Holocaust'.[16] Thus, in the course of pursuing an alternative conception of transcendence, Adorno and Levinas devise what we might consider to be a 'minimalist' conception of transcendence and *perhaps* a 'minimalist' conception of God. Levinas maintains that 'no relation with God is direct or immediate', the Divine can only be accessed through the human other to whom the self is infinitely responsible.[17] That is to say, '[t]he Divine can be manifested only through my neighbour'.[18] Fiona Ellis, both an admirer and critic of Levinas's work, suggests then that according to this, 'God is absent from the world and could be present as a thing within it (or alongside it) only by ceasing to be God.'[19] We will explore Ellis's concern in due course but first we turn to Adorno, who similarly offers a non-traditional (negative) conception of transcendence.

Adorno does not reject *all* thoughts of transcendence, but rather only 'affirmatively posited transcendence', that is 'transcendence conceptualized as having an original, self-sufficient content through which it can be distinguished from everything belonging to merely material, contingent existence'.[20] In *Minima Moralia*, Adorno refuses to offer any consolation, in regard to his active pessimistic attitude post-Auschwitz, thus avoiding any false consolations of knowledge, whether scientific or theological.[21] But in the same breath offers his sense of transcendence: a 'standpoint of redemption'.

Moreover, Adorno offers a 'middle ground', that is a tentative space that oscillates between formalization, abstraction and openness, on the one hand, and materialization and concretion, on the other.[22] This 'third way' (*tertium datur*) leading 'beyond' the fruitless alternatives of standard naturalism and classical theology, he thought, reveals to us that Adorno does not simply wish to 'overcome' nihilism but to evoke a space that 'demands hope'.[23] Furthermore, this oscillation or tension between transcendence and immanence in Adorno's philosophy is carried forward into another variant of 'minimalism' which came later from de Vries.

De Vries also poses the question: What is it that can be asked of traditional theology 'after Auschwitz'? He explores the significance of this question through the work of Adorno and Levinas, which he expresses as 'theology in pianissimo', namely an attempt to navigate between classical (biblical/dogmatic) theology and theological non-realism (a 'science' of God) constituted by the *trace of a transcendent Other*. De Vries holds out hope for the trace of the Other, the transcendent, the 'new' 'minimalist' understanding of the absolute 'which no longer either can or should resemble or represent the highest being . . . [and] must remain (almost) meaningless and unsusceptible . . . that which incessantly breaks away from any solid or definite context of meaning and action, judgement and expression'.[24]

Another variant of 'minimalism' which also explores the strange abyss between immanence and transcendence, more specifically naturalism and transcendence, is Ellis and her theory of *expansive naturalism*. Ellis argues against the 'temptation' to suppose that (scientific) naturalism is the default position and the idea 'that we are forced to choose between either science or God',[25] in other words: theological realism or religious seriousness. Rather, Ellis defends a distinct form of naturalism, one that is theistic in nature and 'can accommodate the distinction – and indeed, the relation – between God and nature'.

Ellis asks us to re-envision God as lovingly 'wholly other',[26] whose existence or 'presence' in the world can be illustrated by the 'knife-edge that exists between secular expansive naturalism and its theistic counterpart'.[27] Inspired by Levinas, this 'knife-edge' can also be described as rejecting any 'worlds behind the scenes' and, equally, any attempt to reduce God to something that can be adequately grasped in thought.[28]

Ellis's God is not necessarily or strictly the God of CPT. In *God, Value and Nature* Ellis does insist upon (at least) the compatibility of a Christian framework and the God of Christianity. '[T]he Christian God plays a morally motivating role similar to that of Levinas's God' says Ellis, the loving God that she wishes to uphold can be understood through the Incarnate God, insofar as 'the Christian's talk of God bears some resemblance to what Levinas is saying'.[29] However, it is the 'otherness' of God that Ellis defends; that is, God is 'not a member of the larger household of all reality' but that God 'stands in the most intimate connection with things' and has 'the power to inwardly transform those beings who are human'.[30] Inspired by Rahner, Ellis tells us that God is 'the most radical, the most original, and in a certain sense the most self evident reality'.[31] This sounds closer to a more 'minimalist' conception of God than the perfect God of CPT, and she gives us further reason to suspect this.[32]

It is important to note that what will be offered in this book is not a 'soft middle' way ('between' or 'beyond' traditional realism and standard non-realism) but a serious alternative to a 'full-blown' classical conception of God and its full-blown realist ontology. I offer a meaningful conception that resonates in a real way with those who feel the strain of the theological realism/religious seriousness impasse.

With that being said, the 'minimalist' conception offered here does, to a significant extent, have its roots in the classical theistic tradition. God, in this distinctive minimalist sense, is thought to be something along the lines of a suitably qualified version of Anselm's 'that-than-which-a-greater-cannot-be-conceived', a formula which is often viewed as the focal point of perfect being theology, and derives the traditional omni-attributes of God from it. Certainly, for Anselm, God as 'that-than-which-a-greater-cannot-be-conceived' does infer the omni-properties (and perhaps some further ones, such as timelessness and necessity), in accordance with the classical doctrine of divine simplicity. The book looks to avoid such inferences and not commit the post-traditionalist to them, insofar as post-traditionalism *does* look to borrow the Anselmian formula *without* necessarily adopting the omni-properties ipso facto. Therefore, this book will use a bare, minimalist, apophatic interpretation of Anselm's formula as a popular monotheistic understanding of God without defending the entirety of Anselm's theological system.[33]

Moreover, I will suggest that there might be a genuine way to reinterpret this: to defend God who is 'the most radical, the most original and in a certain sense the most self-evident reality' without committing to a 'full-blown' classical, philosophical conception of the perfect God. The best way to explain the distinctive minimalist conception of God as 'that-than-which-a-greater-can not-be-conceived' might be to answer this question: What are the important differences between this conception and the other conceptions?

Semantically, this distinct conception of God resonates more with the standard non-realist's more nuanced conception of God, rather than the traditional realist and fictionalist God of CPT. This is because it agrees with the non-realist's tentative reflection of the perfect God, choosing to place emphasis on God as *the* ideal, *the* guiding star rather than stress any specific omni-characteristics. Ontologically, however, the distinct conception of God differs from the non-realist's conception because it is the realist that describes God as existing outside of human language, concepts and social forms, having some type of objective, external existence 'out there'. Thus, the wonder and realness of 'God' is preserved by this distinct, 'minimalist' conception. It is a type of realist conception.

Some of the ways in which this distinctive, minimalist conception of God differs will come to light when I lay out the second axis. This will include a discussion on the type of religious believer who might be interested in this conception, for whom the 'perfect God', the 'fictional God' or God as a 'leading' idea is not satisfying, perhaps this is because it is not 'serious' enough or fails to reflect a genuine alternative to what classical theism offers. We will now turn to the second axis.

Axis two: From standard non-realism to post-traditional realism

The second axis shows *a spectrum of commitment* that goes from standard non-realism through to traditional realism. I tentatively use the classification of

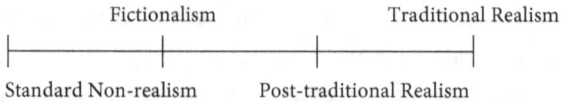

Figure 2 Axis two: A spectrum of commitments to God. © Jessica Eastwood.

'spectrum' again here to describe what is going on in this second axis, because although these certainly are discrete positions that I map out, what justifies the order of the positions is their increasing openness to a 'thicker' ontological commitment. And when it comes to the concept of 'commitment', it might appear initially misleading as one might expect to find degrees of 'belief' or 'acceptance' to be measured on the spectrum, something like this perhaps: full belief, to non-doxastic acceptance, to resistance, to outright rejection. But this is not what is being shown here, rather it is to do with *ontology*.

To clarify, what I am interested in is distinctions, some of which are nuanced and cross-over each other. So, for example, the chart with an x axis (axis two: spectrum of commitment) and y axis (axis one: spectrum of conceptions) is not really a 'spectrum', but a depiction of conceptual zones, some of which are quite discrete from each other, even though some positions are closer than others.

This book will pay close attention to the textures of reality that might lie between these two positions. They include the fictional reality posited by the religious fictionalist and the distinct reality ascribed to the 'minimalist' conception of God posited in this book, a commitment that I will refer to as *post-traditional realism* (otherwise, post-traditionalism). An illustration of what the axis might look like is shown in Figure 2.

The threefold structure of this section will begin by providing a definition for standard non-realism and traditional realism and set out their relationship through Christopher Insole's typology. Then it will explore the textures of a realism that might lie in between these two positions: the first will be *fictionalism* (semantic realism), and the second *post-traditional realism*, namely the space that is 'passed over' too quickly, this book will argue. Let us turn then to clarifying what we mean by (traditional) realism and (standard) non-realism.

Standard non-realism and traditional realism

It is important to identify exactly what I mean here, and throughout the book, when I use the phrases 'realism' and 'non-realism', and to demarcate the differences between these two philosophical views. One helpful way to draw the realism/non-realism distinction is to classify four broad categories or specific sets of interests. Those categories might be: ontological, semantic, epistemological and cognitivist construals of the distinction.[34] In this first part, I follow Insole's typology. Other typologies are available, and I am not making any original claims in this part, but setting out a typology provided by Insole which allows us to focus on the first of these two categories that this project is particularly interested in (those being, ontological and semantic). For this reason, I will give only a brief description of the final two categories (namely, an epistemological and cognitivist construal) before expounding what an ontological and semantic construal of the realism/non-realism distinction might look like.

To frame the *cognitivist* construal of the realist/non-realist distinction it might be useful to ask about the truth-apt function of a religious utterance such as 'God exists'. Is it a descriptive or prescriptive/expressive utterance? In other words, 'is the utterance x a statement that is capable of truth or falsity?'[35] The realist will answer: *yes*, utterance x is capable of truth and falsity. Whereas, the non-realist will deny this possibility.[36] The *epistemological* category is concerned with the relationship between truth, our access to it (whether we can or cannot know it/ rationally believe it) and the role our mind (our beliefs) plays in accessing truths. More specifically, the epistemologist is asking whether 'religious utterances about x [are] true or false independently of our minds thinking about x/ our beliefs about x/ our evidence for x/ our epistemic practices for discerning the truth or falsity about x?'[37] On this construct, only the realist will answer: *yes*, we can have access to some truths about x independently from our minds thinking about x / our beliefs, our evidence for, our epistemic practices for discerning the truth or falsity about x. The question of the mind and its relationship to x feeds into the next category: ontology.

Ontological construal of the realism/non-realism distinction

The question of mind-independence and mind-dependence is central to the *ontological* construal of the realist/non-realist distinction (and to this book), namely whether x exists (or does not) independent of mind (or not). One is a realist about x if one responds that x does exist *in*dependently of mind. Conversely, the non-realist will reject this notion of independence and suggest, instead, that x's existence is dependent on the mind. So far so good. But, as Insole shows, things can get a little more complicated when we ask what sort of 'reality' might be substituted for x in 'does x exist independently of mind?'

When we talk about *x*, are we talking about an 'entity'? By this I mean, a singular term with or without a referent – that is, pandas, goblins, flowers.[38] Some philosophers of religion and theologians feel anxious when talking about God in terms of an 'entity'. Insole tells us that one reason for this concern might be that such language pulls us towards a 'paradigm of discrete, contingent (spatially and temporally) extended, created things'.[39] However, where I would nuance Insole's treatment is to suggest that this description is not universal, and it is not representative of the many different ways that the term 'entity' might be used in reference to *x*.

What I mean by this is that a case could be made that not all entities are as static in nature and obviously present to the subject (regarding their spatio-temporal whereabouts) as the description suggests. Not all entities can be described as 'medium-sized dry physical objects'.[40] For example, as I will argue in Chapter 6, abstract mathematical objects (such as numbers, sets and functions) are not discrete, contingent, extended, nor, arguably, 'created' in any obvious way. Rather, such mathematical entities are widely considered by many mathematicians (namely mathematical realists) to lack spatio-temporal location, to be inaccessible to the senses and acausal.

A second point to mention about the ontological construal of the realist/non-realist debate is the danger of 'pushing doctrines' concerning God (such as 'God is simple/the creator ex nihilo/perfectly good/triune/incarnate in Jesus Christ') 'through the mesh' of the realist/non-realist debate.[41] That is to say, 'lumping together' things that should be separate. The fear is that by adopting a realist ontological position that God is mind-independent, one is *also* committing oneself to a whole host of doctrines concerning the nature and character of God (as simple/the creator ex nihilo, etc.). I have referred to this traditional realist conception of God as the perfect God of classical philosophical theism, and it will appear a lot in this book as we compare it to the post-traditional believer's conception of God, as a 'stripped-back' minimalist interpretation of 'that-than-which-a-greater-cannot-be-conceived'.

There have been plenty of challenges to traditional theism (realism) that are purely rooted in its ontological thesis, namely that the perfect God of CPT exists objectively. For example, 'there is the well-known problem of evil, or suffering: how can the evident fact of suffering, indeed intense suffering from which no adequately compensating good seems to ensue, be reconciled with the existence of God as traditionally conceived: a God who loves us, knows about our suffering, and could have prevented it?'[42] For many religious people the existence of evil *and* the perfect God of CPT are irreconcilable, and since they feel they cannot deny the existence of evil, they relinquish their realist belief in God. Perhaps feeling the intensity of the theological theism/religious seriousness impasse, the traditional believer may then 'slide down' the second axis towards fictionalism or standard non-realism. They may even slide off the axis completely into atheism. Notably, the traditional realist often 'passes over' 'post-traditional' realism as a meaningful response to the impasse as they make their way down the axis. The aim of the book is to highlight 'post-traditionalism' as a genuine realist alternative to non-realism (and atheism), one that may even provide a satisfactory response to the problem of evil.

In Chapter 3 we will explore why a religious person might choose a fictionalist approach to apprehending God and religious discourse. In Chapter 6, however, we will turn our attention back to 'ontology' as we will in a position to compare the 'thickness' of fictional reality to the sui generis reality ascribed to 'God' by the post-traditionalist, through an analogy that will be drawn with the kind of sui generis reality ascribed to mathematical objects (such as numbers, sets and figures) by some mathematicians.

The purpose of this analogy will be to highlight a texture of reality that might exist 'between' traditional realism and fictionalism, and how it might provide a satisfying religious approach to apprehending God in a way that is 'religiously serious' but not 'traditionally realist', a reality that is both non-traditionally realist by nature and serious by disposition. That is, a post-traditional, realist reality.

Moreover, the post-traditional minimalist proposal goes beyond fictionalism, but without affirming a conceptual space beyond a richly conceived naturalism. This is what is being driven at by the suggestion of a sui generis conceptual texture: it is a relatively underexplored 'zone' in the literature – beyond fictionalism but not beyond naturalism – although, arguably, some 'minimalist theologies' in the wake of Adorno (e.g. de Vries) are working in this space, they do not try to work it out very analytically. Naturalism is enough for genuine (not fictionalist 'as if') belief in God, but such naturalistic belief does not set limits to what is believed in (because of epistemic limitations and the intrinsic complexity of what is believed in). That naturalism is enough for belief in God does not mean that we know God to be exhausted by the naturalistic. This is the space beyond fictionalism that does not go beyond naturalism, but which does not, in principle, claim that naturalism sets the limits of what could be real. The above is not an unknown or unprecedented conceptual space, and I will apply insights in other branches of philosophy to suggest that they provide a helpful analogy.

Semantic construal of the realism/non-realism distinction

The second category that I will focus on in this book regarding the realist/non-realist distinction is known as the semantic construal. The semantic category could be captured by presenting the conflicting responses from the realist and the non-realist regarding the following question: '[I]s the meaning of the statement x exhausted by the conditions under which we are justified in asserting x?'[43] The non-realist will maintain that our understanding of the meaning of x is exhausted by the conditions under which we were justified in asserting x. Put another way, the non-realist holds that our understanding of a statement (about x) 'is given entirely by the conditions under which we are justified in asserting the statement'.

Conversely, the realist will defend the notion that (at least part of) the meaning of a statement (about x) 'is given by what would make it true, [that is] independently of the conditions under which we are justified in asserting the statement'.[44] Moreover, the difference comes down to which conception of truth one holds. Furthermore, it might be the case that we are dealing with a debate between 'two thinkers who confess belief in God, but who disagree about what a belief is . . . disagreeing philosophically about what constitutes such truth [that there is a God] because they disagree about what constitutes truth as such'.[45]

An important note to make on this particular semantic construct is that 'semantic non-realism does not directly say anything about ontology'.[46] To this extent it is possible to have a realist semantic view (about x) and also hold a non-realist ontological thesis (about x). What this means is that if we do not want to say that the semantic non-realist *really* believes that 'there is a God', 'we need a way to distinguish a person with this sort of general non-adherence to a particular conception of truth from someone who holds a realist conception of truth but does not *really* believe in the truth of the Christian faith'.[47] In other words, there is a difference between belief in 'religion' and belief in 'realism'.[48] The two are not the same.

To demonstrate what I mean by this, I invite you to imagine the possibility of a subject who believes that the meaning of the statement x *is* exhausted by the conditions under which we are justified in asserting x (thus, holding a non-realist semantic position), but who *also* continues to engage in a religious community and actively participate in its practices (through their belief in 'religion'). Belief in 'realism' represents a more traditional commitment to both a realist semantic view and a realist ontological view. Having now provided a definition of (standard) non-realism and (traditional) realism and set out their relationship through a nuanced version of Insole's typology, we will now move on to explore textures of reality that might exist 'between' these giant pillars, the first will be 'fictionalism' (or semantic realism).

Fictionalism and the realism/non-realism distinction

Now that we have an idea of how one might draw a distinction between realism and non-realism in a religious or theological context, for the purposes of this book it is also important that we look at this distinction in relation to religious fictionalism. Fictionalism, as we know, is the philosophical view that religious discourse is best interpreted as intellectually stimulating and morally enlightening *fiction*. This means that *ontologically* the fictionalist holds the same position as the non-realist – that is, in regard to x, x's existence is dependent on mind. *Semantically*, however, the fictionalist will hold a similar thesis to the realist because of their unique conception of truth, insofar as the fictionalist will assert religious statements such as 'God is omnipotent' but in the context of *theological fiction*, and not a reality 'out there' as the realist does.

In other words, the fictionalist understands that religious statements are made in a context of make-believe. A fictionalist who says that 'the world was created by God' will assert this as part of the game of 'make-believe' and is, thus, *pretending* to assert, not actually asserting, that the world was created by God. Moreover, God-talk is capable of being true (or false), but they are only true (or false) within a specific fiction. They are fact-stating, but the facts they state, because fictional, are not attitude- or convention-independent.[49]

We will talk a lot more on fictionalism throughout the book (particularly in Chapters 3–5) but for now it will be useful to remember that (i) fictionalism is a branch of no-realism; therefore (ii) the fictionalist does not hold a realist ontological commitment to God; however (iii) the fictionalist does hold an alternative type of semantic commitment, as they believe religious language to be (fictionally) truth-apt. Moreover, they do not hold exactly the same semantic thesis as the traditional realist, because the traditional realist takes God-talk to be truth-apt, irreducible and objectively fact-stating.[50]

We will now look at the second texture of reality that this book looks to defend, *post-traditional realism*, which I argue is a distinctive conceptual space with a unique ontology that is passed over too quickly when measuring 'where it is' that believers can exist on 'a spectrum of commitment'. Before we explore this space, it will be useful to present the graph and its two axes: (1) *a spectrum*

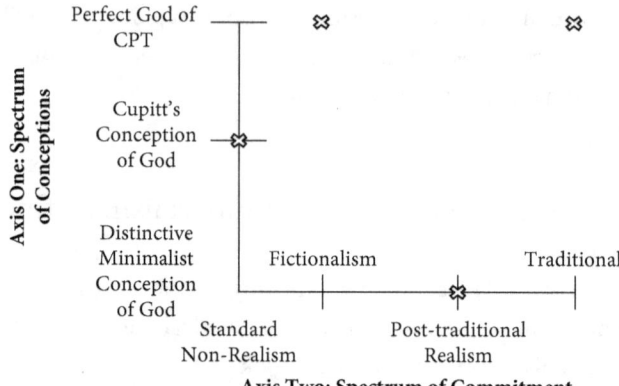

Figure 3 Axis one and two combined. © Jessica Eastwood.

of conceptions of God from the perfect God of CPT to a 'minimalist' conception of God, and (2) *a spectrum of commitment* from standard non-realism through to traditional realism (Figure 3).

I have plotted on the graph four types of 'religious commitments' with their respective conception of God. From left to right along the second axis we have:

- Standard non-realism and Cupitt's conception of God.
- Fictionalism and the perfect God of CPT.
- Post-traditional realism and a distinctive 'minimalist' conception of God.
- Traditional realism and the perfect God of CPT.

Having now visualized what the realist/non-realist debate could offer with the addition of 'post-traditional realism' plotted between fictionalism and traditional realism, we will further explore what this sui generis conceptual space could provide the religious believer, for whom the search for a 'religiously serious' and 'genuine' type of faith continues.

Post-traditional realism and the realism/non-realism distinction

Earlier we described post-traditional realism as a 'minimalist' or 'stripped back' kind of realism (compared to traditional realism). If we refer back to the second axis on the graph (a spectrum of commitment) we can see that post-traditional realism sits 'between' fictionalism and traditional realism. It sits to the 'right' of fictionalism because although it agrees with the fictionalist that God is 'that-than-which-a-greater-cannot-be-conceived' (but will not then ascribe other omni-characteristics that make up the God of CPT) the post-traditional realist ascribes 'that-than which-a-greater-cannot-be-conceived' some kind of distinctive, external reality. That is, a reality that exists 'outside of' any kind of fictional reality conjured by the human mind.

The distance between post-traditionalism and traditional realism hinges on two elements of a traditional realist position that the post-traditional believer does not wish to commit themselves to. First of all, the post-traditional believer does not commit themselves to belief in the CPT conception of God, but rather that God is 'that-than-which-a-greater-cannot-be-conceived' in its simplest sense. The second difference is that post-traditionalism could not also be referred to as 'religious platonism', as traditional realism can be. This is because the post-traditionalist does not wish to commit themselves to the belief that God ('that-than-which-a-greater-cannot-be conceived') has an *unconditionally necessary* existence, which means that God's existence is not in any way conditioned by the way that the world actually is, and exists *wholly (mind-) independently*, that is not say that God does not depend in any way on the existence of us, human beings, as the traditional realist does. I will comment further on these facets of a traditional realist or platonic reality in Chapter 6.

The reason why the post-traditional approach might be centre-right of the spectrum (between fictionalism and traditional realism) is because it can be described as both an '*inflated fictionalism*' and a '*deflated realism*'. By the former – inflated fictionalism – I mean that because post-traditionalism looks to go 'beyond' the fictional realm ascribed to God (of CPT) by the fictionalist, and 'beyond' the kind of ontology that fictional characters might possess, post-traditionalism ascribes an 'inflated fictional reality' or 'fictionality plus'. What does this 'inflated reality' look like? To colour this curious texture of reality we will enter in the world of philosophy of mathematics.

As briefly mentioned before, in Chapter 6 we will explore the strange realm that some (realist) mathematicians ascribe to abstract mathematical objects (such as numbers, sets and functions). For those mathematicians who understand these abstract objects to have some kind of independent existence 'out there', they posit a sui generis realm where they might exist. We will ask whether this strange conceptual space posited by some mathematicians can help us to *develop* the theologically distinctive conceptual space that the post-traditionalist wishes to ascribe to God and *defend* its possibility.

Drawing on the ontological thesis of these mathematicians will also help us to draw an important distinction between post-traditionalism and traditional realism, specifically in regard to the 'additional' facets ascribed to the latter, namely *unconditionally necessary* and *wholly independent*. In the world of philosophy of mathematics, mathematicians who ascribe this kind of existence – *unconditionally necessary* and *wholly independent* – to abstract mathematical objects are known as 'mathematical platonists'. By comparing mathematical platonism and traditional realism and the kinds of reality that they ascribe to their 'abstract object' (so for the platonic mathematician this might be natural numbers, and for the traditional realist this will be the God of CPT) we might get a better sense of why post-traditional realism is a '*deflated*' kind of realism.

Post-traditional realism might also be described as *deflated realism* because of its quasi-apophatic approach to the perfect God of traditional realism. That is to say, the post-traditional realist is hesitant to commit to God as (also) omnipresent, omniscient, omnibenevolent and, thus, Creator, Sustainer and moral Judge. This is because this says more about 'God' than the idea that God is certainly 'that-than-which-a-greater-cannot-be-conceived'. Instead, it describes the God of traditional theism. Thus, post-traditional realism can be described as a kind of 'deflated' (post-traditional) realism, as it posits a 'deflated' (post-traditional/'minimalist') conception of God.

At this point in the chapter, we have introduced the 'post-traditional' conceptual space that this book defends and its adjoining distinctive, 'minimalist' conception of God by setting out two axes. The first axis looked at different conceptions of God from the God of CPT to this 'minimalist' conception. I plotted the distinctive, 'minimalist' conception of God on this axis 'below' the God of CPT and Cupitt's God to reflect the subtle but important distinction between the former conceptions and God as 'simply' 'that-than-which-a-greater-cannot-be-conceived' existing in some sui generis kind of external reality. The second axis looked at the spectrum of 'religious commitments' from standard non-realism to traditional realism. I plotted post-traditional realism between religious fictionalism and traditional realism, because post-traditionalism offers a more 'robust ontology' than fictionalism does, without committing to classical theism.

Chapter 1 (*What Does It Mean to Have Belief? Conceptions of Belief and Faith*) will focus on the second axis (a spectrum of commitment) as we look at what might be four different types of religious 'faith'. Specifically, we will focus on the two components that make up these commitments, namely 'belief-that'/'belief-in' and the voluntariness of these components. Thus, the chapter's twofold structure will explore the question: 'What does it mean to have belief?' I will present three propositional and *in*voluntary accounts of belief by David Hume, Richard Swinburne and Gilbert Ryle. Then, I will examine three non-propositional and voluntary conceptions of belief, including theological work of Plantinga and Swinburne, Aquinas and finally Rudolf Bultmann and Richard Braithwaite. The purpose of this chapter is to give a comprehensive presentation of different types of religious faith and to demonstrate that there is room here for a 'post-traditional' account of religious commitment.

Chapter 2 (*Standard Non-realism and the Nature of 'God' à la Don Cupitt*) will focus on a particular variant of one of the four types of 'faith', that is non-realism as construed by Don Cupitt.[51] We will draw on both axes, this time with a sole focus on that which Cupitt contributes to the realism/non-realism debate. That is to say, we will assess, both, his conception of God (and his position on axis one) which, as we will come to see, might feel a bit like 'chasing after the wind', and his particular strand of non-realism (which will clarify his position on the second axis). To do this we will take a whistle-stop tour through some of Cupitt's works from the late 1970s to the late 2000s, with the aim of suggesting that although Cupitt certainly opens a gate onto a larger conversation on how we can understand the reality of God, the path on which he looks to lead us might lack the same promise as his opening of the gate initially sparked. That is to say, this body of work is, in part, inspired by Cupitt's unabashed attempt to re-envision 'who' God is, and 'where' God is, so that the 'doubting traditional realist' might find a 'new' way of apprehending God that resonates or aligns more coherently with their worldview.

With that being said, the chapter will conclude with the understanding that if the so-called doubting traditional realist does ultimately find Cupitt's final non-realist position as lacking the same spark that ignited their quest to re-explore what divine reality is, then we will need to continue our search for an *intellectually*, *emotionally* and *spiritually* coherent philosophical approach to apprehending the nature and reality of God. In Chapters 3–5 we will explore another variant of a non-realist type of faith that might provide such an account, that is *fictionalism*. As a brief sketch, we will investigate the extent to which fictionalism can offer a variant of religious non-realism that is *intellectually* coherent, by this I mean that its belief system is found intelligible (in Chapter 3); *emotionally* coherent, in the sense that it holds emotional engagement in religious discourse as an important aspect of 'faith' (in Chapter 4) and *spiritually* coherent, insofar as it allows for an element of the 'unknown' to resonate with meaning and a sense of connecting to a larger reality that we believe exists (in Chapter 5).

We will find that fictionalism does appear to deliver a coherent account of 'faith' in regard to the first two cases but, as we will see, it will be fundamentally lacking spiritually.

The overarching question that Chapter 3 will be asking is: *'Can Faith Without Belief Be Meaningful?'* This question, which is also the title of the chapter, asks how a religious person/commitment/book can be genuine without a standard commitment (belief-that) God exists objectively 'out there'? I will, therefore, be focusing on the second axis in this chapter by way of exploring this type of faith through religious fictionalism. To begin, I will give three reasons (1) *why a person might choose to adopt fictionalism*. The crux of this section however will be to argue that fictionalism is 'intellectually coherent', by this I mean that its appeal might be its non-commitment to metaphysical claims of traditional theism.

To argue for the intellectual coherence of fictionalism I will, first, address the potential concern: (2) *does faith require 'belief-that'?* by replacing the concept of 'belief-that' with the concept of 'assuming' and 'steadfastness' in light of the following philosopher's work: Daniel Howard-Snyder, Brian Zamulinski, Elizabeth Jackson and Lara Buchak. After this I will explain how fictionalism might be said to be (3) *'reframing' God* (in light of Simon Blackburn) and why this might help to build a bridge between a scientific picture of the universe and a type of faith, through the works of Le Poidevin, Peter Lipton and Wittgenstein. The aim of Chapter 3 is to present a number of cases which suggest that fictionalism is an intellectually coherent kind of (alternative) religious faith.

The purpose of Chapter 4 (*Are Our Emotions Toward Fiction Real?*) is to argue that fictionalism is 'emotionally coherent' insofar as the fictionalist has a coherent view about the emotions, in that the fictionalist is not simply confused if they allow religious narratives to shape their emotional lives. I will do this by first exploring *the nature of fictional emotions* by challenging the so-called paradox of fiction, premise by premise, starting with *(P1) we are genuinely moved by fiction*. I will draw on Kendall Walton and Le Poidevin to demonstrate how our emotional response to fiction might not be 'genuine' (insofar as they are not brought about by that which we know to be true/the case) but nevertheless powerful and meaningful. The second premise: *(P2) we do not believe that fictional entities exist* will be tried against potentially compelling arguments to suggest the opposite. The first argument concerns the *fleetingness of belief* (in fiction), and the second looks at *the nature of general truths*, by this I mean how fiction can generate emotions by presenting historical or common facts.

Then we will turn to the final premise which states the following: *(P3) to be moved, we must believe that fictional entities exist*. In response to this I will mention three thinkers and their theories to demonstrate how this premise might be overcome, these being Katherine Tullman's theory of HOT emotions, Tamar Gendler's coining of 'alief' and Michael Weston's notion of fiction as a work of art. I will end this chapter by suggesting that fictionalism might be emotionally coherent to an extent.

Chapter 5 (*Fictionalism and 'The Humane Turn'*) will also attend to the second axis and present a contemporary 'humane' model for philosophy of religion, a movement that promotes the connection of the subject more closely with the moral and spiritual sensibilities that shape religious belief. The threefold structure of this chapter will begin with an exploration into the 'humane' turn through its key proponents, namely John Cottingham and Eleonore Stump. After which I will examine the extent to which religious fictionalism can be said to honour the movement by exercising the same epistemic virtues. Finally, I will ask whether we have, in fact, pushed fictionalism to its edge. By this I mean, I will suggest that fictionalism *might not be* compatible with this type of 'humane' philosophizing because it might require a realist worldview, a worldview that the fictionalist is not inclined to hold. Therefore, I will offer three reasons why the humane turn and fictionalism are, perhaps, not a match made in heaven, and that rather than 'jump' to a traditional religious realist worldview, that we might stop and explore another texture of realism that might exist.

Chapter 6 (*God and Numbers: A Minimal Realism*) will explore this reality. Here we will discuss both axes, the first axis will be referred to in relation to how we conceptualize objects which are considered abstract, specifically mathematical objects in the world of mathematics and 'God' in the world of theology. The second axis will be addressed as we consider the kind of reality ascribed to these mathematical objects and to 'God'. I will suggest that a helpful analogy can be drawn between the kind of realism ascribed to mathematical objects by some mathematicians and the kind of realism ascribed to a distinctive 'minimalist' conception of God by the post-traditional realist. Thus, the chapter will conclude by stating the following claim: mathematical realism and its ontology about abstract mathematical objects might help the theologian (and philosopher of religion) think about broadening the scope of religious realism and the potential adequacy of a conceptual reality such as that posited by 'post-traditional' religious realist to ascribe to a 'post-traditional' conception of God.

In the Conclusion chapter (*Post-Traditional Realism and a Distinctive 'Minimalist' Conception of God*), we will reflect on the previous chapters and what they taught us, like a prophetic photo album: cleverly and carefully constructed and taking us on a purpose-led journey. Starting from the first axis, I will point to each type of conception of God and explain its relationship to the conception that is defended in this book, which is a distinctive 'minimalist' conception of God. The same will be done with the second axis; I will address each form of commitment and compare it to the commitment espoused in this work, which is 'post-traditional' realism. The overall conclusion of the book will be this: if we want to overcome the apparently unavoidable impasse of traditional realism *or* standard non-realism, I propose that we dig a little deeper into the possibility of latent textures of reality that might exist 'between' traditional realism and standard non-realism and ascribe this sui generis reality to a distinctive 'minimalist' conception of God as 'that-than-which-a-greater-cannot-be-conceived'.

I will now gesture, very briefly, to the wider and deeper historical tradition of philosophical theology, with a particular focus on the choice of the phrase: 'post-traditional' (realism). The tradition that I come after with my 'post-traditional' conception is recent in analytical debates around CPT. But what I am calling '*post*-traditional' may, from other perspectives, resonate with aspects of the philosophical and theological tradition more broadly conceived. For instance, Insole's interpretation of the 'Kantian movement', specifically Kant's argument that 'reality' can be in some way mind-dependent but objective.[52] Peter Singer's interpretation of Hegel's philosophy might also open up the 'post-traditional' space argued for in this book. Singer says that '*Geist*' 'has a spiritual or religious flavour' which suggests that 'in some sense there's a reality above and beyond my individual mind...Mind with a capital "M", not just mind in the sense of individual minds'.[53] Thus, Hegel's concept of 'ultimate reality' might share similarities insofar there exists some kind of sui generis space that is somehow tethered to persons but exists 'beyond' the subjective nature of an individual mind.

The 'post-traditional' space might also resonate with the theological work of Karl Rahner and the idea that we cannot know God in the same way that we know other things in the universe. That is, if there were a list of things in the universe God would not be the first one or the final one or somewhere in the middle. Rather, God is 'absolute mystery'.[54] Similarly, Paul Tillich presents a non-traditional conception of God in his *The Courage To Be* as he apprehends a 'God above God', that is, 'God above the God of theism'.[55] I am perfectly comfortable with the idea that this 'post-traditional' concept might resonate with these historical philosophical and theological strands, but I make no particular claim here.

The aim of the book is not exactly to propose this conceptual space as 'compulsory'. It is not an 'argument for the post-traditional existence of God'. It is more modest: a claim that there is a conceptual zone (not necessarily on a spectrum) beyond fictionalism that does not go beyond naturalism, but which is open to epistemic humility, in such a way that does not affirm that naturalism is the final word. Just as I will argue that fictionalism has a coherence and salience, without arguing for fictionalism as such, I will argue that this post-traditional stance has a type of coherence and salience.

1

What does it mean to have belief?

Conceptions of belief and faith

Theologians have often looked at religious faith as two types of beliefs interacting in a certain way, namely 'belief-that' and 'belief-in'. Traditionally, 'belief-that' (henceforth, also referred to as simply 'belief') might be described as holding true a conception of God (of CPT) as existing objectively 'out there', that is, as having some kind of external existence. It is, therefore, a type of realist commitment. By extension, 'belief-in' might describe a personal connection to God (of CPT), if the person holds certain positive propositions about God's nature. A person of faith is traditionally seen as having both 'belief-that' and 'belief-in' the God from CPT.

In this chapter we will be looking at the relationship between these two conceptions of belief when it comes to other types of faith as well as the traditional conception. Thus, we will also explore the way in which these beliefs interact with one another when the conception of God is *not* from CPT. For instance, we will look at the kind of faith that the post-traditional believer might have, given their ontological commitment to a distinctive 'minimalist' conception of God. In this case, 'belief-that' will describe holding true a conception of 'God' (not necessarily of CPT) as existing objectively 'out there'. This is, then, still a form of realist commitment. And, 'belief-in' will describe their personal connection to God (again, not necessarily of CPT).

Additionally, there is another important factor to consider when looking at what might constitute religious faith, and that is the *voluntariness* of one's beliefs. Is one's 'belief-that' a *voluntary* belief or an *involuntary* belief? That is to say, is one's belief-that oriented towards that which 'cannot help but' be believed and is, therefore, a type of 'involuntary' belief? Or is it, rather, a conscious, pragmatic or purposeful choice and is therefore a type of 'voluntary' belief? I suggest that classical faith held by the traditional realist might be described in the following way, once we now also include the voluntariness of their beliefs: *involuntary* 'belief-that' and *voluntary* 'belief-in'. That is to say, the traditional realist 'cannot help but' believe that God (of CPT) exists objectively 'out there' (*involuntary* '*belief-that*'), and they choose to worship and trust in this God (*voluntary* '*belief-in*').

In this chapter I will describe four different types of relationship between 'belief-that' and 'belief-in', both voluntary and involuntary. Along the way I will plot the four types of religious commitments presented in the previous chapter and plotted on the second axis (a spectrum of commitment). Before I do this, it is important to clarify what I mean by 'faith'. For our purposes, faith will mean 'belief-in'. There are two further things to note here, the first is that 'belief-in' is always voluntary, which ties into my second point. The second type of 'faith' we will look at does *not* have a 'belief-in' component; however, I shall still refer to it as a type of 'faith'. The reason being that one variant of this account *is* referred to as a form of 'faith', and the traditional understanding of faith, as having both 'belief-that' and 'belief-in' the God from CPT, might only be a guiding template from which other, less traditional, forms of faith can evolve. Moreover, I argue that traditional realism (Christianity, for example) is not the only type of religious commitment that has (a kind of) 'faith' element (i.e. voluntary belief-in). Rather, post-traditionalism, standard non-realism, fictionalism and more pragmatic forms of religious commitment can all be referred to as 'a type of religious faith', more broadly conceived.

The presence of a 'belief-that' component will also be important to our project here, particularly whether it is held voluntarily or *in*voluntarily. By establishing the nature of one's religious belief, it will illuminate the major difference between standard non-realism and fictionalism, and post-traditionalist realism and traditional realism. Namely that the former *does not have an involuntary (nor a voluntary) belief-that component*, whereas the latter *both have an involuntary belief-that component*. Thus, interestingly, what we will find is that post-traditionalism is a variant of faith as it is classically conceived, which suggests that the post-traditionalist position is perhaps not that radical or restrictive, but in fact values the intensity of a kind of belief that 'cannot help but' be held, *and* how this belief is played out through a personal connection to 'God'. In light of these forecasts, I present the following four types of 'religious faith'.

I. *Involuntary 'Belief-that' and Voluntary 'Belief-in'*. I suggest that this best represents (Ia) **traditional realism** and the God of CPT. When the traditional realist 'cannot help but' believe that God (of CPT) exists objectively 'out there' and ascribe a reality that is '*un*conditionally necessary' and 'wholly independent' (*involuntary belief-that*), they choose to worship and trust in this God (*voluntary belief-in*).

II. *Involuntary 'Belief-that' Without Voluntary 'Belief-in'*. This might correspond with a type of unconcerned and neutral assent to religious truth claims, such as what Aquinas calls 'the devils' faith'. That is, a 'cannot help but' belief that God (of CPT) exists objectively 'out there' (*involuntary belief-that*), but they do not adjust their life according to this belief-that (*without voluntary belief-in*).

III. *Voluntary 'Belief-that' and Voluntary 'Belief-in'*. Such a commitment might depict William James's 'Will to Believe' (a pragmatic argument for the adoption of a belief without prior evidence of its truth). Thus, more broadly, it might describe when one chooses to believe that God (of CPT) exists objectively 'out there' (*voluntary 'belief-that'*), and one also chooses to live according to this truth (*voluntary 'belief-in'*).

IV. *Voluntary 'Belief-in' Without Involuntary 'Belief-that'*. This might be the (IVa) **standard non-realist** type of commitment (and maybe even religious agnosticism).[1] Insofar as it might describe when a person chooses to actively and positively engage with religious discourse and God (a nuanced version of the CPT conception) (*voluntary 'belief-in'*), but they do not believe that this God exists objectively 'out there' (*without involuntary belief-that*).

It also represents the (IVb) **fictionalist** type of commitment, as it describes a person who chooses to actively and positively engage with religious discourse and God (of CPT) (*voluntary 'belief-in'*), but they do not believe that God exists objectively 'out there' (*without involuntary belief-that*).[2]

I will discuss each of these four types of 'faith' in turn, and I will locate post-traditionalism. I suggest that post-traditionalism is *not* a variant of (II), (III) or (IV), instead it will turn out to be a variant of (I). Thus, I argue that post-traditionalism can be described as something along these lines:

I. *Involuntary 'Belief-that' and Voluntary 'Belief-in'* also represents (Ib) '**Post-traditionalism**' and its distinctive, 'minimalist' conception of God. When the post-traditionalist 'cannot help but' believe that this God exists objectively 'out there' and ascribe a reality that is 'conditionally necessary' and 'semi-independent' (*involuntary belief-that*), they allow their belief to positively impact their life (*voluntary belief-in*).

It might be safe to assume that those who exercise a pragmatic approach to religious discourse (in relation to the former account) seek to 'weigh up' whether or not they feel that they can commit to *a religious discourse*, rather than a purely philosophical discourse. 'Post-traditional' realism is not a strictly religious position but rather a philosophical one, until (or if) it is paired with fictionalism for instance. Thus, if one were to pragmatically *choose* whether to believe that God exists, one might choose to 'believe' (Jamesian minimal realism) or 'imagine' (fictionalism) the existence of the omni-God of CPT, rather than the philosophically nuanced and somewhat nebulous conception from post-traditionalism (see my 'reframing', rather than 'reconceptualizing', argument in Chapter 3). Henceforth, it will be assumed that post-traditional realism (qua the conception in this book) certainly contains an involuntary belief-that component.

The mission of this chapter will be to defend the location of post-traditionalism as a variant of (I). To do this we will need to explore each of these four types of 'faith' and, in particular, highlight the number of possible variants of each of them. This will help to defend the possibility and the plausibility of post-traditionalism as a variant of faith classically conceived, namely *involuntary 'belief-that' and voluntary 'belief-in'*. With that being said, the layout of the chapter will proceed as follows. There will be four sections, with each focusing on one of the four types of 'religious faith'. For each faith-type I will do three things: (1) give a brief description in light of the presence or absence, and voluntary or involuntary nature of its belief components; (2) provide some examples of that faith; and (3) suggest whether or not this faith is representative of post-traditionalism, and why.

Beginning with section one on (I): *involuntary 'belief-that' and voluntary 'belief-in'*, I will suggest that this type of faith is most commonly associated with traditional religious realism.

However, to demonstrate not only the number of ways that 'involuntary belief' can be interpreted, but the number of ways that this faith can be understood, we will focus on the broader question on the nature of belief and ask, 'What does it mean to have belief?' In answer to this question, we will explore two interpretations of involuntary belief-that.

The first will include three *propositional* analyses of belief: one non-religious account from Hume, and two traditional, religious accounts from Swinburne and Plantinga. The second will include two *dispositional* analyses: one non-religious account from Gilbert Ryle, and one non-traditional, religious account from Wittgenstein. Although dispositional attitudes are often thought of as a sort of 'belief-in' rather than belief-that, I argue that assent to a proposition (belief-that) is demonstrated by virtue of showing certain dispositions. In light of demonstrating the varying examinations of 'involuntary belief-that' and what might be different variants of (I), I will argue that post-traditionalism is also a variant of faith as *involuntary 'belief-that' and voluntary 'belief-in'*, while highlighting the difference between the objective reality ascribed to God by the traditional and the post-traditional realist.

In section two we will look at the second type of faith, that is (II) *involuntary 'belief-that' without voluntary 'belief-in'*; here I will give two examples of different variations of this type of faith, after giving a brief description of its nature. Namely, as a non-committal and unemotional belief that God exists objectively 'out there'. The first variant will come from Aquinas and his understanding of the kind of faith that the devils have about God. Then we will look at a less sensational example from Lily; Lily is an imaginary character who 'cannot help but' believe that God exists 'out there'; however, she does not act on this belief. Thus, Lily is a laxed realist. I will then explain why post-traditionalism is *not* representative of this type of faith. The reason being that the post-traditionalist will have an '*involuntary belief-that*' component to their religious commitment, a component that is absent from (II).

What follows in the third section is a discussion on the third type of faith, namely: (III) *Voluntary 'Belief-that' and Voluntary 'Belief-in'*. I will outline this type of faith, before giving William James's pragmatic approach to religious belief as an example of (III). Then I will explain why I will refer the reader to chapter three of this book (*Can Faith Without Belief Be Meaningful?*) and its exploration into fictionalism, and variants of (III) that look to replace the '*voluntary belief-that*' component with other forms of commitment, such as 'steadfastness' or 'assuming'. I will finish this section by explaining why post-traditionalism is *not* a variant of (III), in view of the fact that the post-traditionalist's '*belief-that*' is '*involuntary*' in nature, thus it would be inappropriate to describe post-traditional religious belief as '*voluntary*'.

Then in the final section we will explore the fourth type of religious faith: (IV) *voluntary 'belief-in' without involuntary 'belief-that'*. I will explain why this position might be most commonly associated with (standard) religious non-realism. The focus of this section will be on what might be two variants of (IV), those being Rudolf Bultmann and his approach from *necessity* (*müssen*), and Richard Braithwaite and his approach from an attitude to storytelling. Afterwards, I will argue that these theologies and their understanding of 'faith without belief' have been carried forward and explored further in more contemporary literature through the work of fictionalism. That is to say, Bultmann and Braithwaite's material can act as a sort of deep background piece on the fictionalism that we will go on to explore. I will end this section by confirming that post-traditionalism is *not* a variant of (IV), and the reason for this is because (IV) does not have the *'involuntary* 'belief-that" component, a definite counterpart to that which constitutes post-traditionalism.

Finally, the chapter will conclude by affirming post-traditionalism as a distinctive variant of (I), thus drawing attention to the involuntary nature of *'belief-that'* and the necessity of adjoining *'belief-in'* 'God'. Moreover, we will have explored what might be four different types of religious faith, located post-traditionalism as variant of faith, classically conceived and clarified what it is that constitutes or 'makes up' not only traditional realism and post-traditionalism realism (I) but also standard non-realism and fictionalism (IV).

Involuntary 'belief-that' and voluntary 'belief-in'

I. *Involuntary 'Belief-that' and Voluntary 'Belief-in'*. I suggest that this best represents (Ia) **traditional realism** and the God of CPT. When the traditional realist cannot help but believe that God (of CPT) exists objectively 'out there' and ascribe a reality that is *'un*conditionally necessary' and 'wholly independent' (*involuntary belief-that*), they choose to worship and trust in this God (*voluntary belief-in*).

The threefold structure of this section will allow us to first get to grips with these two belief components ('belief-that' and 'belief-in') and how they fit together and form religious faith as it is classically conceived. It might be helpful, however, to begin by looking at involuntary 'belief' as it is more broadly considered. Therefore, we will look at Hume's *propositional* account of belief, followed by two accounts of religious belief from Swinburne and Plantinga. Thus, giving two variants of (I). Then we will look at involuntary belief as it is more broadly conceived again as we explore Ryle's *dispositional* account, followed by a brief exploration into Wittgenstein's dispositional account of religious belief (or at least, not strictly propositional). Again, giving another variant of (I), but this time *not* as it is traditionally conceived. Lastly, and in light of having explored numerous accounts of involuntary belief-that from Hume and Ryle, and how these accounts of belief can be found to describe religious belief, by Swinburne, Plantinga and Wittgenstein, we will return to exploring the nature of (Ia). Here

I will explore the similarities and the differences between (Ia) and (Ib) and put forward the argument that post-traditionalism is a variant of classical faith: '*involuntary "belief-that" and voluntary "belief-in"*'.

Hume's propositional account of belief

Philosophical theories concerning the nature of belief can be roughly classified into two groups: those which pertain to the concept of belief as a special sort of mental occurrence, and those who understand belief as a dispositional attitude. Hume is classically referred to as an exponent of the former group.[3] Commentators on Hume's philosophy concerning the concept of belief are often divided on whether Hume thought that 'belief' *can* be defined since he provides a definition in *Treatise*, or whether its nature is too complex[4] which is why we receive a perplexing array of terminology (in both *Treatise* and *Enquiry*).[5]

It is my understanding that what largely connects the numerous and potentially ambiguous commentaries that Hume gives regarding the concept of belief is that, at least to a significant extent, belief is (a) involuntary, (b) propositional and (c) psychological. I will now argue that Hume's account of belief does demonstrate these elements and, thus, draw out the conclusion that his description promotes a psychological, deterministic and involuntary understanding, demonstrative of the complex nature of belief.

Hume's account of the mind is the window into Hume's account of belief. To understand what Hume thought it might mean to hold a belief, we must understand the first distinction (of three) he makes among our conscious mental episodes or 'perceptions'. That is, the division of *ideas* (or thoughts) and *impressions* (or feelings). Impressions are the 'sensations, passions and emotions, as they make their first appearance in the soul',[6] that is, the first appearance of basic emotions or feeling and bodily sensations. Ideas, by contrast, are 'the faint images of [impressions] in thinking and reasoning';[7] namely, they are pale copies of 'lively and vivid' impressions.[8] For example, seeing the colour red and the feeling of anger are impressions, but the *memory* of seeing the colour red and feeling angry are ideas, as they are secondary to the primary impression.

The second distinction Hume makes branches off from his conception of ideas, namely ideas of the memory and ideas of the imagination. The latter, then, breaks down further still, into the final distinction: ideas of the *fancy* ('imagining' or 'mere fiction') and ideas of *judgement* or *beliefs*. What separates beliefs from 'mere fiction' is a difference of *assent*, or what we would call the subjective confidence or degree of belief, and beliefs hold a stronger feeling of assent than fiction.

Thus, 'belief' is characterized by the way in which an idea (from an impression) is *conceived* by the individual. For Hume, an idea is static; that is to say, two people can share the same idea, but it is how the idea is conceived by the individual that dictates whether the idea *ascends* to the status or feeling of belief. If the idea is felt strongly by the agent, specifically possessing a particular felt quality or a special feeling that intensifies the idea, then *this* is what qualifies a belief, and, therefore, what makes it differ from an 'incredulity' (i.e. 'disbelief' and/or merely to 'entertain an idea'). Hume sometimes refers to this feeling that enlivens an idea as *sentiment*.

Sentiment is the passion that enables the mind to know what it believes, and what is believed is what causality and experience have led it to believe. Thus, Hume's 'sentiment-based' epistemological approach to 'beliefs' suggests that they are involuntary insofar as beliefs have 'more force and influence', appear of 'greater importance' and are 'the governing principles of our actions'.[9] Beliefs can and do actuate the will, to the extent that many of the 'basic' beliefs that the majority of people hold are propositional, and at the same time involuntary. Beliefs such as these:

- There is an external world, which exists whether we perceive it or not.
- Some events are caused by other events.
- We are, in any sense, the same person today as we were yesterday.
- In the simplest inferences from our experience to the predictions about the immediate future.[10]

Hume describes belief to be 'more properly an act of the sensitive, than of the cognitive part of our natures',[11] confirming Hume's account that beliefs are involuntary, propositional and part of the inner mechanics of our human nature. Moreover, Hume's theory is highly deterministic.[12] He presents 'belief-that' as something in which the individual makes little conscious contribution. To that extent, 'belief-that' is defined as something that 'happens to us', rather than something we are constantly seeking to ascertain. It is a process of our past experiences being triggered by a present impression and raising the idea into a belief through their feeling of 'force and vivacity'. In other words, the whole process is automatic: 'impressions in, mechanism whirrs, beliefs out', Edward Craig describes Hume's theory in this way, as a 'somewhat primitive psychological theory'.[13]

With this in mind, we can now understand why Hume has been celebrated as a proponent of 'Occurrence Analysis'. The Occurrence Analysis of belief is the more traditional understanding of belief, and its chief claim is the analysis of assent. The Occurrence Analysis will say that what we assent to is a proposition: something that is true or false. And to assent to a proposition is more than just merely entertaining an idea; it is an inner inclination to commit to the idea (over another idea perhaps), and it is how one conceives the impression. Furthermore, belief is a mental occurrence.

Hume says that fiction is powerful. It is indubitable that the imagination is vigorous and colourful. So much so, in fact, that it can inhibit one's ability to distinguish truth from falsehood. Fiction can have the 'same influence as the impressions of memory, or the conclusions of judgement, [it] is received on the same footing, and operates with equal force on the passions'.[14] But, there *is* a crucial difference. And, again, the difference will come down to *sentiment*. How we tell the difference between belief and fiction is not a result of faith or applying some a priori standard, but a feeling or sentiment resulting from examining the situation. It is our experience of the situation that helps us to determine the difference between fiction and belief.

It is no surprise, then, that mistakes can happen; that belief can be mistaken into believing what turns out to be fiction. But Hume's position is that 'fictions cannot be believed and remain fictions'.[15] In addition to the difference in sentiment, Hume also identifies a difference when it comes to the voluntary/involuntary nature of beliefs and ideas of the fancy. As we have established, Hume understands (justified) belief as *involuntary* in its nature. On the other hand, it is possible for an idea to be *voluntarily* assigned to fiction:

> The mind has authority over all its ideas, it could voluntarily annex this particular idea [of reality] to any fiction and consequently be able to believe whatever it please; contrary to what we find by daily experience.[16]

Further,

> the difference between fiction and belief lies in some sentiment or feeling, which is annexed to the latter, not to the former. . . . Whenever any object is presented to the memory or senses, it immediately, by the force of custom, carries the imagination to conceive that object, which is usually conjoined to it; and this conception is attended with a feeling or sentiment, different from the loose reveries of the fancy.[17]

In summary, Hume's account of belief is of an introspectable happening: a justified occurrence that is propositional, involuntary and can be understood through an examination into the psychology of human nature. Hence, Hume is often identified as an occurrence analyst. Another contemporary philosopher who also attempts to unpick the concept of involuntary belief as propositional is Swinburne, but this time in the context of religious belief. Thus, by exploring Swinburne's account, we will be exploring one variant of (I) from the classical, philosophical theistic tradition.

Swinburne's propositional account of religious belief

In many ways Swinburne's account of belief is similar to Hume's, but there are also some key differences. Apart from the obvious difference that Swinburne's account is used to describe traditional *religious* belief, Swinburne's account is less 'deterministic' and more a question of degree. Similarly, however, Swinburne's analysis of belief also depicts 'belief' as an involuntary mental act, but Swinburne's account is given in terms of *probability*. That is to say, Swinburne treats 'belief' as a matter of logical probability rather than psychological contingencies. Thus, at the heart of Swinburne's notion of what it means to believe is 'epistemic probability'. That is, to measure the extent to which evidence renders a proposition likely to be true. We will begin by exploring Swinburne's secular account of belief, before seeing how it relates more explicitly to religious belief, and importantly as a variant of (I).

Swinburne regards belief as a 'contrastive notion', meaning that one believes *this* proposition as against *that* alternative proposition.[18] Within his concept of belief, there exist the following two core elements: (i) the concept of believing so-and-so (i.e. that 'today is Monday' and 'there is a God'), and (ii) the concept of acting on the assumption that so-and-so (i.e. that today *is* Monday and that there *is* a God).[19] So what is it to believe that today is Monday? And, that there is a God? It is here that Swinburne demonstrates his argument from probability: that the primary concept of belief is to believe so-and-so is *more probable* than such-and-such.

The first core element (i) dictates that so-and-so is *more probable* than such-and-such. In other words, '*S* believes that *p*' entails '*S* believes that *p* is more probable than not -*p*'. If S^{20} thinks that *p* (so-and-so) is more probable than not -*p* (such-and-such) then *S* believes that *p*, and not -*p*. *S*'s belief in the former (that *p*) amounts to depending on the latter (that not -*p*). In other words, you believe in one proposition as against another proposition since the former is more probable than the latter.

The second element (ii) is also part and parcel of Swinburne's very definition of belief. That being, to believe something is to act in accordance with or for that something. It is within *S*'s interest, says Swinburne, to fulfil their purpose or to carry out the proposition. That is to say, belief has consequences for action. To the extent to which nothing will count as belief unless it is compatible with the way in which the believer seeks to realize their purposes. Ultimately, Swinburne's account of belief is this: belief is an 'inner attitude towards propositions which is manifested in action and often evidenced by public criteria, but which may exist independently of its manifestations and of evidence shown in public behaviour'.[21]

This account of belief, especially this particular account given in 1981, faced an array of praise, as well as criticism. Philosopher William Alston gave a rather critical response to *Faith and Reason* (1981), finding it 'untenable'.[22] For Alston, Swinburne's reliance on probability to define belief is largely problematic. The ability to evaluate probabilities, to the extent to which various propositions are rendered more or less probable, is not an ability or a skill that all persons possess, affirms Alston. Comparative probability judgements are too sophisticated for many believers.[23] Swinburne took Alston's feedback seriously and altered his account of belief.

Hence, the original definition altered from the 1981 definition: 'believing in so-and-so is *more probable* (or more likely) than believing such-and-such',[24] to 'believing so-and-so *as against* such-and-such'.[25] This is the definition given in the second publication (2005). This 'watered down' description removes the concept of probability from the very definition *itself*, thereby removing the claim that probability is at the very centre of what it means to believe.

It becomes clear, however, as one reads Swinburne's *Epistemic Justification* (2001) (another significant publication that looks into the nature of belief), that the application of probability filters all the way down through Swinburne's theory of belief. And, we can see this by looking at the points that we have just touched upon, namely matters of negation and matters of action. In the first instance, if we were to take the revised definition of belief (believing in so-and-so *as against* such-and-such) Swinburne immediately follows this statement by stating that usually the normal alternative with which a belief is contrasted is its negation (as we saw earlier).[26] For example, the negation of a proposition p is the proposition not -p or 'it is not the case that p'. From these two instances, probability, as a way in which to help define the concept of belief, is clearly at the centre of Swinburne's understanding of the very nature of belief.

In terms of belief as involuntary, Swinburne defines propositional belief as an 'involuntary responses to experiences of the world or apparent truths of reason, or to evidence in the form of other propositions which seem to make the belief probable';[27] moreover, a person cannot *choose* what to believe in any given circumstance; rather, 'believing is something that happens to someone, not something that [one] does'.[28] Otherwise referred to as the Occurrence Analysis.

Swinburne does, in fact, refer to Hume and establishes how he agrees with his account, and where their differences lie, namely that what Hume 'does not bring out is that [belief] is a logical matter, not a contingent feature of our psychology. For if my arguments so far are correct, then a person believes that p if and only if he believes p over against not -p because he believes that his evidence supports p rather than not-p'.[29] We will now explore how Swinburne's propositional account of belief plays into his account of *religious belief*, and, more specifically, as a variant of (I). To do this, then, we will also look at the second component, namely 'voluntary belief-in'. What it means to have *involuntary belief-that and voluntary belief-in* is to have belief in and to trust in God through one's belief that, not only does God exist, but God is Almighty and all loving and should, therefore, be trusted in. Hence, belief (that God exists objectively 'out there') *with* faith (in the goodness of God and the power of orientating one's life towards this goodness). Swinburne defends theistic belief that God exists and finds it equally reasonable for the believer to claim trust in God based on their 'belief-in'. He draws this conclusion from different standpoints that we have belief in God because God is *more probable* than not.

Swinburne makes the distinction between believing that a certain proposition is true and believing *in* certain propositions. The distinction lies, he says, in the difference between believing that something is true, which he identifies as 'belief-that', and to trust, to rely on and to have faith *in* something, which he identifies as 'belief-in'. Faith, then, is a matter of 'belief-in'. Swinburne says that this is demonstrated by the Creeds of the Church, which always start with 'I believe . . .' or 'We believe in . . .', not 'We believe that . . .', because it is through these proclamations that one is declaring one's trust *in* God and the Church.

The voluntary aspect of 'belief-in' is shown through Swinburne's asking: 'If you are uncertain of whether there is a God or not, is it sensible to put your trust in God?' Swinburne says, yes. He uses a similar argument to Plantinga to suggest that it is more than reasonable to believe that God exists, but it is important to put one's trust in God. Thus, faith, or 'belief-in', is voluntary to the extent that 'belief-in' is a secondary belief after 'belief-that'. It is not necessary but it is important for a well-rounded belief. The Christian who has trust and faith in God will *want* to and *will* wholeheartedly believe in the almightiness and loving nature of the God who works in favour of humanity, and will act accordingly.[30]

Confusingly, Swinburne does state, repeatedly, that 'belief' tout court is an 'involuntary state',[31] and we cannot help but hold the beliefs that we do at any given time. However, Swinburne also proposes that the best kind of faith is 'rational faith'. Rational faith is described as when an agent pursues a 'religious way which is good to follow and the best one to follow given the different probabilities on the agent's evidence, obtained after adequate investigation, that the creeds of different ways are true'.[32] This seems to suggest that religious faith involves some decision making which does not 'just happen' involuntarily. Furthermore, Swinburne claims that to exhibit faith is to act on an assumption,[33] and may be compared to various actions which may be said to be rational. Thus, a faith will be rational to the extent to which 'it begins to approximate to that ideal rational faith'.[34] Now I will give a final propositional account of involuntary belief-that by Plantinga, thus also giving a second variant of (I), also from classical philosophical theism.

Plantinga's propositional account of religious belief

Plantinga, much like Swinburne, defends theistic belief that the perfect God of CPT exists and finds it equally reasonable for the believer to claim trust in God based on their 'belief-in'. However, unlike Swinburne who draws this conclusion from probability, Plantinga's notion is that to have belief *in* God, the believer will also have an involuntary belief *that* God exists, and that this belief is 'properly basic'. Plantinga makes the distinction between 'belief-that' and 'belief-in' by defining belief-that as simply accepting a certain proposition as true, namely that there is such a being as God. Belief-in, however, describes the intimate relationship between an agent and God, where the agent is '*trusting* God, accepting God, accepting his purposes, committing one's life to him and living in his presence'.[35] The believer will see the love of a family, the greatness of mountains and the surging ocean as gifts from God, for example.[36] Thus, believing in God is an additional element to the propositional component of belief-that God exists.

That being said, it follows that one must hold true the propositional belief that God exists, if one is to also believe in any additional characteristics or subcomponents of God pertaining to 'belief-*in*'. Plantinga explains this by suggesting that it is impossible to believe that God created the mountains and the seas and the love between people (additional characteristics or subcomponents of God) if one's belief-that God exists is not married to a belief-in God's all-loving nature. The idea that 'belief-in' requires 'belief-that' is referenced in the New Testament, 'He who would come to God must believe that he is and that he is a rewarder of those who seek him' (Heb. 11.6).

Plantinga identifies *faith* in the Calvinistic sense as a *cognitive* state or activity.[37] However, it is not merely a cognitive state or activity, because it also involves the affections and the will of the agent. Faith is, then, *at least* cognitive. It is also a matter of 'knowledge' and, thus, involves believing in propositions about God's benevolence. And, so, the 'propositional object of faith is the whole magnificent scheme of salvation God has arranged'.[38] This belief is *more* than simply believing that there exists a being called God. Moreover, for Plantinga, to have faith is to believe that there *is* such a scheme but also, and most importantly, to believe the scheme to be personal and available to *me*; that Christ died for *my* sins and it is, therefore, possible for *me* to be reconciled with God.[39] Faith, as a matter of knowledge, means that faith is not like 'a leap in the dark'.[40] Rather, because the subject has sure and certain 'knowledge', and is convinced of what she reads in the Gospel, there is no leap in the dark. More than that, faith is not an 'involuntary' or 'unwarranted' act; instead, Christian belief is rational and warranted and, by extension, somewhat voluntary.

Plantinga stands by the idea that 'belief-that' can be translated as a certain type of knowledge and can therefore be warranted; he does not argue that 'belief-in' God (or 'the greatest things of the gospel') has 'warrant' because, although he thinks that theistic and Christian beliefs can indeed have warrant and are *true*, Plantinga denies having the ability to show their truth by way of arguments that commend themselves to everyone.[41] Therefore, belief in God is (to this extent) a voluntary belief, insofar as belief in God, for example, cannot be argued for in the same way as 'belief-that', but is nonetheless strongly 'adopted' by believers as part of their overall belief system. We will now explore another way of understanding involuntary belief-that, that is, as a dispositional attitude, and we will explore this position through the work of Ryle, and later as a variant of (I) from Wittgenstein.

Ryle's dispositional account of belief

The dispositional analysis promotes the concept of belief as an attitude; the attitude of holding a proposition as true, or thinking it to be the case. Thus, beliefs are considered to be propositional attitudes, insofar as, if an agent believes something, they will bear a certain attitude towards the proposition (i.e. the attitude of 'holding to be true'). Moreover, the dispositional analysis will assert that for someone to believe some proposition *p*, that person must possess one or more particular behavioural dispositions pertaining to *p*. For example, 'Mary believes that *p*' is a dispositional statement about Mary, and this is equivalent to a series of condition statements describing what Mary would be likely to do or say if *p* were to arise.[42]

But, before we further explore this account, you may be thinking at this point, what difference does it really make which of these two analyses of belief – if either – is the correct one? Who cares whether Mary's belief about *p* is describing a mental occurrence or whether it is, in fact, a dispositional statement about Mary? But, in order to demonstrate the variation of how 'involuntary belief-that' can be construed, and, thus, how many accounts of religious belief can constitute faith as *involuntary 'belief-that' and voluntary 'belief-in'*, it might be helpful to ask: 'What kind of statement is: "Mary believes that *p*"?'

Ryle in his *The Concept of Mind* (1949) challenged the Occurrence Analysis of belief and the view that belief is a mental event. Instead, Ryle argued that much of what passes as mental is best construed as *dispositional* in character. Rather, the former account of belief as a private, even 'ghostly' 'occurrence', 'happening' or 'episode' can be given dispositional analysis. Thus, many of our ordinary psychological concepts should be construed as dispositional in nature.[43] Purposely avoiding references to internal states and occurrences, Ryle defines belief as a determinable and dispositional verb (like the words 'know', 'aspire' and 'clever').[44] It was thought that one's belief(s) could be located inside the agent's 'secret grotto' or mind, but Ryle stresses that this is mistaken.[45]

Believing or 'to believe' does not take place in some type of 'limbo world', says Ryle.[46] But, 'to believe that' describes a propensity to make certain theoretical, imaginative and executive moves or decisions, as well as to have certain feelings. And, all these elements hang together on a 'common propositional hook'.[47] By this Ryle means that to believe is more than to act 'as if' one has knowledge of something (e.g. that the ice on that lake is dangerously thin), but it also propels the agent to act and think differently about the affair (to skate wearily). The dispositional analysis of belief, demonstrated through Ryle's account, undermines the former analysis by doubting the secrecy or special character of the mind.

To explain this, Ryle says that not only is 'belief' a determinable and dispositional verb, but it is also a *tendency* verb (describing a person's disposition towards something) and, in this way, it is also in the family of 'motive words'. Thus, belief answers those *why* questions: *why* does *x* do so and so?[48] To this end, Ryle argues that the mind is not a 'secret grotto' to which only the keeper has privileged access, so its former status as a 'queer place' with special priority ought to be dispensed with.[49] Belief is, however, still somewhat an involuntary act, as both the occurrence analyst and the dispositional analyst cannot help but act according to their feelings towards the propositions or situation that the proposition or situation arises in them.

Is there an account of *religious belief* that pertains to a dispositional account of belief? One might argue that Wittgenstein's approach to belief in a religious context coincides with a dispositional analysis.

Wittgenstein's dispositional account of religious belief

Chon Tejedor tracks Wittgenstein's early treatment of religion (and ethics) from his *Notebook 1914–1916* to his altogether different approach in the *Tractatus*. Tejedor draws our attention to Wittgenstein's move towards religiosity, namely a move away from the view that religiosity is conditioned by a transcendental subject and, instead, endorses an understanding of the religious attitude as non-transcendental. This shift, Tejedor argues, is reflective of a dispositional attitude (rather than emotive): one that is bound up in language, thinking and action, and yet, at the same time, ineffable.[50]

Opening her account with the following quote from Ryle – 'To impart propositions without giving their justification is to try to persuade, not to try to teach; and to have accepted such propositions to believe, not to know' (Gilbert Ryle, 'A Rational Animal' (CP II, 428)) – Danièle Moyal-Sharrock makes a similar case, that Wittgenstein's non-propositional attitude to belief is reflective of his ruling out of the kinds of belief which characterizes one's 'unquestioning attitude', that is, one's religious attitude as a *propositional* belief.[51]

D. Z. Phillips also seems to depict Wittgenstein's approach to religious belief as dispositional, as he quotes him in his essay 'On Really Believing' on the practical implications of theoretical belief.[52] He mirrors Wittgenstein's understanding of the complex relationship between the following two matters. The first, denying that religious beliefs are logically independent of religious actions and relevant affective attitudes. And, on the other hand, both he and Wittgenstein appear to be implicitly assuming the logical independence of these things when talking.[53]

Through our discussion of two types of involuntary belief that from a *propositional* analysis (with Hume) and a *dispositional* analysis (with Ryle) I hope to have demonstrated three things. The first is to show the various ways that involuntary belief-that can be construed. The second is to illustrate how different types of faith that might otherwise be placed in opposition (namely, Swinburne and Plantinga's traditional account of faith and Wittgenstein's non-traditional account) might, nevertheless, *all* be considered variants of faith as: '*involuntary "belief-that" and voluntary "belief-in"*'. Third, and what I will do now, is to argue that there is another variant of (I) that ought to be discussed, and that is post-traditionalism.

Difference between traditional belief and post-traditional belief?

If we can go back to the descriptions of (Ia) and (Ib) I gave, the reader will notice a difference in the language used to describe the kind of objective reality ascribed to 'God'. With the former describing the reality as '*unconditionally necessary*' and '*wholly dependent*', and the latter: '*conditionally necessary*' and '*semi-independent*'. As a quick caveat, remember that in each case the conception of God that is ascribed to these kinds of realist realities is different. With the traditional realist ascribing the former reality to the perfect God of CPT, and the post-traditionalist ascribing the latter to their distinctive, minimalist conception of God as 'that-than-which-a-greater-cannot-be-conceived'.

Focusing on the former first of all, what exactly does it mean for God's existence to be considered 'unconditionally necessary' and 'wholly independent'? The traditional realist understands the nature of God's reality (or God's existence) as not only necessary, in the sense that God could never have *not* existed, but that God would have existed even if the world was not the way that it is. And, 'wholly independent' suggests that God's existence is not only independent in the sense that God exists independent from human persons and their beliefs, values and feelings, but that God would have existed whether or not humanity existed. So, what about the post-traditionalist's nuanced version of these conditions?

The post-traditional realist understands the nature of God's reality as necessary, in the sense that God certainly exists, but they refrain from suggesting that God's existence is *un*conditionally necessary; rather, they argue that God's existence is conditionally necessary. This means that they hesitate to suggest that if the world *had* been different, God would certainly have existed. They argue, instead, that God's necessary existence is in some distinct way conditioned by our human existence. And, what I mean by '*semi*-independent' is that rather than adopting the stronger strain of '*wholly* independent', the post-traditionalist will (only) want to say that God exists independently from us human beings insofar as God was not 'invented', but God's existence is, in some distinct way, tethered to us. That is to say, the post-traditionalist will not stake the claim that God would have *definitely* existed if humanity did not exist.

As these qualified terms (of 'conditionally necessary' and 'semi-independent') are crucial for understanding the position in conceptual space that post-traditionalism is gesturing towards, and to confidently know the difference between 'full-blown' realism and this distinct type of minimal realism, it is important that we go into a little more detail. Particularly as these terms will be the focus for Chapter 6, when the book will draw an analogy between the ontology ascribed by the religious post-traditionalist to God (qua a suitably qualified version of Anselm's formula) and the sui generis but very real ontological space that some mathematical realists ascribe to abstract mathematical objects (such as numbers, sets and functions). Let us begin with God (qua a suitably qualified version of Anselm's formula) as 'conditionally necessary'.

It might be helpful to compare unconditionally necessary truths to contingent truths. An example of an unconditionally necessary truth is '1 + 1 = 2', to deny that '1 + 1 = 2' implies a contradiction as such truths of reason have an absolute or metaphysical necessity. Moreover, said truths hold across all possible worlds. For the traditional religious realist, to deny that God (of CPT) as unconditionally necessary is metaphysically paradoxical. It is the case, on the contrary, that God exists in all possible worlds.

On the other hand, contingent truths are conditionally necessary, such as 'King Harold II was defeated in 1066'. Given that, in this case, the individual monadic substance (King Harold II), of whom the truth is predicated on (that he was defeated), *exists*. To deny such truths does not lead to a logical contradiction; however, these conditionally necessary truths do imply some other proposition from which it logically follows. Such truths do not hold in all possible worlds as the 'condition' on which the conditionally necessary truth supervenes on might not exist in all logically possible worlds. The question now is: 'How does this link to religious post-traditionalism?'

The post-traditionalist's understanding of God as conditionally necessary reflects the belief that God might not exist in all logically possible worlds but, rather, God supervenes on *something* that is contained in this world and all other possible worlds like this world. What is the 'condition' on which God might supervene? Perhaps frustratingly, the post-traditionalist does not claim to know the 'condition' on which God supervenes. What can be said with confidence is that God might be conceived of supervening on something that exists in the actual world (including human minds), and all other possible worlds like this one. That is not to say that the post-traditionalist denies that God is independent, nor are they able to confirm it. Nor are they able to say that God is dependent on human minds. Rather, they are querying the difference.

This is all to say that, for the post-traditionalist, God irreducibly supervenes on a whole possible world which contains human minds, but it cannot be known for certain which part of the whole world (including human minds and that which is encountered through the human mind) God supervenes on. Thus, exercising epistemic discipline and humility is an essential part of post-traditionalism, particularly when responding to the enquirer of that which God supervenes on, which might be met with the following response, 'what I say I am saying and beyond that I do not wish to confirm or deny more'. Put another way, the exact 'condition' on which God supervenes cannot be identified without assuming or claiming to have more knowledge than is accessible.

The notion of 'conditional necessity' is acknowledged in the literature, and we can refer to the following analogies. The first is given by Brian Leftow in his *God and Necessity* when he talks about the following paradigm case. A certain gravitational force which exists between the Earth and the Moon is necessary *given* the laws of nature, but not unconditionally so, since those laws could (in some logically possible world) have been different. The analogy here is that the post-traditionalist would say that God exists necessarily *given* the way the world is (including the existence of human minds) but not unconditionally so, since the world could have been different (in some logically possible world).

A further example might be drawn from non-naturalistic accounts of morality. Morality is not unconditionally necessary (in every possible world) but this world, and other possible worlds like it where there are human minds, there is morality. That is not to say that morality is dependent on minds, nor is it to say the contrary. It is to say that given the way that this world is with human minds (and all possible worlds like ours) there exists morality.[54] The final analogy that I will draw, and will be more fully explored in the sixth chapter of this book, is from the philosophy of mathematics. Some realist mathematicians will say we did not 'invent' numbers, but in a world unlike this one (including the absence of human minds) would numbers exist? We cannot be sure. Let us now turn to the second qualified term, 'God' (qua the Anselmian formula on my account) as 'semi-independent'.

At first glance, God described as 'semi-independent' sounds like an outright contradiction. To say that *x* is independent of *y* is to say that *x could* have existed in the absence of *y*. To say that *x* is dependent on *y* is to say that it *could not* have existed in the absence of *y*. There is, surely, no third possibility here. The question is, then, what is 'semi-independence'? If it means that God is *both* independent of *and* dependent on us, then this is logically inconsistent. If God was not created by us, there is no reason at all to suppose that God came into being at the same time as us or will go out of existence at the same time as us. So, what is being suggested to avoid this contradiction? To answer this, we will compare the views of traditional realism to post-traditional realism on the matter of dependence.

The traditional realist will make (at least) the following two claims about God (of CPT) when it comes to God as 'wholly independent'. The first is that God was not simply 'invented', and the second is that God is entirely, fundamentally, ontologically independent from, not only the attitudes of intelligent agents (e.g. believing in Him) but the very existence of intelligent agents (and their language, thought and practice). The post-traditional realist agrees with the traditional realist that God was not 'invented' by human persons and is thus committed to the weaker vein of the classical ontology that God is, therefore, (mind-) independent (in some sui generis way). However, the post-traditionalist will not wish to commit to the stronger vein of the ontology and agree that, therefore, God is entirely, fundamentally, ontologically independent from intelligent agents. Instead, the post-traditionalist adopts a weaker ontology which will not claim much more other than to agree that God *exists* and God *was not simply 'invented'*. They cannot commit to the stronger ontological claim without assuming too much.

It is worth highlighting the fact that the reality ascribed to God (minimally construed) by the post-traditionalist is *'semi'* independent and not *'quasi'* independent, and that there is a reason for this specific qualification. The reason being, '*quasi*' can often describe an 'as if' kind of reality, and this is *not* the type of existence that the post-traditionalist suggests that God has. Which is to say that the post-traditionalists do not ascribe a kind of 'as if' reality to God; 'as if' God exists in some kind of mind-independent reality; 'as if' God has some kind of 'real' existence. Rather, the post-traditionalist *does* believe that God exists in some kind of mind-independent reality and has a *real* existence. Thus, insofar as '*quasi*' implies 'as if', it would be inappropriate to use this term of qualification, therefore I use '*semi*' instead.

In both cases, that is, (Ia) and (Ib), it is the second part of their nature, namely the additional characteristic that 'thickens' the ontological commitment, that the post-traditionalist is hesitant to commit to. Therefore, they nuance the nature of the reality, thereby ascribing a less 'weightier' ontology. We see this as the necessity of God's existence goes from being '*unconditional*' in nature to being 'conditional', as the post-traditionalist avoids making the commitment that *God would have existed even if the world was not the way that it is*. We also see this as the independent nature of God's reality goes from being 'wholly' independent to being '*semi*' independent, and this is because the post-traditionalist holds a 'lighter' ontology, which does not commit them to the idea that *God would have existed whether or not humanity existed*.

Moreover, this nuancing '*involuntary "belief-that"*' as it is classically construed by the traditional realist demonstrates how and why post-traditionalism (its conception of God) is a variant of (I). Furthermore, faith as '*involuntary "belief-that" and voluntary "belief-in"*' is not a one size fits all. Rather, as we have seen, there are different variants of this type of faith, including faith from classical philosophical theism, and, as I have argued, post-traditionalism. The post-traditionalist 'cannot help but' believe that God exists (*involuntary 'belief-that'*) and choose to actively engage with God (*voluntary 'belief-in'*). We will now move onto the second section of this chapter, as we focus on the second type of 'religious belief'.

Involuntary 'belief-that' without voluntary 'belief-in'

II. *Involuntary 'Belief-that' Without Voluntary 'Belief-in'*. This might correspond with a type of unconcerned and neutral assent to religious truth claims, such as what Aquinas calls 'the devils' faith'. That is, a 'cannot help but' belief that God (of CPT) exists objectively 'out there' (*involuntary belief-that*), but they do not adjust their life according to this belief-that (*without voluntary belief-in*).

In this section we will look at (II), and two variants of faith as '*involuntary "belief-that" without voluntary "belief-in"*'. One from Aquinas and his understanding of the kind of faith the devils might have, and a less sensational account of a 'cannot help but' belief that God exists from Lily the laxed realist, who is, as we remember, an imaginary character who holds an involuntary belief-that God (as *at least* that-than-which-a-greater-cannot-be-conceived) exists objectively 'out there' but she does not often think on nor act on this belief. On this account, I will draw a clear distinction between Lily's 'cannot help but' religious belief' and Polly the post-traditionalist's 'cannot help but' religious belief. When engaging in God-talk Polly (another imaginary character) takes these statements about God to refer to a real, mind-independent being minimally construed.

First of all, let us clarify what this type of faith looks like. Perhaps it might be helpful to compare it to (I). The difference between (I) and (II) is that the latter does not include a 'faith' element, insofar as faith, here, pertains to having 'belief-in' God. Thus, another way to describe (II) might be '(religious) belief without faith'. What I mean by this is that this type of religious belief is *not* life altering, in the sense that the believer does not necessarily orientate their life in acknowledgement of, or in favour of their sure belief that God does exist in some objective reality. That is to say, their involuntary belief that God exists 'out there' does not lead them to meaningfully engage with God. In order to better grasp this type of faith, I will now present 'the devils' faith' as a variant of (II).

Aquinas and 'the devils' faith'

The Thomist account of faith features a discussion of this particular type of faith as *involuntary belief-that without voluntary belief-in*. It is important to note that for Aquinas, this is a denatured and disordered type of faith, and it is not his main account of it. That said, for our purposes here, we will focus on Aquinas's description of (II), and not his own account of faith which is different.[55] Thus, to have 'belief-that', according to Aquinas's discussion on (II), God exists without 'belief-in' any additional characteristics of God. This kind of religious belief has been presented in the following way: 'with one addition and two qualifications, to have faith in God is simply to have belief-that, to believe that God exists'.[56]

The *one addition* which Aquinas adds to faith as 'belief-that' is this: that one must also believe *certain other propositions as well*, such as what God is like and what acts God has performed. The *first qualification* is: that *'belief-that' does not amount to scientific knowledge*. That is to say, for Aquinas, that faith is a form of mental certitude about absent realities that cannot be qualified through scientific enquiry.[57] The *second qualification* is: that faith as 'belief-that' *is not intrinsically meritorious*. By this Aquinas means that faith as simply 'belief-that' is not religiously virtuous because it is not a faith formed by love or charity. Nevertheless, it *is* possible to have faith without testifying other propositions about God. Aquinas called this 'the devils' faith'.

'The devils' faith' is *involuntary belief-that without voluntary belief-in*, or faith as simply 'belief-that'. This 'faith' is formed because devils have enough true beliefs about God to hold 'belief-that' God exists, and Aquinas acknowledges the devils' 'belief-that' as religious faith. The Letter of St James is quoted by Aquinas, which he interprets to suggest this type of faith: 'You believe that God is one; you do well. Even the demons believe – and shudder.'⁵⁸ However, according to the second qualification of his account (faith is not intrinsically meritorious), 'the devils' faith' is *not* a meritorious faith. A meritorious faith is another type of faith that Aquinas speaks of, namely the 'true', religious faith (henceforth, *ideal* faith). That is, faith that will be rewarded with salvation. The 'faith of the devils' is not meritorious for two reasons.

The first, as we have mentioned, is that it is not formed by love or charity but, rather, Aquinas writes that 'the devils' faith' is, so to speak, forced from them by the evidence of signs. The second concerns the nature of 'belief-that', namely whether it is a voluntary or involuntary matter. The faith of the devils is based on *involuntary* 'belief-that', and according to the Thomist view, this type of faith cannot be valuable. In order for faith to be meritorious, it must come about through *voluntary* 'belief-that' God exists.

However, the 'faith of the devils' is interesting. Aquinas *does* recognize the devils' 'belief-that' as equivalent to a type of religious faith, but not as the *ideal* faith. The *ideal* faith is formed by a *voluntary* decision to believe in other propositions about God (such as, what God is like and what acts God has performed) on the grounds that God has revealed them. 'The devils' faith', in contrast, is forced upon the devils by the evidence of signs and, thus, not in any way to the credit of their wills.⁵⁹ Aquinas concluded that the devils could have faith in God but, because it is *involuntarily* formed by signs to evidence and not from love or charity, it is not the *ideal faith*. Faith as 'belief-that' is not the *ideal* faith in which one can expect salvation. Now we will move onto the second variant of (II): Lily's 'cannot help but believe that'.

Lily the laxed realist

Imagine that Lily is totally convinced that there is a God (because of *x*, *y* and *z*),⁶⁰ but as a result of Lily's conviction that God exists, she feels in no way compelled to 'live-out' this belief by following and trusting in this God. She does not have a particular attitude towards God, nor does she feel a compulsion to act on her 'belief-that'. Lily defines her religious faith as *involuntary belief-that without voluntary belief-in*. One reason why Lily chooses to identify her religious commitment as 'belief without faith' is because she is not convinced of the Christian doctrine (for example) on life after death. Sometimes, Lily thinks that there might be some type of afterlife, but she does not draw upon Christianity to tease out her curiosity. It is simply *that*; a curiosity, that she does not spend a lot of time thinking about. Moreover, for Lily, possible belief of some type of afterlife does not act as an a priori element to her religious commitment (the reason for her 'belief-that' God exists), nor does it act as an a posteriori element to her religious faith (compels her to have 'belief-in' God). Rather, Lily believes that God *exists* but she does *not* believe in any additional elements that may come with 'belief-in' God.

Is Lily's faith plausible? Aquinas would say no. Lily and Aquinas agree that 'belief-in' is *voluntary*; however, Aquinas argues that 'belief-in' defines 'true' religious faith, but Lily disagrees and bases her faith solely on her belief that God exists. To summarize, Aquinas would deny the plausibility of Lily's religious faith because it is not a faith formed by love nor by evidential signs of God's existence, and therefore it must rely on 'belief-in', which it doesn't. Thus, Aquinas thinks that this is a possible position but disordered; it is certainly not proper faith. For Aquinas, faith as simply 'belief-that' is 'the devils' faith', and since Lily is not a devil, Lily's faith is not a true religious faith.

However, is it possible that Lily's faith *is* plausible? I think we can answer 'yes' to this question, to the extent that religious faith as 'belief-that' is not inherently contradictory *if* one does not believe in any 'additional characteristics' of God or any 'extensions' of the Christian faith. That is to say, Lily's faith is plausible if it can be described as something along these lines: a 'cannot help but' type of belief that there is some kind of divine reality or being, but this belief does not significantly impact or alter Lily's life, to the extent that it does not inform her decision making, nor does she attend to practices, or reflect on this belief very often.

Difference between Lily the laxed realist and Polly the post-traditionalist?

The reader might be wondering at this point whether Lily's religious belief sounds similar to that of the post-traditional believer. I suggest that they are not the same, and to demonstrate why I will compare Lily's 'cannot help but' religious belief to Polly's 'cannot help but' religious belief.

What do they have in common? Both Polly and Lily have an 'involuntary belief-that' 'God' exists. In other words, Polly and Lily are equally convinced that there exists an objective 'God' somewhere 'out there', beyond the contours of our minds. But, do they hold the same conception of God? I suggest that Lily is more likely to hold a traditional conception of God, whereas we know that Polly has a distinctive minimalist conception of God as 'that-than-which-a-greater-cannot-be-conceived'. However, as we saw with (I), it is possible for Lily and Polly to be described as holding different variants of the same type of faith if their conception of God is different. Ergo, this is not a contributing factor to my argument that Polly does not hold (II). Rather, *it is what Polly does with her certain belief that God exists* that separates her faith from Lily's religious belief.

Although you might not find Polly in church, for instance, with the traditionalist realists (and some fictionalists), she will, in quiet, reflective moments when she might seek guidance or grief counselling, connect with God and draw strength on the knowledge that there exists something good, something that is greater and more mysterious than she. This is where she directs her 'belief-in'. You are even less likely to find Lily at church, maybe at a Christmas and an Easter service as part of a cultural or family commitment. Lily is not particularly interested in furthering her belief that God exists; her belief does not lead her to a state of curiosity about whether engaging with God would be beneficial for her, in the sense that Lily is less likely (than Polly, Reginald the realist and Fiona the fictionalist, who we will meet later on) to indulge her certain belief that God exists. The reasons for this (I am hesitant to say lack of curiosity) might range anywhere from once having 'belief-in' and finding it be to be 'less than fruitful' or 'unrewarding', to simply feeling that she is too busy, with work, childcare, and so on, to explore what a full-on committed religious life might offer.

It is at this stage that we might find that we have offered a response to an important question for this investigation, namely, 'Why is belief-in *not* all that matters?' However, we will later find two well-established variants of faith *without involuntary belief-that*, and for whom voluntary belief-in *is* all that they 'have'; it is what constitutes their 'faith'. Do we want to say that their faith does not 'matter' or that it is not genuine? This question of what makes for a 'genuine' faith will come up again and again in this book, but for now I wish to say the following on the question about whether belief-in is all that matters in regard to the types of faith that we have looked at: (I) and (II).

For the traditional realist and the post-traditional realist, belief-in is *not* all that matters; rather, it is a combination of belief-in and involuntary belief-that. Whereas for the devils, and for Lily (and for those who might identify with Lily) belief-in might be all that matters, insofar as they feel no major obligation, desire, necessity or want to delve deeper into their belief that God exists 'out there'.

The type of faith that we will explore now, (III), will add an interesting dimension to how we respond to this question, as it does include a 'belief-that' component to its account of faith as well as a 'belief-in' component, *but* its 'belief-that' component is *voluntary* in nature. Will adherents to this type of faith respond to this question differently to those who adhere to (I)? We shall find out now.

Voluntary 'belief-that' and voluntary 'belief-in'

III. *Voluntary 'Belief-that' and Voluntary 'Belief-in'*. Such a commitment might depict William James's 'Will to Believe' (a pragmatic argument for the adoption of a belief without prior evidence of its truth). Thus, more broadly, it might describe when the will chooses to believe that God (of CPT) exists objectively 'out there' (*voluntary 'belief-that'*), and one also chooses to live according to this truth (*voluntary 'belief-in'*).

Previously we have looked at (I) and (II), both of which have an 'involuntary 'belief-that'' component, in other words, a 'cannot help but' belief that God (however construed) exists. Now we will turn to a type of faith where this 'belief' component is *voluntary*. This means that the believer 'chooses', for lack of a better word, to believe that God (usually the God of CPT) exists objectively 'out there'. That is to say, for whatever reason, this realist attitude is not innate or visceral for those who hold (III).

For instance, the lack of 'evidence' for the existence of God (whatever this evidence may be) does not stifle the believer and refrain them from believing that God exists. They are, in fact, willing to take the 'risk' and believe anyway, because the potential gains from belief are so large.

Thus, it is an epistemological 'weighing up' of whether or not to believe-that God exists 'out there'. Not only this, but to make the decision whether to also believe-*in* God by engaging with this God and religious discourse. Moreover, we might say that those who pertain to (III) live 'as if' God (of CPT) exists 'out there' ('*voluntary "belief-that"*') and that it is worth participating in religious practice ('*voluntary "belief-in"*').

To get a better handle on this type of 'faith', I will give a brief presentation of what might be one variant of (III), namely James's account of pragmatic theism, before stating why post-traditionalism is *not* a variant of (III).

James and 'The Will to Believe'

There is a simple argument for the conclusion that it is wrong to believe that God exists, and it goes something like this:

P1) There is no evidence that God exists.
P2) If there is no evidence that God exists, it is wrong to believe that God exists.
C) It is wrong to believe that God exists.

The first premise of this argument is highly controversial, and many people (particularly traditional realists) might argue that there are copious amounts of evidence that prove the existence of God: evidence from prayer, from Scripture and so on. But if we can put this question aside, important though it is, and focus on (P2), and ask whether it is true that 'If there is no evidence that God exists, is it wrong to believe that God exists'?

There was a famous interchange on this topic in the nineteenth century between William Clifford, who believed that belief without evidence is immoral, and William James, who believed that it is sometimes acceptable to believe without evidence. Let us briefly look into Clifford's argument for (P2), before I offer James's defence of 'religious belief without evidence' and his adjoining account of faith as a possible variant of (III).

As a critic of religion, Clifford's most famous topic on whether evidence is needed for genuine faith can be found in his work, 'The Ethics of Belief'. It is here that Clifford illustrates his ethical stance on this argument (supra) with a story, which goes something like this: the owner of a ship knows that his ship is rather old, and worries that it is no longer seaworthy. However, through fear of the cost of repairing the ship, the owner manages to convince himself that the ship is in perfectly good working order. Thus, as the ship leaves the harbour he has no concern about whether the ship is in good condition. However, the ship is not in good condition, and on its voyage, it sinks and takes its passengers with it.

This story demonstrates, for Clifford, that 'it is wrong always, everywhere, and for anyone, to believe anything upon insufficient evidence'. It is the ship owner's fault that the passengers died, he says; his belief that the ship was in good condition was not justified, and he should not have believed otherwise. Clifford used this story to motivate his attack on religious beliefs, writing with all the pomposity of a Victorian moralist: imagine a religious person who stifles doubts about his faith, the life of that man is one long sin against mankind.[61]

In response to this and in a famous paper called 'The Will to Believe', James gave his own story to defend his counter-argument that it is OK sometimes to believe without evidence. Here is a Jamesian-style example of an instance where belief that something is true without evidence is OK. In the final round of a job interview, Amy (the candidate) needs to take an unseen examination that she cannot prepare for. Amy has no evidence to suggest that she will do well, as she has no idea what will come up on the examination. However, in spite of this, she chooses to believe that she will do well. This is because she knows that if she can convince herself that she will pass, she will be more relaxed and the examination will go more smoothly. In this case, it would seem to be a good idea for Amy to make herself believe that she will pass the examination if she can, at least it does not seem that it would be wrong for her to do this. James used stories like this one to cast out on Clifford's claim that it is always wrong to believe something without evidence. And he carried this over to his account of *religious* belief.

James's theory of religious belief can be understood as 'managing risk'. That is to say, for James, the nature of belief-that is 'voluntary' insofar as he insists that only each person can themselves 'weigh up' whether belief-that (and belief-in) God is a 'risk' that they are willing to take. It is a risk on the basis that there is no conclusive evidence for God's existence. Moreover, according to James, it is all about 'managing risk': by believing that God exists you risk believing a falsehood, if you refrain from believing that God exists you risk missing out on a truth. Ergo, it makes sense for some people to believe that God exists even in the absence of evidence simply because the possible gains from belief are greater. Furthermore, I suggest that James's account of faith here is a variant of (III), namely *'voluntary "belief-that" and voluntary "belief-in"'*.

To round up this third section on (III) I will explain, although it might be clear by this point, why post-traditionalism is *not* a variant of (III). There might be four differences to highlight, three in relation to the nature of 'belief-that' and one on the second belief component, namely how 'belief-in' is 'lived out'. The first is that the post-traditionalist does not ascribe an objective reality 'out there' to the perfect God of CPT as the traditional realist does, but rather to a distinctive minimalist conception of God. I argue that those who hold (III) are more likely than not to ascribe an objective reality to the classical conception of God instead. The reason being that their belief-that is based on the potential benefits of taking a 'risk' that God's existence is true, and the factors that contribute to this 'weighing up' will, arguably, be looked for in Scripture, testimonies of answered prayers, and so on.

This brings us onto a second difference. If the holder of (III) is more likely to 'voluntarily' believe that the perfect God of CPT exists, then they will be ascribing a reality to God that is 'wholly independent' (God would have existed whether or not humanity existed) and *'un*conditionally necessary' (God would have existed even if the world was *not* the way that it is). Comparatively, as we know, the post-traditionalists adhere to a less 'weighty' ontological thesis, as they ascribe a reality to (their conception of) God that is, instead, '*semi-*independent' (God's existence is, in some distinct way, tethered to us) and 'conditionally necessary' (God's existence is true insofar as the world is the way that it is).

Third, the post-traditionalists 'involuntarily' believe that God exists in this sui generis reality, whereas it might be better described as a 'voluntary belief' in a (probably 'thicker') divine reality for those who adopt (III). In the sense that it is not strictly speaking a 'cannot help but' kind of belief, and more of a rational, responsible, responsive, prudential or practical willingness to believe that.

The fourth difference in relation to the second belief component, 'belief in', is this. Although it is the case that both those who pertain to (Ib: post-traditionalism) and (III) believe in the goodness of God and the benefits of engaging with God, the way in which each religious believer will 'live out' and 'practise' their faith (belief-in) differs. The latter will most likely have adopted the belief that the perfect God of CPT will, thus, engage in Scripture, prayer and religious discourse to show their trust in God. Or, they will dive into these texts and practices if and when they seek guidance, perhaps. Whereas, the former (the post-traditionalists) might perform prayer-like practices, enter into meditative-like states and even communicative in some way with God, all by way of 'tapping into' a divine reality, but their understanding of who God is and what belief in (their conception of) God can offer them is different from classical philosophical theism and the omni-God.

We will now turn to the final section of this chapter on what might be a fourth type of faith. We will look at the nature of what it means to, again, (voluntarily) believe in the goodness of God and the benefits of engaging with God (however conceptualized) *without* believing that God exists in some kind of objectively reality.

Voluntary 'belief-in' without involuntary 'belief-that'

IV. *Voluntary 'Belief-in' Without Involuntary 'Belief-that'*. This might be the (IVa) **standard non-realist** type of commitment (and maybe even religious agnosticism). Insofar as it might describe when a person chooses to actively and positively engage with religious discourse and God (a nuanced version of the CPT conception) (*voluntary 'belief-in'*), but they do not believe that this God exists objectively 'out there' (*without involuntary belief-that*).

It also represents the (IVb) **fictionalist** type of commitment, as it describes a person who chooses to actively and positively engage with religious discourse and God (of CPT) (*voluntary 'belief-in'*), but they do not believe that God exists objectively 'out there' (*without involuntary belief-that*).⁶²

It is in this final section that we will return to an earlier question: 'Why is belief-in *not* all that matters?' I suggested that belief-in is *not* all that matters, as it is our mission here in this chapter to locate post-traditional realism which we know has an 'involuntary belief-that' component. However, I said that we will later find two well-established variants of faith *without involuntary belief-that*, and for whom voluntary belief-in *is* all that matters; it is what constitutes their 'faith'. And do we really want to say that their 'faith' is not genuine? I suggest that we will not, given that we will explore, here, two well-known theologians and their well-respected accounts of faith that, arguably, could be described as 'faith without belief' or *voluntary 'belief-in' without involuntary 'belief-that'*. Bultmann and his approach to faith from *necessity (müssen)* and Braithwaite and his account of faith from having a certain attitude to story-telling have pioneered this type of faith (IV) as they speak of religious belief, or faith, in such a way that believing in God is not about holding any such propositions at all. That belief in God is not necessarily in conjunction with the belief that God exists in any traditional sense.

We will explore each theologian in turn, in the hopes of demonstrating, more specifically, how their material acts as a sort of deep background piece on the fictionalism that we will go on to explore in great detail later in the book. This type of faith – *voluntary 'belief-in' without involuntary 'belief-that'* – can be found in more contemporary literature in accounts on religious fictionalism. At the end of this section, I will explain why post-traditionalism is not a variant of (IV).

Bultmann and his approach from *necessity (müssen)*

Bultmann explains⁶³ that when we talk 'of God' we are *not really* talking 'about God' as we think we are. For as soon as we attempt this style of speaking, in which God (*Gegenstand*) becomes an object of thought, God has been lost. The true reality 'of God' cannot be reached through asserting propositions about God, and since 'belief-that' entails that the believer holds certain propositions about God, Bultmann suggests 'belief-that' is not the way to God. Persons who hold positions concerning God's way and reality do not understand the true reality 'of God'. Therefore, it makes no sense to move from 'belief-that' (based on a false understanding that we can speak 'of God') to 'belief-in' God. Instead, when we speak about God, we must understand that we are really talking *about ourselves*. In fact, 'if it be asked how it is possible to speak of God, then it be answered, only by speaking of us'.[64]

Moreover, to have 'belief-that' God exists is to take a position about God, as if God were apart from us. God, then, that is God's existence, becomes 'a thing' towards which we can develop an attitude. But, 'God is nothing *toward which* something or other can be undertaken', says Bultmann, for God is w*holly other* (to the human person, but over and beyond).[65] Thus, for Bultmann, faith is *voluntary*, but what of faith as '*belief-in*'? Bultmann says that 'faith can only be the affirmation of God's acting upon us' and, arguably, this means that 'belief-in' God is the only type of belief or faith that we can have, '[w]e *know* nothing of God; we *know* nothing of our own reality; we have both only in faith in God's grace'.

Keen to preserve the religious values of the Christian faith that remain *after* any and all supernatural elements are discounted, Bultmann stresses that faith cannot arise from 'belief-that', for example by any historical warrant. Instead, faith can only rise through *voluntary 'belief-in'* the *kerygma* (proclaimed message) in the Gospels. It might be said, then, that Bultmann's account of faith represents faith as *voluntary belief-in without involuntary belief-that*. Insofar as, he does not think believing certain propositions about God can lead to true faith. Rather, it is our free choice to 'believe-in' God and through our acceptance and embracing of our human finitude, we can show obedience to God through '*necessity*', that 'compels thee' (*tua res agitar*).[66]

Braithwaite and his approach from an attitude to story-telling

Similarly, Braithwaite did not equate religious faith with 'belief-that'. Rather, Braithwaite[67] suggests *voluntary 'belief-in'* God, insofar as religious beliefs are a person's individual, or a religious community's, intention to *behave* in a particular way. Thus, the importance lay with acting 'as if', and not asserting 'belief-that'. Moreover, Braithwaite was not looking to defend the 'truth' or 'reasonableness' of religious beliefs. Instead, he was interested in the problem of *meaningfulness*. That is to say, as we have seen before with the accounts of 'belief' with or without 'faith', Braithwaite has changed the focus and asks: 'What *meaning* can religious beliefs hold in the face of scientific methods for meaning?'

He found that religious beliefs could not be 'tested' by the classic trichotomy of methods. Religious assertions cannot be examined through *empirical facts* (part of the definition of God is that God is not directly observable), *scientific hypobook* (religious statements cannot be about the actual world but also irrefutable in any possible world), nor can they be *logically necessary statements* (for this would not allow them to make any assertion of 'existence').[68] To get around this problem, then, Braithwaite treats religious assertions like *moral* assertions. In that, by still implying *empiricism* but in a way that a statement 'need not itself be empirically verifiable, but that it is used in a particular way is always straightforward empirical proposition'.[69]

Moral assertions are used to express 'an *attitude*' of the person making the assertion.[70] They are not used to assert the proposition that the agent *has* an attitude; rather, it is to show forth or evince the agent's attitude. Thus, the theory is more *conative* than emotive. Braithwaite applied this to his theory of religious belief. Religious belief, then, is '*given by its use in expressing the asserter's intention to follow a specified policy of behaviour*'.[71] One's intentional or *voluntary* behaviour is based upon a basic set of wants, and the only way to define a universal (or '*typical*') definition of religious belief is 'to specify the form of behaviour which is in accordance with that one takes the fundamental moral principles of the religion in question'.[72] Of course, what one person (or one's religious community) deems as 'fundamental' will differ from others, due to different wants. Therefore, Braithwaite identifies a set of fundamental moral principles as the 'story' or set of stories.[73] A *story* is a set of empirical propositions. There is the Christian story, the Buddhist story and so on. Therefore, we must add a second element to the definition of religious belief: a '*religious assertion will, therefore, have a propositional element [. . .], in that it will refer to a story as well as to an intention*'.[74]

It is apparent at this point that the Braithwaitian account of religious faith does not endorse 'belief-that', but what about *voluntary belief-in*? Here the situation is different, as Braithwaite insists that 'belief-that' is *not* essential for religious faith, but he also suggests that 'belief' tout court is not necessary for religious faith to have *meaning*.

> [I]t is not necessary, in my view, for the asserter of a religious assertion to believe in the truth of the story involved in the assertions: what is necessary is that the story should be entertained in thought i.e. that the statement of the story should be understood as having meaning.[75]

Moreover, religious faith is not about *involuntary* 'belief-that' statements that are strictly 'true' but, arguably, it is about some type of *voluntary* 'belief-in' the powerful nature of religious statements. So much so, that they fulfil a role that only a meaningful *story* could invoke. Braithwaite says two main things. The first: religious beliefs are, rather, 'assertions' or 'convictions' and not 'beliefs', as such, because he found 'nothing which can be called "belief" in the sense of this word applicable either to an empirical or to logically necessary position'.[76] Hence, his account is being called here *faith without belief*. The second is his argument that the importance and influence of fiction literature upon life has not been given 'sufficient weight' by theologians and philosophers of religion.[77]

Now that I have hopefully demonstrated how Bultmann's and Braithwaite's account of faith might be considered a variant of (IV), and an early indicator of what fictionalism will later come to offer those without 'involuntary belief-that', I will address a question that the reader might, rightfully, have at this point.

Conclusion

In this chapter we have explored what might be four different types of religious faith; identified the two components that 'make up' that faith, namely 'belief-that' and 'belief-in'; given a couple of examples of this particular type of faith; and then suggested why post-traditionalism is or is not (or can or cannot) be represented by that type of faith. To very briefly summarize, we said that post-traditionalism is a variant of faith as it is classical conceived, namely '*involuntary "belief-that" and voluntary "belief-in"*'. The nuanced form of (I) that the post-traditionalist holds can be identified by the following alterations:

1) Their conception of God is a distinctive minimalist conception of God (and not the God of CPT).
2) The objective reality ascribed to (their conception of) God is '*semi-*independent' (rather than 'wholly independent').
3) The objective reality ascribed to (their conception of) God is 'conditionally necessary' (rather than '*un*conditionally necessary').
4) The way in which their belief-in is 'lived out' is through less structured and organized forms of engagement (although it might include such engagement) and is more likely to include personal moments of reflection.

I also paired our religious commitments offered in the previous chapter with a type of religious faith offered in this chapter:

- Traditional realism: (Ia) *involuntary belief-that and voluntary belief-in*.
- Post-traditionalism realism: (Ib) *involuntary belief-that and voluntary belief-in*.

- Standard non-realism: (IVa) *voluntary belief-in without involuntary belief-that.*
- Fictionalism: (IVb) *voluntary belief-in without involuntary belief-that.*

What we have found then is that post-traditionalism is a variant of traditional realism, and fictionalism is a variant of standard non-realism. Before we go on to explore fictionalism further, we will now explore standard non-realism through the work of Cupitt.

2

Standard non-realism and the nature of 'God' à la Don Cupitt

The previous chapter ended with an exploration into *'voluntary belief-in without involuntary belief-that'*; we looked at a representative case of this type of commitment with the theological writings of two twentieth-century theologians. Bultmann suggests that 'belief-that' is not 'the way' to God. God is 'wholly other', so as soon as we ascribe any propositions to God, we 'lose' God. Le Poidevin describes Bultmann as favouring an alternative way of interpreting theological language which effectively 'disavows a traditional conception of talk about God as being, literally, talk about a transcendent being'.[1] Braithwaite's concern with 'meaning' led *him* to suggest that we should treat religious assertions like *moral* assertions.

On the same reading of Braithwaite, Le Poidevin says that what Braithwaite is recommending is 'clearly a non-realist account of religious discourse', because on Braithwaite's proposal sentences expressing 'practical commitments (I undertake to do such-and-such) are not capable of being true or false. If the meaning of religious sentences (or at least, a set of related religious sentences) is wholly given by their use in expressing such commitments, then replacement by a non-religious language without loss of factual content is possible'; thus, his conception of religious discourse is 'an expressivist one'.[2] What I wish to do in this chapter is to continue to explore *'voluntary belief-in without involuntary belief-that'* but through the lens of standard non-realism, specifically Cupitt's account of non-realism. Here is how the discussion will proceed.

The twofold structure of the chapter will allow us to first track a shift in Cupitt's conception of God (thus, in relation to the first axis: a spectrum of conceptions of God) and to identify three phases that can help to map Cupitt's unusual root to the God of CPT. 'Phase one' will mark Cupitt's interpretation of 'transcendence' and how his early philosophy (1970s) sought to tentatively defend the God of CPT. 'Phase two' will demonstrate a shift from Cupitt's strange allegiance to the

God of CPT to then supporting who he believes this God to 'now' be (post-Enlightenment and post-metaphysics), namely the 'God of language'. 'Phase 3' will reveal a further shift away from the CPT conception in terms of what 'God' amounts to, which is, at this even later stage (2000), a powerful idiom. After tracking this move away from the God of CPT and revealing Cupitt's nuanced, and somewhat more 'minimalist' conception of God, we will move on to discuss Cupitt's religious non-realism, in relation to the second axis (a spectrum of religious commitment).

In the second section of the chapter, we will notice that in comparison to Cupitt's ever 'shifting' or evolving conception of God, there is *not* a shift in his religious commitment, that is, 'standard' non-realism. Nor does his commitment to this commitment shift. Thus, we will be exploring the second axis: a spectrum of commitment. I will suggest that Cupitt does not extend this plenitude, this 'imaginative openness', that we will see in regard to the first axis, when it comes to the second axis and his religious non-realism. That is to say, Cupitt does not explore different textures of reality insofar as, for Cupitt, it is either 'this' or 'that': traditional realism or standard non-realism. He appears hamstrung. I will argue that Cupitt does not properly explore fictionalism, in the sense that he does not reflect on the 'weightiness' of a fictional realm in which to imagine God (whether it be his initial CPT conception or a later, more 'minimalist' of sorts conception). I will put pressure on Cupitt and question his lack of explorative methods when it comes to different types of religious commitment and the kinds of reality that are explored within those commitments.

For example, D. Z. Phillips (another twentieth-century religious non-realist), and his arguably more subtle approach to the realism/non-realism debate on the reality of God, asks the question: 'What kind of reality is divine reality?', rather than 'Is God real or not?'[3] The latter might be said to reflect Cupitt's 'this' or 'that' approach. I am in favour of the first question and believe that this should be our approach to discussions on the reality of God. Although this question was certainly on Cupitt's mind, if one looks through his works (certainly from the 1980s onwards) it is evident that ascribing any kind of 'reality' to God is not a priority, nor a concern, for him. Rather, Cupitt sought a philosophy that enabled him to 'keep up with' what is known as the 'linguistic turn' of the twentieth century.

It is not my aim to suggest that unless one ascribes a 'mind-independent' reality to God it is a meaningless type of religious commitment. Rather, I am suggesting that there is something to be said for the 'imaginative' shift that we witness in Cupitt's strange defence of the God of CPT, to him then defending a nuanced conception (in relation to axis one). Compared to a lack of 'imaginative' exploration, perhaps, when it comes to exploring possible conceptual realities that might be ascribed to 'God' (in relation to axis two). By examining Cupitt's static, 'standard' non-realist position, we will look at a crucial impasse that he presents: 'theological realism or religious seriousness?' Ultimately, I will use Cupitt as a springboard for what comes next, fictionalism, and eventually 'post-traditional' realism.

Cupitt's shifting conception of God

The way in which Cupitt addresses God and grapples with the question of what it means when someone says 'I believe in God' or 'I believe in *this* God' changes from his early publication period in the 1970s, to his last publications in the 2010s. It changes as his concept of God changes. It shifts from a central concern about the God of CPT, to a focus on how we ought to accept a more 'minimalist' and purely metaphorical conception of God. This shift is reflected on the first axis (a spectrum of conceptions of God), as his conception is 'plotted' between the God of CPT and the distinctive, 'minimalist' conception of God that this book defends. What we will do in this section is identify moments in Cupitt's philosophy where we can see this shift occurring.

Reflecting on Cupitt's conception of God is of value to this book because, in attending to the shift, it allows us to explore the different possible conceptions on the axis. Cupitt tells us that '[p]eople have been struggling for too long to hold on to a meaning of God which is passing away, no doubt because they think that this meaning is *the* meaning, the only possible meaning'.[4] More specifically, it will help demonstrate why it is that I have placed Cupitt's conception of God 'beneath' the God of CPT and 'above' the distinct, 'minimalist' conception of God. The works that will act as our timeframe 'bookends' will be: *The Leap of Reason* (1976) and *Life, Life* (2003), with a small number of works published between these two publications, including one of his most notorious books, *The Sea of Faith* (1984).[5] A review of Cupitt's works will allow a consideration of the following questions:

- Why is Cupitt's conception of God not the God of CPT?
- Why is it also not the distinctive, 'minimalist' conception that this book defends?
- In what way is it a type of 'minimalist' conception?
- What should our takeaway point be?

We will begin, then, with Cupitt's *The Leap of Reason* and his conception of God as close(st) to that of the classical philosophical conception of God. Two ways that Cupitt demonstrates a kind of adherence to the traditional conception are seen through his exploration of *the ability to transcend* and *his allegiance (of sorts) to 'the-God-who-is-the-Father-of-Jesus-Christ'*. Let us take a look at how Cupitt's treatment of 'transcendence' led him to the understanding of God that is, for him, bound up in the classical philosophical tradition's conception.

Phase one: God (of CPT) in the programme

The fact that modern society is filled with a variety of 'religions, cultural backgrounds, moral and political opinions, and ideologies' tells us that there exists more than one 'programme', Cupitt tells us.[6] A 'programme', he explains, consists of a whole system of 'basic concepts, models and principles, with which we address ourselves to the world, interpret it, and shape our action within it'.[7] And our societies are pluralistic in this sense.

This idea of a web of programmes relates to a specific understanding of God according to specific religious faiths. The Jew talks about the-God-who-has-revealed-himself-through-Moses, the Muslim talks about the-God-whose-prophet-is-Muhammad and so on.[8] They are different specifications of God, otherwise the 'God-in-the-programme'. 'Admittedly', Cupitt says, 'God as represented in the programme is *not* God absolutely, but only a symbolic representation of God'.[9] So it looks as though, at this point, Cupitt wishes to 'transcend' the 'God-in-the-programme' in favour of an 'absolute' conception of God as spirit. But it is not that simple. For it all comes back around. And it is here that we witness Cupitt's allegiance (of sorts) to 'the-God-who-is-the-Father-of-Jesus-Christ'.

The 'crucial distinction' he tells us is: 'between God-in-the-programme, the God of practical, institutional religion, on the one hand; and the God who is pure transcendent spirit on the other'.[10] And although it sounds as though Cupitt wishes for us to go beyond the former conception, he makes the following claim, 'God absolute, God as pure spirit, can be expressed *only by insisting upon the relativity of even the most comprehensive and powerful religious programme*'.[11] God is *not* then purely 'intra-programmatic', in the sense that God as spirit is bound to the programmatic God of the religious system.[12] So we must choose, says Cupitt. We must choose a religious programme that is most coherent to us. And for him, that is Christianity and the God of CPT.

> I accept the one which, as it seems to me, embodies the idea of spirit in its central myths more perfectly than any other, namely Christianity. God represents

himself to men in human form: but in that form he must die, and we with him. The incarnation of God in Christ, and yet the necessity for the death of Christ, epitomizes the ideas I have been clumsily expounding, and has inspired them.[13]

Cupitt in the 1970s, as demonstrated by *The Leap of Faith*, reveals a strange 'allegiance' or 'acceptance' of the God of CPT, insofar as this particular conception of God aligns best with Cupitt's paradoxical understanding of God that 'transcends' the relative nature of our programmes, only to be understood truly from within one's programme. Now, we will move into the 1990s and compare Cupitt's conception of God during this period, namely through a reading of *The Sea of Faith*.

Phase two: The God of CPT *is* the 'God of Language'

As we just read, in the 1970s Cupitt suggests that doctrine, its symbols and wider religious narratives all gesture towards the 'transcendent', but that it is impossible to accurately represent the transcendent because we cannot simultaneously be 'inside' our programme and 'outside' of it. What I will argue now is that in the 1990s Cupitt's work no longer reflects a philosophy built on (a non-realist interpretation of) the foundation of CPT and its conception of God. Rather, it is reflective of an increasing influence by American thinkers, especially that of Mark C. Taylor and Richard Rorty, and through them French thinkers, including Jacques Derrida and Gilles Deleuze. Thus, our focus here is to mark Cupitt's unusual relationship with the God of CPT and how he begins to move away from this classical conception of God. This will underline the distinctness of the two axes. That is, one can be quite traditional (CPT) on one axis, and not the other. We will primarily track this shift through the death of God movement and the linguistic turn.

For Cupitt it is simple: after the Enlightenment God as a 'higher power' belonging to a 'higher world' was exposed to be an impossible truth, God had been brought 'down to earth' and became *our* God.[14] And so, God's prime reality was altered from a reality 'out there' to our reality 'down here'. But, 'down here', where does God exist? What is our prime reality here on earth? *Language*, Cupitt believes, is our prime reality. Therefore, it is through language that we must come to understand the nature of God in our post-Enlightment era. The 'linguistic movement' in the twentieth century saw the pioneering of French linguistic philosophy with philosophers such as Foucault and Derrida. This critical look at theology from the perspective of linguistic philosophy fostered the notion that there is more than one way, namely the traditional realist way, in which to interpret the nature of God.

Cupitt was inspired by these thinkers. He believed that Foucault signified the importance of the Enlightenment and how it 'recentered the culture upon the finite human subject', and that Derrida contributed to the *de*-centring of mind as independent from secondary influences, namely upon words and other signs.[15] Cupitt's own account of how language and theology are inherently interconnected is as follows. We must come to understand that in the last two hundred years or so it was realized (Cupitt would say that it is already understood) that we human beings invent our own language and that we ourselves are the makers of our knowledge. So, what happened in the early nineteenth century to cause this shift? It was 'the death of God', says Cupitt, the death of the (realist's) metaphysical God of CPT. Thus, for Cupitt, our language or vocabulary surrounding God changed. God-talk began to describe a nuanced conception of God and *not* the God of CPT existing 'somewhere else' (in fiction perhaps). We began to speak about a God who 'works for us', in a post-Platonic, post-metaphysical world. And so, the God of CPT became 'the God of language'.

What we see here is a shift from a strange and complex allegiance to the God of CPT to a defence of what Cupitt believes the God of CPT has become after the 'death of God'. Namely, the 'God of language'. When the old metaphysical God dies, we ought not to keep the God of CPT frozen in time, existing within a fictional world for example. Instead, we ought to alter this very conception of God, because it affects how we interpret the world. Thus, traditional God-talk and its Platonic vocabulary should be(or 'has been', Cupitt would insist) adapted to fit in with our post-Enlightenment worldview. For instance, traditional characteristics of the God of CPT, such as 'Creator' and 'Judge', morph into non-metaphysical attributes and become words which represent *our* view of the world, and what God means to *us* in our particular point in history. Which means that the 'religious object [the God of CPT] may be called life, or may be symbolized as the God of language'.[16]

What we can see here is that, for Cupitt, that which God is totally bound up in our use of everyday and religious language, and our view of the world. Thus, God (the 'God of language') is something like an endless-outpouring. A 'fountain of linguistic meanings that wells up within us and pours out through us on to our world'.[17] This does not exactly sound like the God of CPT. So how are we to understand the 'God of language'? The 'God of language', Cupitt tells us, is a 'dying god who continually pours himself out into communication, not minding what people make of him'.[18] Notice that Cupitt is not saying that it is through language that we communicate and actualize our thoughts and so God is best communicated and actualized *through* language. Rather, Cupitt is saying that God *is* language; that is to say, 'God' *is* a word.[19]

In the second instalment in the trilogy, *The Meaning of It All* (1999), Cupitt explores a range of idioms about 'it', 'it all' and 'everything' (107–118).[20] In the book Cupitt confirms his belief that 'the old realistic metaphysics is dead. . . It no longer carries us up to anything Above us', and a 'consequence of this is that the relation to God has been brought down into the present moment and this world'.[21] Furthermore, what we see in the 1990s are what Cupitt purports to be the most important new idioms about life plotted against the traditional doctrine of God to show to what extent we have transferred the religious focus from God to ordinary *life*. And this becomes all the more apparent as we move into the next decade.

Phase three: Life *is* God

The value of tracking these shifts in Cupitt is heightened even more so as we reach 'phase three' of his continuous nuancing and reconceptualizing of the God of CPT, as we witness a real turn away from those traditional omni-characteristics pertaining to the classical apprehension of God.

What we find in *Life, Life* for example, published in 2003, is a less 'religious' conception of God (coming away from omni-characteristics) and a more generic conception, in the sense that it could perhaps be described as (a type of) 'minimalist' conception. By this I mean that Cupitt presents 'God' as a powerful *idiom*.

Life, Life contains a collection of hundreds of new phrases, noting the overwhelming reference to the word 'life' as the replacement for 'God' and as a new religious object. For Cupitt,

> in our colloquial language practices the 'supra-natural' has died out and has been dispersed into the ordinariness of our lives. We often take recourse to such phrases like 'wrestling with life', 'loving life' or 'having faith in life', which have over time established themselves as standardised expressions through which we have consciously or half-consciously transformed God into the encompassing notion of 'life'.[22]

So what exactly does Cupitt mean by 'life' and how does it relate to 'God'?

Cupitt believes that 'life' is 'simply, everything'.[23] He argues in *Life, Life* that 'the whole of our worldview, our religion, and our morality are currently being reorganized around the idea of life'.[24] By this he means that the way in which we talk about 'life' in ordinary language is becoming more and more reflective of the ways in which we 'used to' (past tense, as Cupitt have it) talk about God through religious language – that is, 'faith in life', 'the call of life', 'life is what you make it'. Some two hundred and fifty life-idioms are listed in this work.[25] 'The new religion of life is simply of *this* life.'[26] Thus, Cupitt's philosophy of language reinforces his religious non-realist philosophy; that is, a non-realist move away from the God of CPT will eventually lead you here. And where is 'here'? To the understanding that '[t]he world and life are one'.[27] He quotes Tolstoy's *War and Peace*: 'Life is everything, Life is God.'[28] So, we know the ways in which 'life' is markedly similar to God, according to Cupitt's non-realism, but how do they differ?

The differences between the idiom of 'life' and 'God' 'arise from the fact that the "omni" attributes of God come out quite differently from those of life'.[29] The God (of CPT) 'is *(or was)* transcendent, simple, unmixed perfection, and sovereign of all things; whereas life is finite, temporal, immanent, and all-inclusive'.[30] The result? '[S]aying "Yes" to life is markedly different to saying "Yes" to God.'[31] Why? Because when we say 'Yes' to life 'we say "Amen" to *all* of it as a package deal', whereas those who say 'Yes' to God 'on the other hand, take sides'.[32] What does this mean? It means that they commit themselves to a 'dualistic view of life, at every point choosing this and rejecting *that*'.[33] So, how does our tracking of Cupitt's shifting conception of God emphasize why the first axis (a spectrum of conceptions of God) has the God of CPT 'at the top' of the spectrum and Cupitt's conception lower down towards a distinctive 'minimalist' conception?

One of the major indicators that confirm Cupitt's move away from the God of CPT is his abandonment of the classical omni-characteristics, to the extent that he does not wish to 'keep' these characteristics to describe God even from a non-realist perspective. Instead, he gradually presents us with an image of God that is less and less representative of the classical philosophical tradition and arguably more and more representative of a 'minimalist' conception of God. However, as we know, Cupitt's conception of God also does not match up to the distinctive, 'minimalist' conception that this book defends. Why is that?

Cupitt's point of orientation away from the God of CPT is not towards the distinctive, 'minimalist' conception of God that this book defends because the latter suggests that if God can be described purely as 'that-than-which-a-greater-cannot-be-conceived' then this God must be objective. This is *not* the same as saying that the distinctive, 'minimalist' conception of God is the God of CPT 'post-death', who then becomes a less grandiose, metaphorical ideal. And to what end does God become 'less and less' the God of CPT? Well, for Cupitt, the God of CPT is eventually described as an idiom that has slowly become replaced. His romantic descriptions of God as 'a guiding spiritual star' soon turn to descriptions of a 'word' that has gone 'out of fashion'. Cupitt's conception of God is not an objective God understood as 'that-than-which-a-greater-cannot-be-conceived'. This is the distinctive, 'minimalist' conception of God.

Cupitt's conception of God is arguably 'minimalist' insofar as he does not wish to make any classical claims about the nature of God, including ascribing to any of the omni-characteristics. But the difference between *his* 'minimalist' conception and the conception that *this book* defends is that Cupitt abandons these conceptions as he abandons objectivity and realism. However, the distinctive, 'minimalist' conception does not incorporate the classical omni-characteristics into *its* conception for a different reason. It refuses to 'give up' the objectivity/reality of 'God' (insofar as 'God' is understood to be 'that-than-which-a-greater-cannot-be-conceived'); however, it does mean that it does not commit its adherents to these characteristics if they resonate too familiarly with the God of CPT, which the adherents have most likely found challenging, intellectually incoherent, paradoxical and so on.

We will now move on to the second part of the chapter which will look at the second axis (a spectrum of commitment) and highlight an interesting difference between Cupitt's fluid and fluxive conception of God and his solid and stable commitment to standard non-realism.

Cupitt's unshifting religious commitment

Before we begin it will be useful to insert two caveats in order to clarify what I mean when I suggest that Cupitt's commitment to standard, religious non-realist philosophy is unwavering. When I refer to Cupitt's unwavering non-realist religious worldview, I am specifically referencing Cupitt's academic work and not his personal life journey. Some context might be helpful here to highlight the difference.[34] Cupitt grew up in a not particularly religious household, but began his religious journey at school when he was fifteen; he was confirmed in the Church of England and worshipped regularly. Later, after arriving as an undergraduate at Cambridge University in the early 1950s, Cupitt underwent an evangelical conversion. Despite his association with the evangelicals lasting little more than a year, by the end of second year he decided to seek ordination as a priest in the Church of England.

He was ordained in Manchester Cathedral in 1959, becoming curate in the parish of St Philip's, Salford. He was fully involved in church life while also publishing theological articles. In 1962, Cupitt was invited to return to Westcott House as Vice-Principal (a role which had been previously filled by John Habgood, later Archbishop of York, and Robert Runcie, later Archbishop of Canterbury), and it was quite possibly expected that Cupitt would become a bishop, or perhaps even an archbishop.

While his involvement in academic life became more and more prevalent, including obtaining tenure as a university lecturer in the Philosophy of Religion in the Faculty of Divinity at Cambridge in 1976, he worked on projects with Anglican theologians in the mid-1970s about the incarnation (which led to the publication of *The Myth of God Incarnate*, 1977). But in 1980, with the publication of *Taking Leave of God*, Cupitt argued for what he called 'religious non-realism' according to which religious discipline should be freely adopted on the grounds of its own intrinsic worth and value, and *not* because it is objectively true.

Unsurprisingly, leading church authorities pronounced his religious non-realism as incompatible with holding a priestly office in the Church of England, thus he was privately and later publicly called to resign from the priesthood. Although his official roles within the Church did not fully cease until 2008, the non-realist philosophy that he professed in 1980 did not soften, but continued to rule his philosophy of religion, unapologetically so. Thus, when I suggest that Cupitt's standard non-realism is unwavering, I am referring to his academic work from *at least* 1980 onwards, although what we will see as I make the second caveat is evidence for this religious worldview developed even earlier.

With that being said, the second caveat I wish to insert is that although Cupitt's commitment to non-realism is not fluid and fluxive (compared to his shifting conception of God), this does not 'define' the nature of his non-realist worldview. What I mean by this is that Cupitt's twentieth-century world-order painted by non-realism is not the same picture painted, according to Cupitt, by 'the older European thought, both Greek and Christian', in which 'the world was usually regarded as a fully constituted system with a relatively stable and determined structure'.[35] 'Now the picture is changed.'[36] Cupitt gives us the following description of the current picture.

> The world-order is not fully determined in such a way. . . . Rather, the determination of the world's structure is completed only by human thought and action. A plastic world interacts with a human conceptual framework to gain a finished shape. But there is no finished shape. Instead, there are a variety of possible constructions of reality. . . . The mind which scans the world, and the meanings which the world so scanned delivers up to the mind, are both constantly evolving in tandem.[37]

This description of what Cupitt deems to be an appropriate worldview is from his 1976 work *The Leap of Reason*. Later in his 2003 *Life, Life*, he points us to the painting that captures his philosophical approach to religion or 'life' as he would have it.

> Life, however, is non-realist. Life is not a great ready-made thing out there. Life is ourselves, life is what we make it, life is a buzz that we generate around ourselves. . . . Life is the ceaseless whirling dance of signs in which we are caught up, Nicholas Pousin's *Dance to the Music of Time*.[38]

Thus, although Cupitt's position regarding how religious discourse ought to be interpreted has not changed since the late 1970s/1980s, his non-realist position is reflective of

> a Fountain, constantly outpouring and renewing in a cycle of beginnings and endings, with no origins, Creators or foundations. The Fountain enables us to reconnect with the life-force that inhabits the very heart of Nature [. . .] we look to immerse ourselves in the onrushing stream of life. [. . .] Instead of regarding this life as a journey through a vale of tears towards a future, happier existence in a world of immortal souls, we should seek to live intensely and fiercely until that energy is spent.[39]

Now that I have clarified these two points, this section on Cupitt's position on the second axis (a spectrum of commitment) will proceed, first, with an exploration into a realism/non-realism impasse which he proposed in *The Sea of Faith* (1984). Second, I will talk in a little more detail about non-realism as a philosophical approach and how it challenges the classical religious worldview, and put an emphasis on 'nihilism' (rather than a determined world-order) and 'immanence' (rather than transcendence).

Lastly, I will reiterate why tracking Cupitt's shifting (and unshifting) thought is of value to this book and its twofold aim. That is, to help flesh out what a distinctive 'minimalist' conception of God might look like (and not look like), and to suggest that there is a potentially neglected conceptual space in the current 'spectrum of religious commitments' that might accommodate this distinctive conception of 'that-than-which-a-greater-cannot-be-conceived'. To begin, then, let us look at the realism/non-realism impasse that underpins much of Cupitt's philosophy of religion.

As we discussed earlier the topic of our inability to completely transcend the 'God-in-the-programme' in *The Leap of Reason*, Cupitt suggests that we cannot know God who is pure transcendent spirit. Rather, we only know

God 'in-the-programme', that being the 'Jewish programme' and the-God-who-has-revealed-himself-through-Moses, for example. Cupitt later develops his thinking and says that we now need to choose between two opposing philosophical approaches to interpreting our 'God-in-the-programme'. This is because Cupitt believes that we have entered a mature, philosophical period where the 'objectivity' of God is at the centre of it all, and the 'goal posts' of religious 'realism' and religious 'non-realism' measure the 'seriousness' of one's 'decision'. Hence, we face a realism/non-realism impasse, which Cupitt formulates like this: 'theological realism or religious seriousness?'[40]

As I stated at the beginning of the book, I am dissatisfied with the link made between theological realism and 'religious seriousness'. But before I can make the claim about why I disagree with this impasse, I will present Cupitt's case for why one cannot be both a realist and have a serious religious disposition. To demonstrate the reality of the 'theological realism or religious seriousness' impasse for Cupitt, he compares the conceptions of God held by two seventeenth-century religious scientists, René Descartes (1596–1650) and Blaise Pascal (1623–1662).[41]

Descartes is described by Cupitt as 'a loyal and orthodox Catholic; but the real interest guiding his philosophy was the justification of scientific knowledge'.[42] According to Cupitt's reading of Descartes, there are potentially two ways to interpret Descartes' attempt to 'establish a basic metaphysical framework by pure speculative argument'.[43] In broad brush strokes Cupitt presents the three entities that make up his framework as: (1) the human mind as a spiritual substance; (2) the mechanistic universe of bodies in motion; and (3) God, who guarantees both (1) and (2).

One way to interpret this framework, Cupitt tells us, is to say that it is an orthodox system. However, Cupitt favours a different interpretation, one which indicates that Descartes was 'merely using God to underwrite something else which was much more important to generate from its own resource of a complete science of nature'.[44] Descartes' understanding of the relationship between (1) and (2) represents a common theme in this period, namely the alienation between the mind (non-spatial and thinking) and the world (matter: spatially extended and unthinking). It was important for him to identify this separation for the sake of doing physics.

Comparatively, although Pascal also believed that the individual mind has a certain primacy, this alienation of mind and world was 'terrifying to Pascal from the religious point of view', Cupitt tells us.[45] Pascal was a 'gifted mathematician and experimenter and a man of passionately intense piety', and it was his piety, says Cupitt, that drove his 'repugnance for what he sees a deep lack of religious seriousness in Descartes thought'.[46] He found Descartes's 'coolly instrumental use of God revolting':

> I cannot forgive Descartes: in his whole philosophy he would like to do without God; but he could not help allowing him a flick of the fingers to set the world in motion; after that he has no more use for God.[47]

Pascal's God was more than this. By this I mean, Pascal's God was more than a 'God of reason'. Rather, his God was the God of the Bible, the God on whom we are to bet on with his famous Wager argument. It is the God revealed by Jesus Christ.[48] Pascal's conception of God, then, is one felt by the heart and through Christ, and not deduced by arguments and proofs. Thus, for Cupitt, the question that ought to be asked next is this: 'Is Pascal's conception of God an expressive one or is it an objective one?' In other words, is Pascal's CPT conception of God from realism or non-realism? Cupitt argues that Pascal's commitment to God as revealed through Christ demonstrates a subtle but radical move from a cosmic conception of God to a more human-centred, Christ-centred conception. Moreover, what we begin to see in the seventeenth century, says Cupitt, is a move towards a more internalized conception and the 'beginnings of a tendency to see God *only* in the human Christ'.[49] What does this mean for Pascal's conception of God? Cupitt insists that in order to answer this question, another question ought to be asked. '[T]he real questions have only just begun.'[50]

Does Pascal believe that all that can be said with certainty about God (of CPT) is that when I speak of this God it is done in a meaningful, authentic and powerful way? In the sense that Pascal is not looking for metaphysical support or for 'reason' to be on his side. That is to say, he is not looking 'out there' to confirm what he feels 'in here'. On Cupitt's reading, the 'expectation' or central purpose of Pascal's view of God is not dictated by any externalities but internal confirmation.

To illustrate this idea, Cupitt asks us to consider the deliverance of a Shakespearean speech. 'To suppose that a Shakespearean speech needs to be checked item by item against things out there in reality in order to have meaning is to miss the point.'[51] Rather, the point is to 'express the thoughts, feelings, intentions of their speakers in magnificent metaphors and rhetorical tropes.'[52] It is expressive, not descriptive. So, what does this mean when it comes to Pascal's conception of God as expressive or objective? Cupitt insists that 'Pascal's rejection of metaphysical reason as a way to God leaves him no way of knowing for sure what the objective position is', not only that, but this therefore implies, for Cupitt, that 'it presumably does not matter to him'.[53] This is not the case for Descartes.

'Descartes has in his metaphysics an objective God'; that is to say, his religious language does, for him, correspond to the existence of real objects existing 'out there', including God.[54] The balancing act of his orthodox Catholic faith and dedication to science meant that his conception of God was objective but quite non-religious, insofar as his conception of God was not strictly the God of CPT (or 'the-God-who-is-the-Father-of-Jesus-Christ'). Rather, his God is closer to a 'God of reason'; a God who created the universe and the human mind, and can thus explain why the universe exists and why it is the way that it is, and the 'capacity of human reason to generate from its own resources a complete science of nature'.[55] And so, Descartes's God is certainly an omnipotent God but is not necessarily God as revealed through Christ.

Cupitt defends Pascal's conception to God. That is, the God of CPT insofar as Pascal's conception is wrapped up in some kind of religious non-realism and a non-committal to objectivity. Pascal's conception, rather than Descartes's, is a reflection of Pascal's 'religious seriousness'. This is because Pascal's apprehension of God demonstrates for Cupitt 'a passionate Christian whose whole life is invested in his faith – but he does not have objectivity'.[56] In other words, and to use the vocabulary of this book, Cupitt identifies Pascal as having a non-realist, CPT conception of God, and Descartes as having a realist, non-CPT conception of God. 'Either', Cupitt says, 'you can claim to have an objective God, like Descartes, or you can have an authentic Christian faith, like Pascal'.[57] Cupitt is suggesting here that a CPT conception of God understood from non-realism is the greater camp. 'It is one or the other: take your pick.'[58]

I am unsure as to whether we really do need to 'take our pick'. In fact, I am certain that we do not need to make a decision as to whether one is a 'serious non-realist' or a 'not so serious realist', I am going to say two things about this point. The first is that I disagree that you cannot believe in the objectivity of 'God' and have a serious religious disposition about God, insofar as who it is or what it is that 'God' amounts to might not be the God of CPT for you, but perhaps God is simply 'something greater than ourselves' that exists objectively 'out there' somewhere.

Second, and drawing us back into the focus of this second section of the chapter, this realism/non-realism impasse is demonstrative of the lack of creativity when it comes to exploring different types of religious commitment besides traditional realism and non-realism. Cupitt's lack of engagement with imaginative modes of interpreting the kind of reality a divine reality might be, becomes more apparent if we compare his unwavering non-realist commitment to his constantly evolving conception of God. From the God of CPT, to a more nuanced, metaphorical conception of God as our highest 'ideal', the 'pearl of great price', the highest religious 'symbol', to non-omni 'God' as a powerful idiom, to 'God' as a word to represent 'it all' that has now gradually been replaced by the word 'life'.

To put it another way, if we were to 'transfer' Cupitt's 'this' or 'that' attitude when it comes to religious commitment to his conception of God, arguably Cupitt would represent a fictionalist position. This is because, according to an either–or attitude: either the God of CPT exists objectively (traditional realism) or the God of CPT does not exist objectively (fictionalism or atheism). But Cupitt does not engage in *this* either–or attitude in this instance. Instead, Cupitt presents a shifting conception of God, one that is *not* simply the God of CPT understood from a non-realist perspective (nor is he an atheist). Now that we have explored the realism/non-realism impasse, we will talk in a little more detail about the 'decision' that Cupitt made, the same 'decision' that he encourages us to all make: to choose 'religious seriousness', that is, non-realism.

Non-realism: Nihilism and immanence

One of the things that we see in Cupitt's work in the 1990s is a greater emphasis on 'immanence' and a non-committal attitude to a God who exists 'out there'. What is meant by immanence is the acceptance of the transience of everything around us. In this mode of existence 'we cease to be separate, self-conscious individuals, standing aside from life – which used to be the paradigmatic behaviour commended as the most suitable for the "citizens of heaven" (Philippians 3:20) by Christian culture for centuries, which on its part fit rather snugly with the presuppositions of modernity around objectivity'.[59] Instead, we allow ourselves to be 'catapulted out of our inwardness and now be put adrift in the flux of language-formed events', as one is encouraged to be 'overcome by the awe of transience, savouring it in a religious experience called Lebensgefühl by Cupitt' (this borders on a kind of 'empirical aestheticism', which includes a kind of consent for being lost in love for the world, for the iridescent flux of phenomena and for all of life).[60] He expresses the following thoughts on 'outsideness' in his 1992 work, *The Time Being*.

> Everything is inside. Nothing is hidden, deep or invisible. There is no better vantage point from which our life can be seen more clearly and judged more authoritatively than we ourselves can see and judge it. any imagined external

reality or standpoint, simply as something imagined immediately relocates itself on the inside there isn't any extra Dimension of the human situation.[61]

Hence, for Cupitt there is no 'outside', there is no structure, there is no meaning, for the world is in a state of constant flux, and we ought to embrace its fluidity. Since Plato we have adopted this realist 'habit' of looking to an eternal order of things behind appearances, a dimension of depth, which supported and stabilized our life, our knowledge and our values. But we need to give up 'all ideas of substance, all absolutes and things outside time' and, instead, give in to the meaninglessness and chaos, so that we may truly lose ourselves in the 'flux of life'.[62] There are no external 'forms' (Plato) and there are no objective concepts (Kant). Thus, any uncertainty or ambiguity that could have been read into Cupitt's works from the 1970s regarding the objectivity (or 'spirit' or 'transcendence') of God has surely dissipated now. His philosophical transition from potential transcendence to total immanence discredits any earlier attempts to explore the possibility. Religion (like morality and science) is 'part of the inside'; that is to say, there 'is no metaphysical extra', Cupitt tells us.[63] Religion is 'internal to the human realm. It is its own practice'.[64] So how does this tie into his position on nihilism?

For Cupitt, nihilism or a nihilistic worldview goes hand-in-hand with an inevitable consequence of a postmodern understanding of history and language, and most important a rejecting or 'letting go' of realism. This means letting go of the concept of the Real, for it is not to be found. What is ultimately true for Cupitt is that the universe is empty of essence or substance or meaning. This is because Cupitt sees the world as entirely language-formed and thus inevitably involving distinctions. His non-realist interpretation of salvation, for example, means coping with nihilism by knowing, accepting and rejoicing in the fact that we are contingent and empty and that we must create our own meaning.[65] However, we must embrace this inevitably with open arms and try to adopt the positive attitude that Cupitt has. One must be warned in the same breath however *not* to reify the 'empty, blissful blue Void'.[66] Cupitt tells us to avoid giving into the 'itch in our loins' for a Real self and a more-Real world-beyond.[67] This is it, he tells us. 'We dance away, we disappear into the Whole and are gone.'[68] Now that we have fleshed out Cupitt's standard account of religious non-realism, I will draw this section to a close by putting section one (on Cupitt's shifting conception of God) and section two (on Cupitt's unshifting commitment) in conversation, thereby giving a clear overall understanding of why Cupitt's plot of the graph is where it is (see filled in 'x' on the graph: standard non-realism and Cupitt's conception of God, Figure 4).

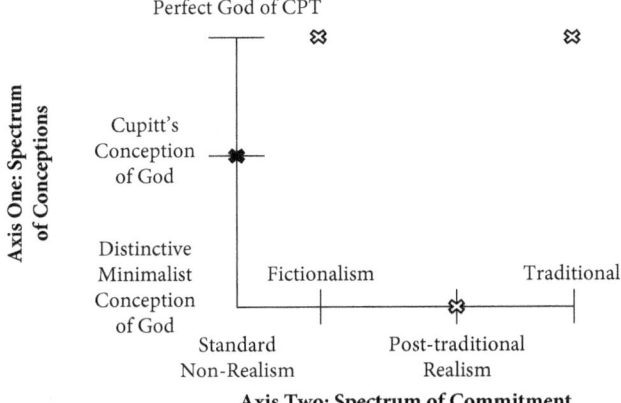

Figure 4 Axis one and two combined and Cupitt's position emphasized. © Jessica Eastwood.

By looking at the graph again it might help to visualize what we have looked at in this chapter. In the first section I suggested that Cupitt's conception of God shifts from the God of CPT to a somewhat 'minimalist' conception of God, insofar as God becomes a guiding 'ideal' and later an old, Platonic idiom that ought to be replaced by the idiom of 'life'. However, Cupitt's later non-CPT conception(s) of 'God' do *not* reflect the distinctive, minimalist conception of God mapped on this first axis. This is because this God is an objective God understood to be 'that-than-which-a-greater-cannot-be-conceived'.

It is also interesting and important to note Cupitt's strange and complex allegiance to classical philosophical theism and its God, from his attempt in the 1970s to retrieve any kind of trance of transcendence, to a speech he gave in 2013 where he professed that 'it's all a great humanly-evolved myth, but it carries precious religious insights and values, and is still the best myth to live by'.[69] Thus, one can visualize Cupitt starting at the 'top' of the axis (the God of CPT) and slowly coming down the axis closer to a 'minimalist' conception, which is why I plot Cupitt's conception of God between the God of CPT and God as 'that-than-which-a-greater-cannot-be-conceived'.

In the second section I suggested that Cupitt's commitment does not shift from a standard non-realist one, therefore this same visualization of 'Cupitt' sliding across the second axis is not the case (as stated previously, in regard to his academic work and personal life since at least the 1970s). That is to say, although Cupitt has been called a 'fictionalist' by some thinkers, I suggest that this does not really encapsulate his (nihilistic) worldview and his shifting conception of

God. Instead, I suggest that the imaginative modes of thinking when it comes to conceptualizing God do not extend to this axis.

To conclude, I wish to comment that I admire what Cupitt did, that is, to open up new ways to understand one's faith. I do, however, feel that I ought to acknowledge a tendency (or a perception of at least) a slight 'flakiness'. By this I mean that over the decades although Cupitt's 'standard' non-realist position has not 'shifted' as it were and this may come across as 'steadiness', his conception of God has wilted, for lack of a better word, as 'God' (of CPT) is reduced to the idiom, 'it all'. I say this because in this book, I hope to also open up new ways to understand one's faith, and to perhaps provide the rigour that one might feel to be lacking in Cupitt's philosophy. But I feel an intellectual and personal inclination to defend Cupitt here and say that with rigour alone, one can miss the lived passion and struggle which Cupitt embodies with an unusual vitality. Cupitt's works have been and continue to be pervasively influential perhaps more so than is widely known, with the following thinkers acknowledging some kind of affinity to his philosophy: myself, Christopher Insole, Robin Le Poidevin, Catherine Pinstock, Clare Carlisle, Dennis Nineham, Gavin Hyman to name a few (see *New Directions in Philosophical Theology: Essays in Honour of Don Cupitt* for more).[70]

As we move on to the next chapter, I intend to use Cupitt as a springboard into the conception of God that this book will defend and the potentially neglected reality that could be ascribed to this God, by putting pressure on his philosophy of religion, in particular the argument that Cupitt does not explore possible textures of reality beyond traditional realism and standard non-realism.

3

Can faith without belief be meaningful?

In Chapter 1 we focused on the second axis as we looked at different conceptions of 'belief' and 'faith'. In particular, we looked at two types of belief: 'belief-that' and 'belief-in', their relationship and whether these beliefs are held voluntarily or not, or even held at all. The following four types of 'faith' were given:

I. *Involuntary 'Belief-that' and Voluntary 'Belief-in'*.
II. *Involuntary 'Belief-that' Without Voluntary 'Belief-in'*.
III. *Voluntary 'Belief-that' and Voluntary 'Belief-in'*.
IV. *Voluntary 'Belief-in' Without Involuntary 'Belief-that'*.

I then suggested which type of faith each of the four commitments might pertain to:

- Traditional realism: (Ia)
- Post-traditionalism realism: (Ib)
- Standard non-realism: (IVa)
- Fictionalism: (IVb)

In this chapter, we are going to traverse (right) along the second axis as we move from 'standard non-realism' to 'fictionalism' and explore *voluntary belief-in without involuntary belief-that* but, this time, as it is construed by the fictionalist (Figure 5).

In doing so we will focus on the following question: 'What, if anything, is lost when one does not have involuntary belief-that?' And subsequent questions, specifically in relation to what it is that variants of (IV), including fictionalism, can offer those without 'involuntary belief-that', such as: 'Is faith as *'faith without belief*, meaningful?' 'Is it 'worthy' of being called 'faith' at all?' Before we continue, I would like to briefly interject and insert a caveat. In this chapter, and throughout the book, I will use the phrase 'doubting realist'. What do I mean by this? I suggest

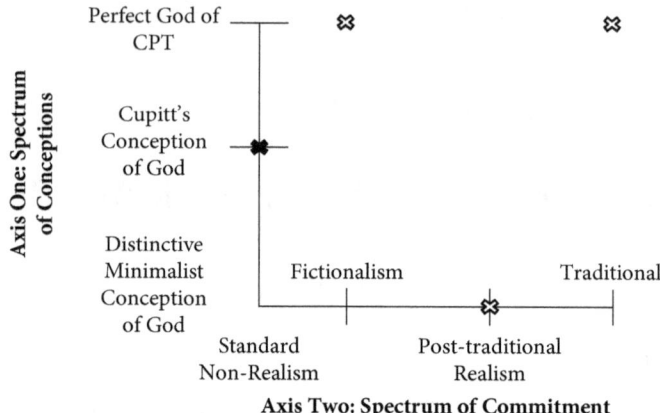

Figure 5 Axis one and two combined. © Jessica Eastwood.

that the 'doubting realist' is (more likely than not) a traditional realist who has come to doubt whether they can continue to commit to faith as (Ia) for reasons *x*, *y* or *z*. For example, if the traditional realist begins to doubt the compatibility of their commitment to the God of CPT *and* a scientific worldview which might close the door to, not necessarily the 'realness' of God but, a God who *must have* created and sustains the universe.

With that being said, the fourfold structure of the chapter will unfold as follows. We will begin by looking at four ways that *voluntary 'belief-in' without involuntary 'belief-that'* has been construed. More specifically, we will explore the different alternative components that have been inserted into (IV) which look to replace 'involuntary 'belief-that', with something like 'assuming' for instance. After which, we will look at a specific variant of 'faith without belief', that is, fictionalism, as we look at what might be three reasons why the 'doubting realist' might come to adopt fictionalism. Then, we will look at four ways of interpreting religious discourse through a 'reframing' of the classical conception of God and the Christian narrative (for example), including three different applications of fictionalist ideas and a non-cognitivist approach. These three sections attend to the first aim of the chapter, namely an examination of different accounts of 'faith without belief', including an exploration of religious fictionalism. In the fourth section we will turn to the second aim of the chapter, as I pose the following question: 'What if the "doubting realist" misconstrued "involuntary belief-that"?' I will suggest that if the 'doubting realist' has incorrectly synonymized 'involuntary belief-that' to mean *only* a 'cannot help but' belief that the *classical conception of God* exists in a *wholly* independent and *un*conditionally necessary existence, then they potentially neglect an account of faith – or variant of (I) – that might better reflect their loss of 'involuntary belief-that'. That is, 'post-traditional' realism. Moreover, we are dealing with the following question that the traditional realist and the non-realist might ask: 'If not the traditional God classically conceived, why bother?'

Faith without belief: Four ways

The 'belief' component of faith has been questioned in the last two decades. One desideratum concerns the need for faith to meet the demands of reason, another prerequisite requires that faith imply hope while excluding despair.[1] It has also simply been described as having 'no interest in a God that has to be believed in'; 'If I am going to have God in my life', explains philosopher of science Nancy Ellen Abrams, 'it has to be a God that cannot help but exist, in the same way that matter and gravity and culture exist. We don't need to believe in these things; they just exist. We can choose to learn more about them, or not'.[2]

In this chapter we are going to focus on those who have replaced the concept of 'belief-that' with some cognitive attitude weaker than belief, such as 'assuming' or 'steadfastness', and ask if they still have a concept of faith that is somewhat recognizable. This is the question that I wish to put forward here in this first section, namely: 'How viable is it that the "doubting realist" can insist that their faith is built on something other than involuntary (or voluntary) belief-that?' I will present here four contemporary cases of just that: 'voluntary belief in and *some kind of commitment to the concept of God*'. We will begin with Daniel Howard-Snyder and Daniel McKaughan's examination into faith without propositional belief.

Howard-Snyder and McKaughan and 'beliefless assuming'

Howard-Snyder and McKaughan engage with this idea of the 'doubting realist' as they pay close attention to the role that 'doubt' might play for the doubting traditional realist. According to Howard-Snyder and McKaughan, the term 'doubting realist' describes those who 'long to live in relation to a God who, for all they know, may or may not exist, and who want to participate in religious communities who will welcome them'.[3] Forms of traditional realism such as Christianity, Islam and Judaism have, Howard-Snyder and McKaughan explain, 'a stake in certain claims about reality', including the claim that 'there is a God who creates, sustains, and acts in and through nature'.[4] Now, on a macrocosmic scale, as we become more and more 'educated and scientifically literate', some contemporary traditional realists might come to have 'serious doubts about claims associated with these traditions' Howard-Snyder and McKaughan suggest.[5] For instance, 'heliocentric astronomy, evolutionary biology, and the vast age of the universe, among other things, might seem incompatible with particular claims they regard as essential to these traditions'.[6]

Moreover, when it comes to twenty-first-century scientific discoveries, some 'doubting realists' might find science successful in 'aiding our understanding of nature and its causal processes that talk of miraculous intervention and experience of God seems superfluous'.[7] Outside the science arena, arguments in philosophy against the existence of God or learning about historical and cultural criticism might also 'lead one to be in doubt about the claims of one's religious tradition'.[8] Stripped of its particularities, and of the emotions, the existential and social crises that can make attending these challenges of pressing practical importance – Howard-Snyder and McKaughan suggest that we can construct the 'doubting realist's' line of reasoning as something like this:

> I am in doubt about some of the claims that are essential to my religious tradition, as a result of encountering severe intellectual challenges to them. But if I am in doubt about these claims, then I lack belief of them. And if I lack belief of them, then I lack faith, too. But if I lack faith, then integrity requires me to stop engaging in those religious practices that presuppose that those claims are true, e.g., worshipping, praying, attending synagogue, church, mosque, etc. And if integrity requires me to stop doing these things, then I should leave my religious community. I should just get out.[9]

How might members of religious communities respond to the 'doubting realist'? Howard-Snyder and McKaughan posit a response which reconfigures what it means to have faith and what it requires. They suggest that faith does *not* require belief of the relevant propositions, as the 'doubting realist' proposed above. Instead, what if 'belief' is not the only positive 'cognitive element' or attitude; is not the only way to 'realize' the relevant propositions?[10] 'Even if you don't believe the basic Christian story', Howard-Snyder and McKaughan argue, you can still '*belieflessly assume*' a range of alternative positive cognitive attitudes towards it. What does it mean to 'belieflessly assume' the Christian story? And why might 'faith without belief' better suit the 'doubting (traditional) realist'?

First of all, it will be useful to briefly explore Howard-Snyder and McKaughan's understanding of 'belief', to check that they do intend to replace 'involuntary belief-that' in their account of faith. 'Belief', they argue, is 'a dispositional state rather than a conscious mental act, occurrence, or process'.[11] Thus, we can confirm that the pair are referring to propositional belief (i.e. belief-that), *and* they posit belief-that to be a kind of 'cannot help but' belief: an involuntary belief. Moreover, we can confirm that Howard-Snyder and McKaughan's account of faith does, indeed, look to replace a 'loss' of 'involuntary belief-that'. Now I will go into a little more detail about belief as a *positive cognitive attitude* according to Howard-Snyder and McKaughan. To believe something is 'paradigmatically positive' (while, disbelieving something is paradigmatically negative, and simply entertaining something is paradigmatically neutral). It is also a *doxastic* cognitive attitude (thus, concerning belief). Moreover, Howard-Snyder and McKaughan are looking for a *positive cognitive attitude* that is *non-doxastic* in nature (therefore, not concerning beliefs).

One or two words on their conception of 'doubt' in relation to belief: both Howard-Snyder and McKaughan argue that 'it is not possible to believe something while at the same time being in doubt about it'[12] for two reasons. First, if you doubt something, then you 'neither believe it nor disbelieve it' and, so, you 'lack belief of it'.[13] Second, if you believe, then you will 'tend to answer affirmatively when asked whether it is the case, and you will tend to mentally assent to it when you bring it to mind', comparatively when you are in doubt, 'you will lack both of those tendencies'.[14]

Now, Howard-Snyder and McKaughan suspect, as many philosophers do,[15] that 'belief is not the only positive cognitive attitude one can take toward a proposition', including religious propositions.[16] To demonstrate how this might be the case, they offer the following two examples.

> The defensive captain. The captain of the defensive team is trying to figure out what play the opposing quarterback will call next. From his experience of playing against him and his coach, and given the current situation, it seems most likely to him that, of the credible options, he will call a plunge into the middle of the line by the fullback. So he acts on the assumption that he will call a fullback plunge and he aligns his defense on that basis.

> The army general. Consider an army general facing enemy forces. She needs to act. Her scouts give some information about the disposition of the enemy but not nearly enough to settle whether they are situated one way rather than several others. So she assumes that they are situated in the way that seems to her the least false of the options she finds credible given the information she has. Then,

acting on that assumption, she disposes her forces in the way that seems most likely to be an effective means to her ends.[17]

They then proceed to make the following six observations about these two cases:

1) We can easily imagine that neither of our protagonists believes nor disbelieves the target proposition. That is to say that both the captain and the general lack the dispositional profile of belief.
2) We can easily imagine that each of our protagonists is in doubt about whether the target proposition is true. As a result, they neither believe nor disbelieve it.
3) Despite their lack of belief and disbelief, and despite their being in doubt, each of them acts on a certain assumption. Thus, there really is some cognitive attitude that each of them acts on. Each of them *assumes* that the target proposition is true.
4) Our protagonists act on the basis of their assumption, and they act in ways you would expect them to act given their aims.[18]
5) We can easily imagine that neither of them believes the target proposition and neither puts it forward as a bit of mental what-if-ery. This sort of assuming exhibited by them is '*beliefless assuming*'.
6) The dispositional profile of beliefless assuming is both different from and similar to the dispositional profile of belief. They are similar insofar as each are 'dispositional states, each are representational, and each have a mind-to-world direction of fit in the sense mentioned above'. They differ in the sense that assumptions lack some tendencies definitive of belief, such as the tendency to affirm p (when you are asked whether p) and mentally assent to p (when p comes to mind).[19]

So now that we understand what 'beliefless assuming' looks like, what does it mean to beliefless assume the Christian story?

The first type of faith that I offered (I) is described as '*Belief-Only*' relational faith by Howard-Snyder and McKaughan, that is 'for you to have (put, repose, maintain) faith in someone, as a thus-and-so, is for you to believe that they are a thus-and-so'.[20] Both scholars suggest that '"Belief-Only" [or (I)] is mistaken', what do they mean by this? Faith as '*involuntary belief-that and voluntary belief-in*' classically construed is suspect for Howard-Snyder and McKaughan; they argue that there are alternative positive, *non*-doxastic cognitive attitudes that can replace 'belief-that' and constitute faith. Moreover, if our only resources for understanding faith make belief a requirement, we miss out on providing an account of faith that better represents one's positive cognitive approach to the propositions. Furthermore, Howard-Snyder and McKaughan propose instead that you have faith in someone, as a thus-and-so, 'only if you have a positive cognitive attitude toward the relevant propositions' (i.e. 'that they are a thus-and-so, or that they are capable as a thus-and-so, or something saliently similar').[21] Moreover, they propose that there are 'multiple ways in which one can meet the positive cognitive attitude condition', and one way is to 'belieflessly assume'.[22]

In a religious context, Howard-Snyder and McKaughan give the example of Saint Teresa's later account of faith. Saint Teresa described her adult commitment 'with nine short words' Howard-Snyder and McKaughan point out: 'to live by faith and yet not to believe'.[23] It is not difficult, they argue, to use Saint Teresa's story as 'someone experiencing severe intellectual doubt . . . and yet we plausibly also see someone resolved to act on the beliefless assumption that the basic Christian story is true, and to keep her vow to serve Christ in the poorest of the poor'.[24]

Furthermore, and despite the 'loss' of an 'involuntary "belief-that"', a response such as this 'can be an important and reasonable manifestation of what it is to be a person of religious faith too', Howard-Snyder and McKaughan argue.[25] More generally then, 'since the cognitive component of your faith is not belief of the basic Christian story, you aren't acting on beliefs that go against your assessment of the evidence'; consequently, they argue, 'there is room for you to act on your beliefless faith with integrity'.[26] And so, Howard-Snyder and McKaughan make the following remark on faith as 'voluntary belief in and *some kind of commitment to the concept of God*', where the 'kind of commitment' (to replace 'involuntary belief-that') is 'beliefless assuming'.

> Indeed, the fact that you care a lot about whether the basic Christian story is true, and the fact that you aim to live in light of that story, and the fact that you are resilient in the face of challenges – willfully resisting the loss of something you hold dear – indicates that you have faith in excelsis. That is what faith looks like in the circumstances that you now find yourself.[27]

Interestingly, Howard-Snyder applies his understanding of 'faith without belief' to fictionalism and asks whether the latter is a good example of the former, namely without '*involuntary "belief-that"*' (2019).[28] In an article titled 'Can fictionalists have Faith?', after distinguishing two types of fictionalists (atheistic and agnostic), Howard-Snyder argues that agnostic fictionalists can have faith, according to his account of 'faith without belief'. However, in this book I assume that the fictionalist is a non-realist and, therefore, I do not make this distinction (i.e. between 'atheistic fictionalism' and 'agnostic fictionalism'). However, I do suggest that the fictionalist who leans closer to realism (and is thereby on the borderline of agnosticism) will have faith, namely (IV): *voluntary 'belief-in' without involuntary 'belief-that'*. Thus, I agree with Howard-Snyder that the atheist fictionalist, or the fictionalist who leans closer to atheism, does *not* have this type of faith (or faith at all), but the fictionalist and the agnostic (or, as Howard-Snyder would have it, the 'agnostic fictionalist') *can* have (this type of) faith. Although, in accordance with this book, I would *not* suggest that fictionalism can replace the 'loss' of 'involuntary "belief-that"' with 'beliefless assuming' because of their non-realist religious philosophy, I argue that this fits the agnostic profile better.

Zamulinski and 'Cliffordian assuming'

Another philosopher who sorts to replace 'belief' with 'assuming' is Brian Zamulinski. Opponents of religion will often justify rejecting all forms of traditional realism by appealing to the ethics of belief, Zamulinski tells us; this means that it is unethical to form beliefs that are unsupported by evidence. But this is not a successful argument *if* the Christian faith is not considered to be a matter of beliefs but, instead, a matter of assumptions to which the faithful person is committed. When it comes to the compatibility of belief and religious faith, Zamulinski uses Richard Clifford's argument that we should avoid believing without sufficient evidence, and act on 'assuming' instead.[29] Thus, Zamulinski applies a 'Cliffordian assuming' method and argues that faith is 'a commitment to a set of fundamental assumptions in the hope of salvation'.[30]

To note, the purpose of the phrase 'in the hope of salvation' as part of Zamulinski's definition of faith (without belief) is to say that 'a person cannot commit himself to a set of assumptions without a purpose in doing so; the absence of a purpose would indicate that no assumptions had been made'.[31] Moreover, Zamulinski's overall aim is to show that 'faith need not be a matter of beliefs but can instead be a matter of assumptions to which the faithful person is committed'.[32] Furthermore, Zamulinski is defending Christianity against this particular attack, namely that faith requires (indefensible) beliefs. So, what exactly is 'assuming' in this case: the component to 'replace' one's loss of involuntary belief-that?

An assumption, says Zamulinski, 'is a proposition that is not believed but is nevertheless used as a guide for action with a view to achieving a particular aim.

We often adopt assumptions when we act under conditions of uncertainty.[33] When it comes to repairing machinery, for example, Zamulinski explains that 'it is often not certain what the cause of the malfunction is'.[34]

> In these cases, the mechanic will proceed by assuming that the problem is such and such. . . . If he had *believed* that such and such was the problem and if the repair had been unsuccessful, he would be puzzled or surprised by the lack of success; in contrast, if he merely *assumed* that it was the problem, he would know that there was a degree of probability that the problem was really something else and he would be neither puzzled nor surprised if the attempted repair failed.[35]

What we can take from this, Zamulinski says, is that making assumptions 'will not have a deleterious effect on our standards of evidence, a person may assume propositions that he should not believe'.[36] More specifically, when it comes to Christianity, Zamulinski argues that 'if faith is not belief but commitment to a set of fundamental assumptions in the hope of salvation, it is simply not possible to use the ethics of belief to make a case against Christianity'.[37] Moreover, Zamulinski tells us that faith seems to include at least the following three elements: (1) it is a propositional attitude; (2) the propositional attitude is not evidence dependent and is adopted voluntarily; (3) its adoption results in the right sort of action.[38]

Another way of explaining what 'assuming' is, is to tell us what it is *not*, and Zamulinski tells us that assuming is *not* 'accepting'. He draws on Jonathon Cohen's argument here that commitment to a set of assumptions is not merely an acceptance of them, where 'to accept that p is to have or adopt a policy of . . . including that proposition . . . among one's premises for deciding what to do or think in a particular context, whether or not one feels it to be true that p'.[39] Thus, on this assumption, '[a]cceptance can be casual or contingent in a way that commitment cannot'.[40] So, how do we translate this when we come to talk about a person of faith? Those who have this 'strongly positive attitude toward the assumptions' will not, says Zamulinski, 'maintain them idly or temporarily, that [one] will not readily give them up, and that [one] is not merely pretending to be a Christian or self-deludingly acting as though he were one'.[41]

So, what is lost when one does not have involuntary belief-that? Zamulinski says himself that his 'redefinition', '[i]ntuitively' speaking, that is 'faith as assuming' 'does not distort faith'.[42] On the contrary, the component of 'assumption' seems to fit better with the nature of faith than beliefs do. Rik Peels responded to Zamulinski's argument and criticizes his attempt to rebut Christian faith as an existential commitment to fundamental assumptions and argues, instead, that non-doxastic voluntarism is not the answer for the 'doubting realist'.[43] Zamulinski refutes Peel's rebuttal and stands by his aims in his original article, that is, to show that the following claims are compatible:

> that it is always morally wrong to believe anything without sufficient evidence; that there is insufficient evidence for some religious propositions; and that it is sometimes morally permissible to take a religious stance that includes such unsupported propositions. I argued that they would be compatible *if faith was not belief but commitment to a set of assumptions* in the hope of salvation.[44]

Moreover, Zamulinski stands by the notion that 'there is good reason for standard Protestant Christians to prefer faith as a commitment to a set of fundamental assumptions in the hope of salvation to "faith" that includes or is reducible to belief'.[45]

> If faith in God involved belief, then, since we cannot believe at will, faith would probably have a deleterious effect on the believer's standards of evidence . . . Since Christianity explicitly commands its adherents to love both God and their neighbour, Christianity implicitly commands them to reject overbelief and therefore requires them to reject faith qua belief.[46]

And, so, contrary to Peels, and in response to a particularly negative reading of our central question, which will focus on that which will be 'lost' when one does not have 'involuntary "belief that"', that is, a genuine account of classical faith, Zamulinski presents the following three reports. All of which begin with '*on the contrary . . .*'

- 'making and acting on assumptions over a long period of time is *not* likely to lead to belief'.[47]

Those lapsed Christians who try, for instance, Pascal's method – to *not* believe that Christianity is true, but rather to act *as if* it is true by reading one's Bible, attending mass on Sunday and so on – 'will probably fail', whereas in contrast, 'a Cliffordian Christian', that is the 'doubting realist', 'would want to avoid becoming a believer'.[48] And, there is 'no reason why a Cliffordian Christian could not be just as successful at avoiding belief'.[49]

- 'faith as assumptions does not involve circularity'.[50]

It is 'logically possible', Zamulinski argues, for someone to 'hear the Christian story, decide that the salvation mentioned was worth seeking, and commit himself to the whole package, including the assumption about the purpose for making the assumptions', guided, Zamulinski mentions, by grace of God 'so there should be no problem from the Christian perspective'.[51]

- 'you do not need to believe in God in order to love Him'.[52]

If, Zamulinski argues, this love is 'the kind that can be commanded' then 'there is no reason why the believer would be at an advantage over the maker of assumptions'.[53] Why? Because both 'can do what they take to be God's will'. And, if the opposite is true, and this love cannot be commanded, there is 'no reason why the believer should be better placed to have what he takes to be an experience of God than is someone who makes assumptions'.[54]

It might be worth noting that while Zamulinski certainly gives an account here of a particular variant of (IV), it is not a form of fictionalism but rather an alternative form of 'faith without belief'.

Jackson and 'rational steadfastness'

In her work on the nature and relationship between belief, credence and faith, Elizabeth Jackson dictates what might be two crucial differences between propositional faith and propositional belief. The first is that you can have belief-that something is true, but you do not have a desire for it to be true. Whereas, when you have faith-that something is true it requires some kind of *desire* component. The second is that faith 'goes beyond' the evidence in a way that belief does not. That is to say that, arguably, you can still have rational faith (and the component of 'rational' is important here too) in something even if you have counter evidence that does not justify you to believe. In other words, faith is consistent with more counter-evidence. We are, of course, interested in how Jackson comes to understand faith, so what we can take from this is that faith might require both a 'desire' component *and* an ability to hold strong against (a certain or significant amount of) evidence to the contrary.

Before we dive a little deeper into how 'desire' and 'rational steadfastness' might work together and constitute a coherent and somewhat recognizable account of faith, including religious faith, we will first need to know what exactly Jackson means by 'belief', 'faith' and 'evidence'. If we begin here with 'evidence', Jackson refers to evidence as the ability to 'raise' or 'lower' the probability of one's credence level. Philosophers often refer to 'credence' in cases when talking about degrees of 'confidence', in layman's terms.[55] Thus, credences are much more fine-grained than beliefs and are often given a value on the [0, 1] interval. For example, 'I have a credence of 1 that $1 + 1 = 2$, a 0.99 credence my car is parked outside, and a 0.5 credence that a fair two-sided coin will land heads.'[56] Now that we know this, we can look at Jackson's understanding of 'belief' and 'faith'.

Belief, says Jackson, is a commitment to the world being a certain way. For example, if you believe that it is raining then you are, in a way, saying that the world is such that it is raining. Faith (i.e. propositional faith) can be one of two things, Jackson tells us, as she assesses the rationality of each. Faith can be understood as (a) a mental state, which is a combination of a certain credence (or confidence) level and a desire component. Or faith can be understood as (b) some kind of commitment act. In order to assess how it is that faith, as construed as either (a) or (b), can 'go beyond' the evidence but maintain a 'rational' status, we need to look at the difference between 'belief' and 'credence'.[57]

Put simply, it is, according to Jackson, relatively easy to change one's credence level (for instance, the value on the [0, 1] interval), as one's credence will 'increase' or 'decrease' in accordance with the evidence (or counter-evidence) available. However, up until a certain or significant point, despite the evidence (or counter-evidence) available, it is entirely possible and plausible, Jackson argues, that one's belief will stay the same. By this Jackson means that belief can remain 'steadfast' in light of these evidential changes, and this is rational. Interestingly for us, Jackson says that faith actually does something very similar.

Faith, like belief, Jackson says, also possesses this 'rational steadfastness' insofar as evidence may shift our credence levels 'up' and 'down' but nevertheless we can still retain our faith that something is true. Additionally, because Jackson thinks that faith might 'go beyond' the evidence (which is not necessarily the case for 'belief'), faith can remain steadfast even though one's confidence levels can be all over the map. And, importantly, faith can remain rational. Now, this is all in relation to faith understood as a mental state. What about faith understood as an act?

There can be cases where we think something is very likely but nonetheless to act as if it is true is not necessarily what is best. For instance, if your cat goes missing and you have pretty good evidence that they are dead but it is not conclusive evidence. In this case, it can still be rational to act as if they are alive and to put up 'missing' posters, and to go and search for them and to do your best to find them, even though you have pretty good evidence that they are dead. What is the reason for this? The reason for this, or at least one plausible reason for this, Jackson argues, is *your desire* to find your cat, that is the relief and the happiness you will feel when you know that they are safe. What this shows is that whether you should act as if something is true does not just depend on whether you are confident that it is true, but it also depends on what is at stake and the way that your desires look. Now, what does all this mean when it comes to religious faith, specifically?

In light of what we have just looked at, Jackson continues by arguing that it can be rational both to continue your commitment to God and to participate in a religious community even when your credence levels get really low. And, perhaps more controversially, Jackson suggests that even those who did not have that kind of (strong) commitment in the first place (namely, traditional realism), one can still make some kind of religious commitment despite their credence level that God exists not being very high. In other words, if one does not have, or has 'lost', their involuntary belief-that. It can even be rational if their desire is to enter into (or maintain) a relationship with God. To explain this Jackson defends Pascal's wager.[58]

Simply put, Jackson defends the following position: faith combined with a desire component and rational steadfastness. Moreover, Jackson suggests 'that faith can both be rational and can also "go beyond the evidence" ... by arguing that rational belief is more sensitive to some parts of a body of evidence than other parts, and that the same can hold true for faith without compromising its rationality'.[59] Thus, one's faith might sound something like this: 'if God exists and I do pursue this relationship with God, that would be a good thing and worth making the commitment, even though I do not have a very high credence level that God exists, or that Christianity is true'. Hence, Jackson's interest in defending a Pascalian approach to faith.

Now, at first glance, this might sound like a 'doubting realist', namely a person who has lost their 'cannot help but' belief in the objectivity of God (however construed), and here is why. Jackson asks us to '[s]uppose instead that faith does not entail belief', given her argument that 'faith can go beyond the evidence in a way that belief does not, as faith may be even more steadfast in light of counterevidence than belief'.[60] Moreover, she says that '[d]efenders of the view that faith doesn't entail belief have argued that this can give faith a unique steadfastness in the face of counterevidence; one might receive counterevidence such that they can no longer rationally believe p, but this need not rule out rational faith that p'.[61] Now, the reader might be thinking, hang on, is this claim not in tension with Jackson's attention to rational belief? Why do we need to give so much attention to rational faith, if faith does not entail belief?[62]

In response, Jackson says that what she has argued is this: 'faith and belief share a certain necessary condition that involves sensitivity to evidence. This need not rule out the idea that it is possible to have faith that p without believing that p; the attitudes can otherwise come apart in many ways'.[63] Might it be the case then that Jackson provides us with a coherent type of faith without involuntary belief-that? I think so.[64] But what about whether her account can coincide with fictionalism?

Like the (Christian) fictionalist, Jackson thinks it is important to preserve (the best one can) the rationality of Christianity. Thus, for both the (Christian) fictionalist and Jackson, it is possible to have a strong commitment to faith that is not based on belief (-that). Jackson draws on Howard-Snyder and his pointing out that

> I may have other attitudes towards p that count toward faith that p: I accept that p, I believe p is not especially improbable, I believe p is more likely than alternatives, I desire that p, etc. Thus, on this view of faith, faith that p can be steadfast in light of significant evidence against p – potentially even more steadfast than belief. There may still be some sense in which belief goes beyond the evidence, but faith does so in a more drastic and significant way.[65]

Can, then, Jackson's account of faith that does not rely on belief-that also defend the suitability of fictionalism as an account of faith? I suggest that it *cannot* for two reasons.

The first reason why Jackson's defence of faith without belief-that cannot defend fictionalism is because of her emphasis on credence. Jackson's account of 'faith without belief' rests on the idea that faith can be held even when one's credence is low, but would we describe the fictionalist's credence level as low? That is to say, would we describe the fictionalist's degree of confidence in whether the God of CPT exists as 'low'? I suggest not. This is because, as I said before, in this book I describe fictionalism as a branch of non-realism (rather than drawing a distinction between 'agnostic fictionalism' and 'atheistic fictionalism').

And, so, if the fictionalist's 'confidence level' were to be measured on the [0, 1] interval, would we say that their credence level is 0.5? 0.25? 0.0001? Any of these answers, I suggest, could potentially underestimate or misrepresent the fictionalist's non-realist attitude, in the sense that they are not necessarily 'agonistic' when it comes to their non-commitment to the existence of God. Which is to say that I would not describe their position as one of uncertainty, but as certain as one can be that God does not exist 'out there'.[66] Therefore, I suggest that this better represents the 'doubting realist' who is leaning towards agnosticism, rather than a fictionalist position.

The second is that as soon as we emphasize Jackson's substitute for belief, namely 'steadfastness' and its role, combined with Jackson's defence of desire, we arrive at Jackson's advocacy of Pascal's wager. Jackson's mission is to save the rationality of traditional realism without having to incorporate 'belief-that' but instead use the attitude of 'rational steadfastness'. Moreover, although Jackson's account of faith is: faith that does not 'have' an 'involuntary belief-that' component, her account, however, does align more with pragmatic theism and agnosticism, I argue, rather than fictionalism.

Buchak and 'acquiescing'

In an article titled 'Can it be Rational to Have Faith?', Buchak speaks about faith as 'going beyond' the evidence, similar to Jackson, and even goes one step further, as she also claims that 'faith requires terminating the search for further evidence'.[67] On the nature of propositional faith (rather than interpersonal faith, i.e. faith in *I*, where *I* is some individual), Buchak says that faith is *not* something like 'believing more strongly than the evidence suggests', or even 'believing without any evidence at all'. Rather, faith is to be willing to take a risk on a claim without looking for more evidence. So, for example, to have faith that your friend will feed your cat while you are away is to be willing to take a risk on the claim that it is true; it is true that you are not going to find a skeleton of your cat upon your return. You also have to be willing to take that risk without looking for more evidence. You are not going to be calling your friend every ten minutes to remind them.

What we have just described is an ordinary example of faith, and the idea that faith does not require more believing than the evidence suggests. Rather, what faith requires is being able to act on the relevant claim without looking for more evidence. To be willing to act on the basis of the evidence that you already have. So, the next question for Buchak is, 'Is this rational?' If, she says, you have a lot of evidence to suggest that your friend is a trustworthy person, it would be rational to have faith that they will feed your cat. In that case, what *are* the conditions that might make having faith rational? There might be two conditions, says Buchak. The first is that faith is more apt to be rational the more evidence you have. The second, and by extension, is that faith is more apt to be rational when the evidence 'out there' in the world is not going to be conclusive. That is to say, when looking for more evidence is not going to help you very much because the evidence 'out there' is not going to make you more certain. So, can these conditions be met when it comes to religious faith? Yes, says Buchak. Insofar as it is perfectly rational to describe religious faith in this same way.

If this is the case then, we can continue to explore Buchak's account of faith, in particular her suggestion that faith statements, particularly 'faith that' statements, which is what we are focusing on, 'typically involve a proposition to which the actor involved acquiesces'.[68] What does this mean? Buchak seems to suggest that belief-that can be replaced with 'acquiesce', that is, 'when a person has faith that p, he acquiesces to p'.[69] Buchak purposefully speaks of 'acquiescing' to a proposition rather than 'believing' it because she is 'not sure that if I have faith in something, I thereby believe it'.[70] Admittedly she says that '[w]hile it sounds infelicitous to say "I believe that ~X but I have faith that X", there may not be anything wrong with saying "I don't know whether X – I have no idea whether I believe that X or not – but I have faith that X"'.[71] So 'as not to prejudge that issue' says Buchak, she makes a weaker claim: 'that having faith involves taking the proposition to be true, that is, "going along with it", but not necessarily adopting an attitude we might describe as belief'.[72]

Buchak's approach to faith was picked up by Malcolm and Scott (2017). In an article aptly titled, 'Faith, Belief and Fictionalism', Malcolm and Scott explore Buchak's replacement of 'belief' for an alternative characterization – 'a positive non-doxastic cognitive state, which can stand in place of belief', that is, 'acquiesce'.[73] In other words, 'instead of involuntarily taking or finding p to be true, that is, believing it'.[74] Acquiescing, they explain, 'involves taking the proposition to be true, that is, "going along with it", but not necessarily adopting an attitude we might describe as belief'.[75] For Malcolm and Scott, Buchak's account of faith is not appealing as they suggest that 'belief is required to maintain a distinction between genuine faith, pretend faith, and fictionalist faith'.[76] Moreover, Buchak's non-doxastic theory of faith, which replaces 'belief-that' with 'acquiesce', can be interpreted as self-deception, and this is not how fictionalism ought to be understood. The religious fictionalist, Malcolm and Scott argue, 'immersed in a pragmatically useful narrative, is *not* guilty of self-deception since she realises (at least when considering the matter in a fully critical way) that she does not believe the religious propositions that she is endorsing'.[77] Thus, they reject Buchak's theory from 'linguistic data' (as they describe it), which is to say that they reject the use of 'faith' in linguistic utterances, particularly in relation to the following claim from Buchak that I previously quoted: 'I don't know whether X – I have no idea whether I believe that X or not – but I have faith that X.'

If we are satisfied with Malcolm and Scott's assessment of Buchak's account of faith, and share their concern, we might well agree with them that Buchak's 'faith without belief' cannot coincide with fictionalism. Nevertheless, her account of faith without belief contributes to this chapter's investigation into whether it is responsible to suggest that a plausible and recognizable account of faith can be put forward which does not require a 'belief-that' component, and I think that Buchak's account is a good example of this.[78]

Now that we have looked at four contemporary accounts of faith without 'involuntary "belief-that"' and how those philosophers might respond to the question, 'What, if anything, is lost when one does not have involuntary belief-that?' Howard-Snyder and McKaughan suggest that one can 'assume' the truth, Zamulinski argues that we adopt a Cliffordian-inspired account of faith, Jackson posits the rationality of holding fast to faith if the 'doubting realist' has lost their 'cannot help but' belief-that and Buchak defends the non-doxastic component: 'acquiesce' to replace a loss of belief-that. We will turn our attention to a particular variant of (IV), namely fictionalism.

The four forms of (IV) that we just explored do *not* strictly advocate fictionalism, as its own variant of (IV), but I suggest that fictionalism is an important variant of (IV) to explore, and it is a branch of non-realism that we focus on in these next two sections of Chapter 3, in Chapter 4 and in Chapter 5. What we will do now, in this second section, is to look at the benefits of fictionalism as a specific variant of faith without involuntary belief-that, insofar as I will offer three reasons why the 'doubting realist' might adopt fictionalism.

Why might a person adopt fictionalism?

Religious fictionalism is a philosophical movement, following the rise of non-realist approaches to interpreting traditional forms of faith (namely, Ia). Its theory is this: that it is both intelligible and morally apt to distil the meaningfulness and usefulness of religious statements *without* affirming the 'truth' of the statements. In other words, statements, particularly about God, are legitimate and worth engaging with, but it is not necessary to '*believe*' the content of what is said.[79] That is, to have involuntary (or voluntary) 'belief-that'. Additionally, fictionalism proposes that it is also legitimate to want to engage in public and private religious discourse and practices. Thus, suggesting that religious 'belief-that' is *not* necessary for a meaningful response and favourable attitude towards religion. This would be a positive definition of fictionalism, as a fictionalist would have it.

It should be pointed out here that this definition of fictionalism does not clearly distinguish fictionalism from non-doxasticism, which is the attitude of denying that justification is exclusively a matter of relations between one's beliefs. The two – fictionalism and non-doxasticism – are often conflated, sometimes purposely and at other times perhaps more clumsily. Collaborative works on fictionalism by Finlay Malcolm and Michael Scott (2017, 2018) seem to treat them as equivalent, as we saw briefly. The difference can be described in the following way: '[b]oth approaches contrast with the traditional view that a religious life must be grounded in religious belief. On non-doxasticism, some weaker cognitive attitude takes the place traditionally held by belief. Fictionalism treats religious propositions as fiction, often conceiving religious life as a game of make-believe'.[80]

A more negative approach to defining fictionalism would inevitably compare it with atheism and crudely suggest that there is no real difference. In this case, fictionalism is 'simply atheism dressed up in a few religious frills, the last refuge for one-time believers who cannot admit that they have lost their faith'.[81] Those who present fictionalism in this way will (more often than not) take the view that if God does not exist as an all-powerful Being 'out there', Creator of the universe, then we should give up all talk of God. I do not wish to endorse this interpretation of fictionalism for two reasons.

First of all, and in relation to this chapter, it is not useful in properly assessing why fictionalism has come about, and why it has become popular in recent literature as an alternative form of religious commitment. In other words, this negative assessment will not help us to understand why fictionalism has arguably become a prevailing alternative for the 'doubting realist' who wishes to, more or less, keep their religious 'lifestyle' and practices, without the ontological commitment. And even perhaps the 'standard' non-realist who also craves this kind of 'traditional' lifestyle without the ontological commitment.

The second reason, more broadly speaking, why I do not endorse this 'negative' definition of fictionalism is because in this book we are looking to investigate what it might mean: (a) to 'believe in' the God of CPT without an adjoining ontological thesis (namely, fictionalism), and (b) to legitimately speak of a non-CPT, objective God (namely, post-traditionalism). These are two very different but interconnected investigations. In this chapter we are focusing on (a), and it is through investigating (a) that we can better explore (b). That is to say, it is through an exploration into what it means to have a non-ontological belief-in the God of CPT (fictionalism) that we can ask *how far fictionalism can take us to post-traditionalism*, and, thus, to look at the legitimacy of speaking about an objective non-CPT God (post-traditionalism).

That being said, there is one question that the negative approach to fictionalism asks that I think can act as a good starting point for our assessment, and that is to ask: 'If not traditional faith, then why bother?' This question will be at the centre of my defence of fictionalism. To clarify, I will defend fictionalism as a thoughtful and meaningful alternative to traditional realism (and standard non-realism). The purpose of this book is to suggest that there is a potentially latent but live texture of reality (a way of 'being real') that might exist somewhere 'between' fictionalism and traditional realism.

Therefore, I will need to, first, assess what it is that fictionalism offers, in order to get to the heart of what might be 'missing' in this type of religious commitment. Furthermore, I will then be in a position to say why drawing attention to a perhaps neglected and distinctive conceptual space could offer a texture of reality that resonates *more* meaningfully for those who cannot long commit to traditional realism, and find fictionalism 'too thin'. Let us now look at three reasons why a person (a 'doubting realist', namely those who assume religious realism to *only* equate to faith as it is classically conceived) might choose to adopt religious fictionalism.

Fictionalism and the problem of evil

One prominent motivation can be the felt strength of the classic version of 'the problem of evil'. A direct challenge to the existence of God, it poses a potential problem for the traditional theist who holds a conception of God from CPT. How can God be all-powerful, all-knowing, all-loving *and* evil exist? The problem, as we know, goes like this: either, God does not foresee the evil (which would make God not all-knowing), God cannot stop the evil (which would make God not all-powerful) or God can stop the evil but chooses not to (which would make God not all-loving).

Le Poidevin (tentatively) points to two reasons why fictionalism might offer an account of faith that can relieve some of the pressure felt by the 'doubting realist' when it comes to the problem of evil. The first is to say that the traditional realist 'feels some pressure to reconcile [their] realist belief in the goodness of God with the evident fact of suffering', while the fictionalist 'is entirely willing to engage with this issue'.[82] The reason being, it is important for the fictionalist that 'the fiction is not isolated from real human concerns', and also 'that the fiction is not (in any obvious way) internally inconsistent'.[83]

The second is that when it comes to satisfactory theodicies, the traditional realist will (most likely) be committed to the existence of a particular successful theodicy. They might be aware that it falls short in some way, in the sense that it 'simply fails to make intelligible some of the most horrific instances of suffering they know about' but, for the traditional realist, 'there is nevertheless a fact of the matter as to which unknown and perhaps unknowable theodicy is the correct one'.[84] For the fictionalist, 'in contrast, there is no fact of the matter as to which theodicy is correct. So there is an explanation in [the fictionalist's] case as to why [they] cannot imagine what a satisfactory theodicy would look like – there is nothing for [them] to imagine!'.[85]

It might already be apparent here, but it is important to highlight the fact that the fictionalist cannot simply 'avoid' or 'side step' the problem of evil. As Le Poidevin points out, any fictionalist who excludes such a salient feature of experience, 'simply in order not to disturb their religious fiction[,] would appear to be indulging in escapism rather than engaging with a process of spiritual and moral development'.[86] The fictionalist will always be wrestling with the paradox *within a theological fictional context only*, and the 'existence' of the perfect God of CPT is not threatened. Rather, (only) the clarity in which one can comprehend the *fictional reality of this God*, because this God was never thought to exist 'out there' in the first place!

Fictionalism and religious community

Is it possible that a former Christian, for example, having lost their (traditional) faith, might very much wish to remain a member of their Christian community, and to follow its more general code of ethics? For some believers, a large part of their faith is inherently connected to wider aspects than their 'beliefs' and 'non-beliefs'. These wider aspects are just as important to them, including the communal aspect, and a sense of purpose that religious practice achieves, such as human flourishing, self-actualization and moral well-being. Thus, adopting fictionalism can allow the 'doubting realist' to participate and meaningfully engage in religious discourse, in all these ways, *without* making 'belief-that' commitments, beyond those that they feel they can make.

Natalja Deng points out the benefits here for those (including the fictionist) who feel an 'affinity with some religions, or with a particular religion', which suggests that in some sense 'they think religious practice has some value', thus, 'we can just take this to mean that they think religious practice achieves something that they value, such as inspiration, comfort, personal or spiritual or moral growth, a sense of purpose, or a sense of community'.[87] Le Poidevin also indicates that those without 'involuntary belief-that' (including the fictionalist) can enjoy these types of benefits, such as 'sing hymns, join in prayers, discuss the sermon ... meet to read passages of the Bible ... and explore the meanings and implications of those passages' rather than, perhaps, adopting a 'standard' (less engaged) non-realist perspective or an atheistic viewpoint.[88] Those being, positions that cannot afford or appreciate how engagement in such activities equally, that is compared to the traditional realist, inspires them, and how they are equally as inclined to relate them to their everyday lives.[89] Which brings us onto a third reason why the 'doubting realist' might choose to adopt fictionalism.

Fictionalism and its framework

The two reasons that I have just stated assume that the 'doubting realist' has moved left along the axis, from traditional realism to fictionalism. However, with this third example, I am now going to assume that the 'doubting realist' is moving *right* along the axis, that is from standard non-realism to fictionalism (Figure 6).

In this case, the 'doubting realist' is probably looking 'for *more*', rather than, with the previous example, not wanting to 'give up' the sense of community that traditional realism provided. I suggest that fictionalism *can* give the 'doubting realist' '*more*' in this sense, insofar as fictionalism can provide a type of commitment that is more holistic and structured in its offering of an alternative vision of traditional faith.

That is to say that the 'doubting realist' (moving 'right' along the axis to fictionalism) might have found standard non-realism and its philosophical perspective too broad when it comes to what it 'means' to have a religious commitment. Insofar as, it may be the case that the 'doubting realist' finds standard non-realism to be lacking in a sure and purposeful direction due to its laissez-faire, of sorts, attitude towards what a meaningful religious commitment and engagement might amount to. Namely, when it comes to the importance of religious engagement, practice, times of reflection and 'go to' sources in search of wisdom and moral coding.

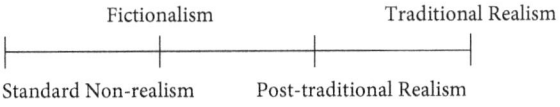

Figure 6 Axis two: A spectrum of commitments to God. © Jessica Eastwood.

Now, in the third section of this chapter, we will continue to attend to our first aim: to see what (IV) can offer the 'doubting realist' by exploring four non-traditional ways of interpreting religious discourse. The first three ways are different applications of fictionalist ideas from Le Poidevin, Lipton and Blackburn, and the fourth way is a Wittgensteinian non-cognitivist approach.

Reframing God: Four ways

Le Poidevin's introduction to Fiona and Reginald

Le Poidevin suggests that the fictionalist, and their reframing of God, can go virtually undetected, insofar as the fictionalist can appear to the average onlooker (and most notably to the traditional realist) to be as engaged and committed to religious discourse and to God as the traditional realist. And arguably *they are* just as involved in their religious community and dedicated to God as their realist counterpart. Le Poidevin makes this point by introducing us to Fiona and Reginald (whom we briefly met earlier), two churchgoers.[90]

Fiona is a fictionalist and Reginald is a realist. They both enjoy singing hymns, joining in prayers, discussing the sermon afterwards and reading passages of the Bible together, to explore the meanings and interpretations of those passages.[91] To the 'neutral onlooker', then, Fiona and Reginald appear to be 'equally engaged in these activities, equally inspired by them, and equally inclined to relate them to their everyday lives'.[92] There is 'nothing to distinguish' their religious attitudes until, upon questioning, each of them will give a 'very different philosophical account of the basis for their behaviour'.[93]

As a realist believer, we might be more familiar with Reginald's basis, namely that he takes statements about God to refer to a real, objective God who exists independent of human belief. But what about Fiona? We might be less familiar with Fiona's basis for her behaviour. As we have heard, Fiona appears to be equally as devoted and inspired as Reginald when it comes to public religious practices, but Fiona does so through her 'reframing of God'. That is, through Fiona's understanding that God, as a real, objective Being that exists independently of human belief, is true *only according to theological fiction.*

Why might this be an intellectually coherent philosophical account? Well, we might say, for instance, that Fiona (as a fictionalist) is looking to build a bridge between a scientific picture of the universe and a type of faith. Both are important and enforce a post-traditional believer's view of the world (a scientific picture of the universe) and their 'worldview' (of hope and morality, through faith) and yet the two are traditionally found to *collide*: a scientific picture and a realist conception of God.[94] But what if fictionalism could provide a type of faith that allows for a *reframing* of God by putting aside 'belief-that' and focusing on 'belief-in'? Thus, the bridge can be built from a scientific picture of the world to faith as (IV). Furthermore, the two can *cohabit*, not *collide*. This is fictionalism, or at least a type of revolutionary fictionalism. Based on the understanding that: the scientific picture cannot be altered, and the significance of faith can only retain intellectual coherence if the post-traditional believer is able to *reframe* God from a realist understanding to a (strand of) non-realist understanding.[95] Peter Lipton argues that we can relieve the cognitive tension between science and religion if we adjust our attitude towards commitment.

Lipton and adjusting our attitude

We have a choice, says Lipton, between '*adjusting content* and *adjusting attitude*'.[96] The former requires us to give up some claims about a discourse (or to reconceptualize). While the latter means keeping the claims by 'changing one's epistemic attitude', and it is the second attitude that Lipton aims to defend.[97] To do so, he identifies three ways in which one could go about the former to manage the tension, only to conclude that he does not find them to be very satisfactory overall. I will explain them here briefly. The first is 'the metaphor view' which suggests that when talking about God what one is *really* talking about is a sense of 'awe' and 'wonder' felt perhaps when admiring nature, and by endorsing this view it affects the way that the Bible is interpreted as *only* metaphorical.

The second is 'the value theory' and to divide science into a category of 'facts' and religion into a category of 'values'. Lipton warns that possible implications of this view include the notion that science is a 'value-free' zone and that religion has no factual content. This is not really what we want to say, says Lipton. Instead, there is a 'third route': 'the selection view'. The selection view is based on epistemic warrant and trying to form a consistent set of factual claims from both science and religion. But Lipton implies that this would still leave unhelpful gaps in religious texts, as a result of removing religious claims that cannot be satisfactorily explained, and seen as 'weaker' than scientific claims that can be verified in some way.[98] In light of this, then, Lipton suggests that we *adjust our attitude*.

Moreover, Lipton is suggesting a revolutionary form of religious fictionalism.[99] That we 'immerse' ourselves fully in the context of the discourse, rather than adopt the belief that *x* exists in reality. His conclusion, then, is that religion without belief is valuable. Moreover, we should

> construe our religious texts literally, we believe only parts of it but we use all of it and we immerse ourselves in the world it describes. The point of exploring this approach is not to persuade those hostile to religious activity that they should repent but to consider a way those who find themselves with a commitment both to religion and to science might have it both ways.[100]

Blackburn and engaging with the 'here and now'

Simon Blackburn looks to promote an 'another direction', or philosophical approach to religious discourse, that is not 'realist' or 'ontologically robust', so that we may open to new approaches to theological discourse which might bring new insight.[101] A Wittgensteinian interpretation of religious language, asking what religious language *does*, can help to promote a new 'direction' in which to approach theology. Blackburn suggests that if we can say that religious language might be 'symbolic or expressive, orientating us towards each other, or towards ourselves, or towards our place in this world', rather than 'representational, giving an account of disconnected parts of the cosmos, regions of space-time', might we, then, say that we are potentially distilling the 'best bits' of religion, the parts that Fiona, for example, fully takes full advantage of[102]

> the social solidarity, the ritual, the confronting of human verities, the communions with the self, piety towards passed generations, resignation of humility in the face of the cosmos, the music and poetry, celebrations of human reason and science, engagement in the here and now of human life and experience.[103]

We will now look at a Wittgensteinian non-cognitivist account, which might be best introduced through Nora, another character of Le Poidevin's who we have not yet met. As a non-cognitivist, when Nora engages with theological discourse she understands said discourse to be 'expressive rather than propositional'.[104] What inspired Nora's approach to religious discourse was reading 'the writings of Wittgenstein', and she feels that 'her view of religious language captures this', namely the view that 'utterances couched in that language (for the most part) simply lack truthvalue'.[105] Unsurprisingly, scholars debate about whether or not this 'tricky exegetical issues' ought to be closely associated with the works of Wittgenstein.[106] In other words, not everyone is convinced that Wittgenstein was a non-cognitivist.[107] If we can say something about the influence of Wittgenstein on forming non-cognitivist accounts of religious discourse, we might say something like the following.

Wittgenstein and playing the language-game

If I ask you to think of what it might mean to engage in 'game-playing', you might, perhaps, suggest one of the following: a child's board game with a pre-mapped board and players' pieces that will be moved around the board according to a set of rules. Or, you might think of a more grown-up game of psychological warfare (a kind of 'I want you to think *this* but I am really thinking *that*', type of game). However, the type of game-playing that we are interested in here is a philosophical and, specifically, a Wittgensteinian type of language-game.

Le Poidevin explains that Fiona is engaging in a rather complex and specifically theological game of 'make-believe'. The rules of the game are these: 'any given theological statement p is true if and only if it is true in the theological fiction that p'.[108] This game of 'make-believe' is a *different* game to the game that Reginald is playing. Reginald is playing the 'God-is-true-by-virtue-of-God-as-a-mind-independent-being' game. The rules for this game are these: 'any theological statement p is to be understood in the context of reality and to have real life implications'. What about Nora? What game is Nora playing? To understand the rules of Nora's game, we might need to first meet Andy, another character introduced by Le Poidevin.

Andy is an anthropological reconstructionist. This means that Andy thinks that 'theological discourse is, despite its surface content, really about human ideals', and because he takes 'theological discourse to be translatable into statements about human ideals' he does not believe that they are 'actually about a transcendent being at all'.[109] Thus, Andy would say that the 'choice between different interpretations of religious doctrine is, if a genuine one, a choice between different ideals', which for the realist is very real, and the fictionalist insofar as every realist dispute has a fictionalist counterpart.[110] Moreover, Andy will take God-talk to '*assert* moral ideals'.[111]

Nora is a variant of Andy, this means that Nora takes God-talk to '*express* those ideals (just as "ow!" expresses pain)', where each statement in God-talk expresses a specific ideal.[112] Based on this understanding, then, we might say that Nora is playing the 'theological-discourse-is-about-expressing-moral-ideals' game, whereas Andy is playing the 'theological-discourse-is-about-asserting-moral-ideals' game. One of the significant differences between the games that Fiona, Reginald, Andy and Nora are playing is how *language* is used, and how the different 'rules' determine how one frames or *reframes* God. In particular, the subtle but important difference between Fiona and Nora's game is that Nora's game does not represent a religious subject matter but instead expresses the speaker's awe, wonder or perhaps some emotion towards God.

We are *all* playing some type of game, says the Wittgensteinian, specifically language-games.[113] Whether it be the 'make-believe' game or the God-is-true-by-virtue-of-God-as-a-mind-independent-being' game, or a different game altogether, because this is how we communicate with one another. And, when we have a breakdown in communication it is because we have failed to recognize that our counterpart is playing a different game to the game that we are playing (with different rules). Which explains why, formally, Wittgenstein understood the function of language to describe, but he later concluded that language is an activity that has many different functions, and it is embedded in different practices which 'answer to and structure our different needs, interests or purposes'.[114]

His later account, then, suggests that we have 'no coherent conception of a world that we can describe by accurately copying it or mirroring it or even representing it in our thought', there are no 'referents "out there" which simply force our conceptions on us'.[115] Instead, concepts, including the concept of belief(-that), are 'aspects of our forms of life'. That is to say, beliefs that Reginald holds are expressions of his experienced life, they are not fixed by any mental conceptions.[116] Moreover, religious utterances are 'not capable of being true or capable of being false'. However, this does not mean that religious beliefs are nonsensical.[117]

Thus, despite the anti-metaphysical strand that is central to a Wittgensteinian account of religion, it is equally central to his account that Christianity cannot be incoherent.[118] For Christianity is a language-game; it is an employment of language embedded in a pattern of human life and, thus, a form of life.[119] Forms of life and language-games cannot be incoherent, illusionary or erroneous. For Wittgenstein writes,

> [i]t strikes me that a religious belief could only be something like a passionate commitment to a system of reference. Hence, although it's *belief*, it's really a way of living.[120]

He continues,

> [i]t's passionately seizing hold of *this* interpretation. Instruction in a religious faith, therefore, would have to take the form of a portrayal, a description, of that system of reference.[121]

I have presented four non-traditional, philosophical ways of 'reframing' religious discourse.

They included three ways from fictionalism, the first was Le Poidevin's claim that Fiona (the fictionalist) and Reginald (the realist) share rather a lot in common, and that their difference of opinion when it comes to the ontology of God need not overshadow the legitimacy of Fiona's commitment to religious discourse. The second, presented by Lipton, suggested that by adjusting one's attitude, like Fiona, fictionalism can be seen to offer a way to relieve the tension between science and religion. The third briefly touched upon Blackburn's insistence that religious discourse promotes positive self and social engagement. Finally, a Wittgensteinian-inspired non-cognitivist account assumed that although religious utterances are not truth-apt one can nevertheless infuse an emotional connection to religious discourse.

Now we will turn to the final section and the second aim of the chapter, as we challenge whether (IV) *is*, after all, the best alternative account of faith for the 'doubting realist'. Or whether, instead, an ontological weaker variant of (I) can provide an account of faith that, in fact, resonates more with the 'doubting realist'.

What if the 'doubting realist' has misconstrued 'involuntary belief-that?'

I want us to now properly address a question that I posed at the beginning of the chapter: 'If not the traditional God classical conceived, why bother?' The reason is that what I am about to suggest will not include a necessary commitment to the God of CPT – understood to exist objectively 'out there' by the traditional realist or in a fictional world by the fictionalist. Rather, this alternative account of faith that I intend to offer the 'doubting realist' ascribes a 'lighter' ontological thesis to God understood, more simply, as 'that-than-which-a-greater-cannot-be-conceived'.

Why am I doing this? Why am I offering an alternative, *realist* account of faith to the 'doubting realist'? For whom, their 'cannot help but' 'belief-that' which formed their traditional faith has been 'lost'? Why does it make sense to offer them a 'realist' account of faith? I suggest it does make sense *if* my suspicion is correct. If it *is* the case that the (average) 'doubting realist' has misconstrued 'involuntary belief-that' to refer *only to* faith traditionally conceived. That is, the God of CPT exists objectively 'out there', in a reality that is '*un*conditionally necessary' (God's existence is not *in any way* conditioned by the way the world is) and '*wholly* independent' (God does not *in any way* dependent on our existence).

I will suggest that a weaker strain of (I) can provide the 'doubting realist' with an account of faith that relieves them of their doubt insofar as it offers: (a) a stripped-back conception of God and (b) a 'less weightier' ontological thesis. In relation to the former, if the 'doubting realist's' doubt stems from them being unable to commit themselves to an omni-God, *and not* the belief that there exists something greater, something divine, namely 'that-than-which-a-greater-cannot-be-conceived', then their 'cannot help but' belief-that might be saved. Further still, once this is understood, the 'doubting realist' might come to realize that it is *not* their 'involuntary belief-that' that has been lost, but their 'involuntary belief-that' *the God of CPT exists objectively 'out there'*. Thus, their 'cannot help but' belief that something greater, something divine could, potentially then, be redirected towards God as, simply, 'that-than-which-a-greater-cannot-be-conceived'. Moreover, there is an argument here that post-traditionalism can revive the 'doubting realist's' loss of involuntary belief-that by offering a distinctive 'minimalist' conception of God instead.

If the 'doubting realist' has now come to accept (a) they can now allow for a weaker ontological thesis (b), one which might provide a more intellectually coherent understanding of God. Namely, God as divine and sui generis in nature, *without then* committing the (former) 'doubting realist' to an ontological thesis that dictates an omni-God that would certainly have existed if humanity did not exist (*wholly* independent) and, if the world were not as it currently is (*un*conditionally necessary). Moreover, if the (former) 'doubting realist' does not wish to make these (larger, 'weightier') ontological commitments (those that are associated with traditional realism, and the fictionalist *only in accordance with theological fictionalism*), then post-traditionalism can offer the following, weaker ontological thesis.

God as 'that-than-which-a-greater-cannot-be-conceived' exists within a conceptual space that is, instead, 'conditionally necessary' and 'semi-independent'. If we remember from the first chapter, I described the former as a commitment to the notion of God as necessary insofar as God exists mind-independently but in some distinctive way conditioned by our human existence. And, what I mean by the latter ('*semi*-independent') is that rather than adopting the stronger strain of '*wholly* independent', one (only) wants to say that God exists independently from us human beings, to the extent of saying that God was certainly not 'invented', but God's existence is, in some distinct way, tethered to us.

Moreover, if the 'doubting realist' agrees with (a) and (b) and adopts these alternative views, then perhaps post-traditionalism, as the proponent of (a) and (b), can provide an intellectually coherent account of faith for the doubting realist, *if* she has misconstrued her loss of 'involuntary belief-that' with her loss of 'involuntary belief-that' God of CPT exists wholly independently and unconditionally necessarily. And, thus, falsely rejects a realist account of faith, thereby neglecting her belief that, by jumping from traditional realism to fictionalism, or a variant of (IV), and skipping a potentially fitting account of faith, namely post-traditional realism.

This is *not* to say that the fictionalist or the person who holds 'faith without belief' is mistaken, or that fictionalism is therefore 'missing the point'. Rather, the reason I point out this potentially neglected type of faith (Ib) is for the 'doubting realist' who feels that they might be 'missing out' on an account of faith that might better attend to that which weighs on their heart. That is, the *realness* of God as, simply, 'that-than-which-a-greater-cannot-be-conceived', and how this sits with them intellectually and, thus, helps to constitute a coherent form of faith for them. And, so, perhaps, it *is* 'worth bothering' to explore God as stripped back from the classical conception if it means restoring one's 'involuntary belief-that' and bringing some intellectual coherence to one's faith.

Conclusion

In this chapter we have attended to two main aims. First, to see what (IV) can offer the 'doubting realist', and, the second, to challenge whether (IV) *is*, in fact, the best alternative account of faith for the 'doubting realist'. The first aim dictated most of the chapter, as we explored three things.

Those being: (1) four ways that *'voluntary "belief-in" without involuntary "belief-that"'* has been construed by replacing involuntary belief-that with different components. Then we look specifically at (2) three reasons why the 'doubting realist' might come to adopt fictionalism, as a variant of *'voluntary "belief-in" without involuntary "belief-that"'*. After this, we looked deeper into fictionalism and (3) how fictionalism 'reframes' the classical conception of God and a religious narrative from a realist framework to a fictional framework.

In our final section here on that which the 'doubting realist' may have misconstrued, I suggested that if the 'doubting realist' has incorrectly synonymized 'involuntary belief-that' and the God of CPT existing in a *wholly* independent and *un*conditionally necessary existence, then they might miss out on a type of faith that can restore their loss of 'involuntary belief-that', if it has been falsely equated with faith *only as it is classically conceived*. And it is here that we attended to the second aim of the chapter: to challenge whether (IV) *is*, in fact, the best alternative account of faith for the 'doubting realist'. I argue that if my suspicion is correct, then the conceptual space that might exist 'between' traditional realism and fictionalism ought to be explored, as it might provide a kind of 'post-traditional' reality that can be ascribed to God as 'that-than-which-a-greater-cannot-be-conceived', if this simpler conception resonates with meaning.

In the next chapter we will revisit the sense of coherence that fictionalism can provide those who feel or experience an emotional connection when they engage in religious practice, even though they do not have 'involuntary belief-that'. Can the religious fictionalist have a *genuine* emotional response to religious discourse? This, we will explore next.

4

Are our emotions toward fiction real?

In this chapter I will argue that fictionalism is 'emotionally coherent'. By this I mean, I will investigate whether (or not) fictionalism has a coherent view about emotions, in order to counter the claim that the fictionalist is simply confused if they allow religious narratives to shape their emotional lives. Thus, I will be looking at fictionalism as a type of religious commitment that might be described as *'voluntary "belief-in" without involuntary "belief-that"'* (IVb). That is to say that fictionalism does not require an 'abandonment' of any emotional connection that one may have as part of their religious commitment because they no longer have (involuntary) belief-that. Nor does it require the fictionalist to stop participating in public or private discourse, just as Fiona (the fictionalist) demonstrates to us.

In the literature, this trade-off between genuine emotion and 'belief' is known as the 'paradox of fiction'. The paradox of fiction contains three propositions: (P1) we are genuinely moved by fiction; (P2) we do not believe that fictional entities exist; and (P3) to be moved, we must believe that fictional entities exist. I will present a series of strong counter-arguments to each of the propositions of the paradox and suggest that there might not be a paradox here at all. What I am suggesting, then, is that it is *not* paradoxical to have an emotional response to fiction. Moreover, if the paradox can be convincingly dissolved, I will argue that the emotional coherence of fictionalism can be defended. Insofar as, if we can say that our emotional response to fiction is not irrational, then might we also say that our emotional response to *theological fiction* is also not irrational? Thus, I will defend the emotional coherence of fictionalism.

This investigation, then, will be into the nature of the emotional states that are evoked by fiction, otherwise referred to as 'fictional emotions'. It is important to note that when using the phrase 'fictional emotions' I am simply referring to our emotions towards fiction. The phrase itself is not making a judgement on the *nature* of our emotions towards fiction, that is, whether they are 'genuine' or not. In turn, I will present each proposition from the paradox followed by counter-arguments to that proposition that look to overcome the paradox.

The nature of 'fictional emotions'

Suppose you are watching a film; it has clowns and creepy music – all the things that you love to hate – so when the clown suddenly appears (!) you jump out of your chair and scream. Or, perhaps, you are more of a 'rom-com' type of person, and you are moved to tears when *he* does finally end up with *her*. Since a much-discussed article was published in 1975, where Colin Radford stated that our apparent ability to respond emotionally to fictional characters and events is irrational, philosophers have pondered, '*Just how is it* that we can be moved by what we know not to exist?' Radford devised what is known as the 'paradox of fiction': an inconsistent triad of propositions that all appear at first glance to be true but cannot all *be* true. And, so, he rules that our emotional response to fiction is puzzling and implausible. Adopted from Radford's article, let us remind ourselves of the paradox:

(P1) we are genuinely moved by fiction
(P2) we do not believe that fictional entities exist
(P3) to be moved: we must believe that fictional entities exist.[1]

And here is one application of the paradox where Anna is the character, Anna Karenina:

(P1) Sally pities Anna
(P2) Sally does not believe that Anna exists
(P3) to pity someone: one must believe that they exist and are suffering.[2]

The paradoxical implication is this: if one could claim to be moved by fiction, they must either admit to believing that the fiction is not, in fact, fiction at all but *real*. Or, that their emotional response is *not* genuine. The former seems to misrepresent our understanding of fiction to be just that, fiction: a separate reality to our own. We know this. But the latter also seems to miss the mark. To say that our emotional response to fiction is not genuine feels like a disservice or downplays the deep emotional connections we have with fictional characters and their stories. Ergo, it seems that we have reached an impasse. Thus, Radford formulates six possible solutions; I will list the solutions here and state how each of these six solutions offered here ties to which particular proposition of his paradox, either (P1), (P2) or (P3).

1. We get 'caught up' in the fiction and 'forget', or are no longer aware, that we are only reading a book or watching a play. This *first solution* is in conjunction with (P2).
2. We do not necessarily 'forget' but we 'suspend our disbelief' while engaging with the fiction. Thus, the *second solution* is tied to (P2).
3. It might not have 'always been the way' that human beings can respond emotionally to fiction and, indeed, not everybody is moved by fiction. This *third solution* does not appear to link directly to one specific proposition.
4. Our emotional response to fiction is not too dissimilar to our emotional response to non-fictional contexts, such as hypothetical scenarios or when caught in a web of 'what ifs'. The *fourth solution* is in response to (P1).
5. The emotion we feel towards a fictional entity is really an emotional response to a real person. This *fifth solution* attempts to counter (P3).
6. 'Belief' is really the only element that separates being moved and 'being moved' (by fiction) and this is not problematic. Hence, the *sixth solution* is a reply to (P3).[3]

Radford is not convinced by any of these solutions. The first and the second solutions, he argues, wrongly undermine our knowledge that we are watching fiction. Radford is unconvinced by the *first solution* and the notion that we simply 'forget' that we do not believe fictional entities to exist. Similarly, the *second solution* and its notion that even though we do not continually remind ourselves of the fact that the fiction is not 'real' (unless we are trying to reduce the effect of the work on us) the paradox is not solved by invoking 'suspension of disbelief' because we are always aware, Radford insists, of what we are engaging with. That is, fiction. The *third solution* (or, rather, 'observation' on how widespread the phenomenon in question is) misses the point, argues Radford, that we *can* be moved and, therefore, does not solve the paradox. The *fourth solution*, Radford suggests, does not account for the scale of probability: the lesser the probability the more likely we are not to feel this way. Thus, it might feel genuine (particularly for a Walter Mitty sort of character whose imagination is so powerful and vivid that, for a moment anyway, what she imagines seems real, that her tears are made intelligible) but we need to believe that the scenario is likely, in order to genuinely respond.[4]

In a similar way, as we move to (P3) and the role of 'belief', Radford explains why the fifth and sixth solutions are not sufficient. The *fifth solution* falsely redirects our emotional response to the character, such as screaming at the sight of a terrifying clown or shedding a tear for the love between two adoring characters, towards a real person and their real story. For instance, 'if and when we weep for Anna Karenina, we weep for the pain and anguish that a real person might suffer and which real persons have suffered'.[5] But this is mistaken, Radford argues. We are, on the contrary, moved by the fictional character, thus this solution does not work because we do, in fact, weep for *her*, we pity *her*, we feel for *her* and our tears are shed for *her*.[6]

This problem remains despite the *sixth solution* and its attempt to measure our beliefs in proportion to our response, because we find that we do *not* need to believe that Anna is real (for instance) to weep for her. Therefore, the question remains: 'How can we be saddened and cry for Anna knowing, as we do, when she dies no one really dies?'[7] It is the argument that we are moved by Anna Karenina: by *her*, not by someone that Anna reminds of us of. Moreover, Radford concludes that our being moved in certain ways by fiction 'though very "natural" to us and in that way only too intelligible, involves us in inconsistency and so incoherence'.[8]

At the time of its publication, that is the paradox of fiction, the judgement theory of emotions was prevalent.[9] The judgement theory looks to explain why when one experiences a 'trembly feeling' in the stomach, for instance, it can be caused by running up a flight of stairs too quickly, but it could also be caused by something cognitive. It could be caused by a *judgement* one makes. The judgement theorist will say that when my love walks into the room the 'trembly feeling' in my stomach is caused by my judgement or belief and, in this case, the belief that my beloved has arrived and that he is the darling of my heart. When it comes to love, we want to say that love is more than this feeling, but it is the *belief* that one has about their love. Ultimately, the judgement theorist does not want to equate emotions with 'feelings', such as the 'trembly feeling' in one's stomach.[10]

Radford, then, clearly adopts this theory of emotion, as displayed by his theoretical commitment to the second proposition. For him, in order to have a genuine emotional response, one must *believe* the object of emotion to exist. The judgement theory of emotions is a cognitive theory because it gives plausibility to the second proposition, namely that a central constituent of an emotion is a cognitive judgement or a belief. In the case of pity, for example, such a judgement (or belief) would be that someone has suffered, or does, or will, or might suffer.

A presupposition of such a judgement is that the object of the judgement has existed, exists, or will, or might exist.[11] We might, crudely, identify this as *'emotion plus belief'*. So where do 'feelings' come into this?

We can and do often use the terms 'emotion' and 'feeling' interchangeably. And, so, for many people the answer to the question 'what is an emotion?' is straightforward: emotions are *feelings*. However, historically – since Aristotle – philosophers have resisted or attacked synonymizing the two and, instead, insisted that emotions are not feelings. Rather, emotions involve cognitions: a belief or a judgement, and feelings are components or even mere 'detectives of emotion'. By this I mean that one can identify the emotion that one is feeling by acknowledging what is happening in one's body: What is one thinking? How is one behaving? Hence, it might be possible to identify one's emotions by acting like 'emotion detectives' who investigate one's own experience of the emotion in the body, brain and behaviour.

This is the cognitivist approach. Notably, William James denied this claim, in favour of a non-cognitive approach. Namely, that emotions are changes of feeling in the body. And this non-cognitivist approach has become more popular since the twentieth century. Ultimately, the term 'feelings' is used indistinguishably to define a psychological response, a physiological response, a combination of the two and strictly one and not the other. And, it would seem that the definition used within a particular account of emotions is dependent upon the user's bias: Are they a cognitivist looking to argue that emotions involve a judgement or belief, or are they a non-cognitivist using the term to promote their argument that when an emotion is felt, the feeling literally is the emotion? This is my impression of the role of 'feelings' in emotion, as tentative; or linguistically fluid.

What the non-cognitivist approach does demonstrate – if we define 'feeling' as a physiological response – is the possibility to have *'emotion plus feeling'* without belief. That is, compared to the cognitivist's *'emotion plus belief'*. Perhaps, then, a combination of the two (cognitive and non-cognitive approach) is required to help explain fictional emotions, that is, a hybrid or neo-cognitive theory of emotion. I will not claim to posit what I consider to be the best theory of emotion, but if I were to take a stand on the viability of the cognitivist theory I would express uncertainty when it comes to any definite requirement in regard to the cognitive element in emotion to be belief. What is important to know is that Radford adopted the judgement theory of emotion, and this pure-cognitive approach to emotions has been questioned as the best explanation of emotions, which of course impacts how we approach fictional emotions.[12] Just to clarify, I am referring here to a cognitivist theory as one which includes belief, as opposed to some other representational but sub-doxastic state.

If, then, belief is sometimes thought of as an essential component of a genuine emotion, how can Sally pity Anna if Sally does not believe Anna to exist? Clearly, it would seem, there is a paradox here. How can Sally feel pity for a woman who felt her life to be so intolerable that she threw herself under a train, when Sally knows that there is no Anna, there is no intolerable situation and there is no train? By tackling different propositions of the paradox, a number of philosophers have devised possible solutions in an attempt to solve the mystery about why is it and how it is[13] that we are moved by fiction and look for an alternative conclusion to: 'our emotions are irrational'.

To begin, I will present opposing arguments to (P1) by Kendall Walton and Robin Le Poidevin. Walton's 'pretend theory' will suggest that fictional emotions are, what he terms, 'quasi emotions'. By this Walton means that our emotions towards fiction do absolutely feel genuine but because of their nature they are *not* brought about by 'beliefs' but by '*make-believing*'. Therefore, they cannot constitute genuine emotions. However, Walton does not conclude, as Radford does, that our fictional emotions are, thus, irrational. They are no less meaningful.

I will then explain how Le Poidevin applies Walton's theory of make-believe to answer the question of how it is that we can become emotionally involved in religious worship. Both Walton and Le Poidevin use the notion of make-believe and quasi emotions to demonstrate how our emotional response to fiction can be 'not genuine' but nevertheless powerful and meaningful. In this way they retain the phenomenological integrity of our emotional response to fiction. Next, I will look at two more arguments presented by Le Poidevin by way of overcoming (P2) of the paradox. Third, in regard to disproving (P3) and dissolving the paradox of fiction, I will explore four theories that each argue against the presupposition that 'belief' is a *necessary component* of genuine emotion.

My overall conclusion will be that this trade-off between genuine emotions and 'beliefs' that the paradox of fiction embodies is not reflected in modern philosophical, scientific and psychological accounts of emotions. What these arguments demonstrate is that it is possible to have, what appears to be, psychological and physiological emotional reactions to fiction in a way that does not require a 'belief component'. I also wish to suggest that the fictionalist's emotional response to theological fiction is coherent, insofar as these arguments have sought to dissolve Radford's conclusion that says our responses are irrational.

(P1) We are genuinely moved by fiction

When indulging in a good book or caught in cinematographic captivity, one can feel an immense bond with the fiction: a deep connection to the characters and their story. And our emotions towards them feel real; they feel genuine. And so, Radford's suggestion that we are genuinely moved by fiction does not, on the surface, appear radical. But it does not take too long to realize the paradoxical implications of this proposition, given the ontological status of fictional entities and the commonly held view that to feel genuine emotion we must *believe* the object of our emotion to exist, to be true, to be *non-fiction*. Radford, therefore, concludes that fictional emotions are irrational. It is irrational to have a genuine emotional response to something you know not to be real, or not to be the case.

In what is often referred to as the 'pretend theory', Walton sought to preserve the integrity of our emotional response to fiction. He did this by rejecting the first proposition. Walton devised a philosophical theory that defines fictional emotions as 'quasi emotions'. Quasi emotions are distinct from genuine emotions that are brought about by *belief*. Instead, quasi emotions are 'constellations of sensations or other phenomenological experiences characteristic of real emotions', but that they are generated *not* by existence beliefs, such as the belief that Anna Karenina really exists. Rather, quasi emotions are brought about by 'second-order' beliefs about what is *fictionally* the case according to the work in question, such as the belief that Anna *make-believedly* exists. Hence Walton is known as a 'pretend theorist'.[14]

Walton, then, draws a separation between our mental lives and 'the mental lives we lead in worlds of our game of make-believe'.[15] Therefore, part-and-parcel with Walton's understanding of quasi emotions that feel genuine is that they are brought about by *make-believing*. By this he means that although we do not *really grieve* for Anna, or *really fear* the shark in *Jaws*, there does exist a 'substantial overlap' of the two worlds (i.e. our world and the fictional world). And so, there are many ways in which 'fictionally we think and feel [in] ways in which we really do so'.[16] Moreover, 'our actual feelings and what fictionally we feel coincide' but, ultimately, there is a clear distinction between 'our psychological games of make-believe and our actual mental lives'.[17] Put another way, it is *fictionally true* that I am 'fearful' of Hannibal Lecter in my make-believe game that Hannibal Lecter is a sociopathic serial killer. I am not *genuinely* fearful. I will explore Walton's theory, also known as a theory of *representation* (of visual arts) and suggest that it is largely satisfying, that is until it is applied to religious fictionalism, by way of explaining one's emotional response to *theological* fiction.

The notion that fiction cannot render genuine emotions (and perhaps only quasi emotions) is damaging to fictionalism. For how can it defend its philosophy as a serious and thoughtful alternative to religious realism if it can only promise 'make-believe' fictional emotions: emotions that feel real but are in fact not? This major consequence gestures at the question yet again: 'If not traditional faith, why bother?' If adopting fictionalism means that I cannot have a genuine emotional response to religious discourse, then why should I consider fictionalism to be an adequate and responsive alternative to religious realism? I will respond to this argument on behalf of the fictionalist and say that the fictionalist's removal of 'belief'(-that) from their 'faith' must go hand-in-hand with an acceptance that their emotional response to religious discourse is not, what is classically considered as, 'genuine' but they *feel* genuine and that, perhaps, is enough or, pessimistically, all they can ask for. Fictional emotions, then, may not be genuine per se but that does not mean that they are, ergo, *not* genuine. I will draw on Walton and Le Poidevin to demonstrate how our emotional response to fiction can be 'not genuine per se' but, at the same time, powerful and meaningful. Thus, retaining the phenomenological integrity of our emotional response to fiction.

Walton and worlds of make-believe

Within a wider investigation into works of art and our relationship to such works, Walton acutely attends to works of fiction. In doing so, he addresses a question that continues to vex philosophers: 'What is the nature of our attitude toward fiction?' Walton attempts to answer this question through his overarching theory of *representation*. Representations (i.e. novels, pictorial art, film, poetry) all function as 'props' in games of *make-believe*. Games of make-believe are best understood as games that are played by children. Imagine,

> two children are pretending to be soldiers. They designate a nearby boulder as an enemy fort and the smaller stones on the ground as hand-grenades. Then they make believe that when they throw the smaller stones at the boulder, they are throwing hand-grenades at the enemy stronghold. In their game, every time one of the stones hits the boulder, there is an explosion in the enemy fort.[18]

In this instance, the boulder and the stones are props; they are *representations* and they function as props in the children's game of make-believe. Works of fiction (such as novels, pictorial depictions, plays and films) are 'things possessing the social function of props in games of make-believe', and their function is to 'generate the fictional material that that we are supposed to imagine', thus appreciating fiction is largely 'a matter of playing games of make-believe with them – games of the sort in which it is their function to be props'.[19] Moreover, Walton examines the role of the *participation* in games of make-believe.

When I read Harry Potter, for instance, I am playing or participating in a game of make-believe; I am imagining that Harry Potter is a wizard. Fictionally I know, then, that Harry is a wizard. Therefore, it is *fictionally true* that Harry is a wizard – that is, in the fiction of my game of make-believe, it is the case that Harry is a wizard. Furthermore, according to Walton's system, it is important to distinguish between the two different types of fictional worlds: 'the world of the prop' (the world of the *representations*) and the 'world of each consumer's game of make-believe' (the world of *participation*). For example, in my make-believe world, it is fictional that *I* see Harry flying on his broomstick, whereas it is *not* an element of the prop world – that is, the *Harry Potter* novels – that it is fictional that *I* (Jessica Eastwood) see Harry Potter flying on a broomstick.

By emphasizing the role of representation and participation through games of make-believe, Walton proceeds to answer the question of just how is it that we can emotionally respond to fiction. We are tempted, says Walton, to equate our emotional response to fiction as *genuine*, that is, identical with the type of emotion we have towards non-fiction (with what we believe to be true). But this temptation should not be confused with what is really going on here. Let us not 'tolerate mystery and court confusion',[20] Walton says, by conflating psychological attitudes with fiction. Instead, let us use the theory of make-believe and 'carve out a new category'[21] for this type of emotional and behavioural disanalogy. According to Walton, the following is an example of the most tempting kind.

> Charles is watching a horror movie about terrible green slime. He cringes in his seat as the slime oozes slowly but relentlessly over the earth destroying everything in its path. Soon a greasy head emerges from the undulating mass, and two beady eyes fix on the camera. The slime, picking up speed, oozes on a new course straight towards the viewers. Charles emits a shriek and clutches desperately at the chair.
>
> Afterwards, still shaken, he confesses that he was 'terrified' of the slime.[22]

Is Charles *genuinely* afraid of the slime? Walton thinks not, and here is why. Can we say that Charles *half believes* that he is in danger and is, therefore, *half afraid* of the slime? Not really, for it would not make sense to accuse Charles of this uncertainty, since Charles is not under any real illusion that the slime is real and, therefore, does not really fear it. And, ironically, the symptoms of fear Charles shows – heart pounding, gasping for breath – are not signs of someone that is 'suspicious' (a *half belief*) but quite the opposite. Yet we know this not to be the case, that is, that Charles believes that he is in real danger. Thus, to say that Charles *half believes* he is in danger and is *half afraid* does not seem to explain what is going on here.[23]

What about the idea that Charles's belief is of a 'unique' kind, similar to that of 'gut' feeling? Walton is not convinced by this either. He compares Charles's automatic responses to that of someone who performs *deliberate* actions to avoid what they fear. For example, one might avoid flying for fear of the plane crashing. One can make sense of someone avoiding flying because of their belief that it is dangerous, so we can postulate beliefs and therefore reason to make sense of this. But we cannot make the same judgement for Charles, one does not have a reason for things that one does not *do* – a pounding heart and gasping for breath – so it would not work to attribute 'belief' to Charles to render his response as reasonable.[24] In another attempt, could it be perhaps that Charles *momentarily* believes the slime to be real and, in that moment, really fears it? Walton is not convinced that this can explain the whole story either, for a 'momentary-fear theory' would not help to explain other cases of different psychological attitudes to fiction, such as pity.[25]

What separates Charles's response to say someone who fears flying is that the object of fear, in this case the airplane, is real and is believed to be so. Whereas, the terrible green slime is not real and not believed to be so. Therefore, 'part of the problem is the notion of *belief*'.[26] Walton stresses that we will 'do better to assimilate genuine fear and genuine emotions generally to belief-desire complexes'.[27] In other words, it makes sense to assimilate make-believe and make-believe emotions generally to fiction complexes. Walton calls *these* emotions (emotions towards fiction) 'quasi emotions'.[28]

Quasi emotions, as I said before, are physiological-cum-psychological sensations. They look (physiologically) and feel (psychologically) like genuine emotions, and typically they do attend genuine emotions, but they are not genuine (belief-driven) themselves. We will come back to the nature of quasi emotions compared to that of (real) emotions at the end of this section and in regard to our overall aim, namely to assess the extent to which we can defend the 'emotional coherence' of religious fictionalism if we can dissolve the paradox of fiction. To bring us back, then, Walton's claim is not that Charles experiences no genuine fear tout court but, rather, that Charles does not fear the slime 'but the movie might induce in him fear of something else'.[29] For instance, if 'Charles is a child, he may wonder whether there might be real slimes or other exotic horrors *like* the one in the movie . . . he may have nightmares about them for days afterwards'[30] but, crucially, this fear is of the 'depiction of the slime, not of the slime depicted'.[31]

Furthermore, Walton describes fictional emotions as physiological-psychological states of quasi emotions. The terrible green slime induced, for Charles, quasi fear, but 'it alone does not constitute genuine fear'.[32] Moreover, Walton's response to the (P1) of the paradox (we are genuinely moved by fiction) will be to say that, on the contrary, our fictional emotions are quasi emotions; they appear to be genuine, but they are in fact not. This does not mean, however, that our emotions towards fiction are, consequently, meaningless or useless. Walton states that 'the magic of make-believe is an extraordinarily promising basis for which to explain representational arts – their power, their complexity and diversity, their capacity to enrich our lives'.[33] Walton hopes to have devised a 'positive account' of one's experiences; 'a well articulated alternative to literal-minded acceptance of ordinary claims' such as to 'fear the slime'.[34] The notion of quasi emotions was picked up by Le Poidevin through his investigation into fiction and the emotions within a wider context of exploring the question: 'Is God fiction?'[35]

Le Poidevin and *theological* make-believe

Through a larger exploration into the concept of 'Religion without God' (i.e. religion without the classical realist conception of God), Le Poidevin defines three different interpretations of religious discourse. The first is *realism*; in stark contrast there is *instrumentalism*, and third, *positivism*. The realist, as we know, believes that statements about God should be taken at face value. Adversely, the instrumentalist and the positivist do not take statements about God at face value. This commonality means that the two theories are often conflated, especially when it comes to 'radical theology' and its alternative approach to theological language and religious practice.[36] But this is problematic, says Le Poidevin, because the theories are 'quite different, and indeed incompatible, philosophical positions'.[37] The tension is this: the positivist agrees with the instrumentalist that God-statements should not be taken at face value but *disagrees* with the instrumentalist that discourse about God is purely fictional. Rather, the positivist (like the realist) agrees that statements about God are either true or false (not fictional). Instrumentalism, then, is one type of fictionalism.

So the question is: 'should we, like the positivist, reduce theistic statements to non-theistic ones and reveal their true meaning?', or would we do better to 'leave them as they are, but treat them as make-believe' like the instrumentalist?[38] Le Poidevin suggests that the latter is the most attractive option. To answer the question, 'Can religion exploit the familiar phenomena of emotions generated by fiction?', Le Poidevin draws on Walton's philosophy of make-believe as the most plausible account to defend the instrumentalist interpretation. If we apply Walton's philosophy to religious discourse,[39] to engage in religious practice is to engage in a theological game of make-believe. We 'make-believe' that there is a God by reciting, in the context of the game, a statement of belief'.[40] And, in doing this, by *participating* in the game of make-believe, we allow ourselves to become emotionally involved in fiction – in religious activity.

> When we become involved in a fictional story, we are engaging in a world of make-believe. Just as a child make-believes that a group of chairs set in a line is a bus, or that, when chasing after a friend, he is chasing after a desperate criminal. . . . In doing so we, as it were, locate ourselves in the novel. We are there witnessing the events. We may even assign ourselves a role, and imagine talking to the characters. . . . Indeed, the make-believe can increase the intensity of the experiences generated . . . and part of the game is to feel something akin to real emotions, though they are not the genuine article.[41]

Le Poidevin identifies three difficulties that may arise for the instrumentalist (particularly from the realist). Here, we will focus on one of these issues, namely the nature of emotions towards fiction. That is, comparing 'these supposedly *ersatz* emotions' to 'their *echte* counterparts': to compare quasi emotions to genuine emotions. Le Poidevin phrases the counter-argument to instrumentalism and the theory of make-believe like this.

> This justification of religious practice seems far less powerful than the one which is available to the realist, for whom prayer and worship really is God-directed, and for whom the emotions thus evoked are real, capable of having a direct effect on one's life. The instrumentalist, in contrast, has to make do with Walton's quasi-emotions: a make-believe imitation of the real thing. Is such a watered down version of religious practice worth preserving?[42]

This response seems plausible. Why settle for a 'semi-genuine' emotional connection when you can have a completely 'genuine' emotional connection to God (through *faith with 'belief-that'*)?

Thus, reverting back to the question, 'If not traditional faith, why bother?' Le Poidevin's response is this. While it is true that the realist believer will be motivated by their beliefs which then render their emotions genuine, it is also true for the instrumentalists that these beliefs are false and can therefore give rise to 'not-genuine' emotions.[43] By this Le Poidevin means, in the case of those who consider realist beliefs to be false, it is plausible to assume that their emotions will also be considered as non-genuine since they are based on false beliefs. Moreover, it seems that Le Poidevin reinforces Walton's theory through a rejection of realism as an unconquerable interpretation of religious discourse.

Le Poidevin, then, can defend fictionalism, through his argument that we can have a meaningful emotional response to theological fiction, by employing Walton's philosophy of representational arts. In turn, this suggests that proposition one – that we are genuinely moved by fiction – mistreats fictional emotions, thus weakening the proposition, the paradox and Radford's conclusion that our emotions towards fiction are irrational. If this is true, then it is crucial that both Walton and Le Poidevin attempt to articulate an alternative conception of fictional emotions without rendering such emotions as 'not genuine' by default. That is, as, perhaps, 'foolish' or 'juvenile'. Rather, they are impactful and important, insofar as they are impactful and important to that particular fiction.

That being said, we began this exploration with the notion that fiction cannot render genuine emotions but only quasi emotions and this is damaging to religious fictionalism. So, what we have done here is to suggest that these emotions are not genuine per se, but are nevertheless meaningful. Thus, I have attempted to defend the 'emotional coherence' of religious fictionalism. However, the issue is I need to show that (i) quasi emotions are constitutionally distinct from (real) emotions and not just emotions which have non-standard causes, in order to argue that quasi emotions offer a solution to the paradox of fiction. Because, if they only differ in their causation then we do not have (ii) an explanation of the behavioural differences between (real) emotions and quasi emotions. I am not convinced that we can show (i) and (ii), therefore we cannot fully defend fictionalism as wholly 'emotionally coherent', but only to the extent that we can have emotions towards fiction that *feel* (to a significant extent, at least in the short term) and *look* (behaviourally, again to a significant extent) real. And perhaps this is enough?

(P2) We do not believe that fictional entities exist

The second proposition of the paradox states that we do not believe that fictional entities exist. That is to say that we, as audience members or readers, are aware that the characters we are engaging with exist *only* in the relevant fictional world. So, 'Harry Potter exists' insofar as 'Harry Potter exists in the fictional world of Harry Potter'. Harry Potter does not exist in the real world, nor does he exist in Peter Jackson's fictional world of 'Middle Earth'. Thus, the only way to overcome the paradox by collapsing (P2) is to say that we *do* believe fictional entities to exist. Here, we will look at two arguments that attempt to argue just this. The first argument concerns the fleetingness of our belief in fiction, and the second looks at the nature of general truths. What I mean by 'the nature of general truths' is that we will explore how fiction can generate emotions by presenting historical or common facts, such as Dickens bringing to our attention the appalling conditions of the poor in Victorian England. Le Poidevin presents both arguments and concludes that neither one of them are very convincing; however, I will argue that if we unpack these arguments further that they are, potentially, quite compelling.

The fleetingness of belief

The first argument is to suggest that 'for a fleeting moment' we forget that we are indulging ourselves in a fictional world, and we believe that we are really being presented with the truth. And it is this belief that causes our emotional response. When reading a novel or watching a film we are so engrossed in the story and the characters that we 'forget' that we are actually engaging in a fictional world – even if the world includes an awkward schoolboy learning spells to defeat a dark Lord. For that time we spend in J. K Rowling's world of witches and wizards, we 'suspend our disbelief'. We leave our world behind and enter into this fictional world of wizards, talking trees and flying cars, where the casting of a spell can turn your mortal enemy into a toad!

A cinema complex only has a couple of rules and they are there to stop anyone or anything from interfering with one's ability to 'enter into' the fictional world of the film.[44] We are asked to switch our mobile phones off and to refrain from talking. And, so, for a 'fleeting time' time when the film is running and we are watching, we believe that Hogwarts is a real school, Harry is a real boy and a real wizard and the dark Lord really does need to be defeated. Le Poidevin does not find this argument convincing. To explain why, he uses the example of watching a horror film.

> Typically, when we feel fear as a result of some belief that, say, we are in danger from the man in *Psycho*, we would take steps to find out where he is operating, or

whether he has been caught. We would take care to keep the doors locked even during the day, and especially when taking a shower. But fiction does not incline us to action in this direct way. We watch the film without running out of the cinema and ringing the police, or buying the paper to find out the latest. We are not fooled,[*] even for a moment, and only instantaneously believe the fiction to be true, then, on this account, our emotional state should be correspondingly fleeting. But, typically, our emotions will not fluctuate in this way.[45]

It seems that there are two arguments here. First, that fiction does not directly affect us, and second, that if we do believe, we only believe for a moment which would mean our emotional response would last for a moment. I do not think that this is the case. I will present both arguments and respond to each in a way that attempts to overcome the second proposition. Fiction does not directly affect us. Le Poidevin arrives at this conclusion from his understanding that we do not physically react to traumatic events 'on screen' in the same way that we do 'offscreen' or, at least, not *directly*. Here, I want to make two counterpoints. First, I would argue that we *do* react in 'real life' to fiction. After watching a horror, we certainly might lock our doors, we might check to see if the film was based on a true story or if anything similar has ever been reported, and I do not think it is far-fetched to imagine a call being made to the police for fear of being in real danger. Granted, the police officer might tell you that 'it's just a story' and that you have nothing to worry about, but how much does that really relieve your fear? Or does it just stop you from calling 999 again for help?

Even if our reaction to the film is based on a past trauma that has been brought to the surface, thus making any reactions 'indirect', does this mean that we do not believe fictional entities to exist? There is, certainly, a difference between believing Harry Potter (a fictional wizard) to exist and believing Michael Myers (a fictional murderer) to exist outside of their relevant fictional worlds, because we do not typically believe in wizards but we do know that murderers exist. And yet, rational or irrational, fantastical or scientific, a belief or 'suspension of disbelief', I find it hard to deny that we do not react to fiction, even in ways that may be irrational.

A love story, for instance, might come with a memorable philosophy, something like: 'I can live without, you but I don't want to, I don't ever want to.' Fans of the television series *Grey's Anatomy* will remember Meredith Grey saying this to her husband and those fans might, after hearing this, live out their lives according to this philosophy (perhaps even unknowingly). Does this not suggest that one such person *believes somewhat* in the existence of these two people in this relationship, or at least the love that they share? You hear people say all the time, 'I'll never forget this one line from this film . . .', or: 'this was one of the best lines I ever heard . . .' Fiction impacts people, it makes us react and I think that it is reasonable to say that there is some belief-act going on here. Moreover, in response to the argument that we do not respond dramatically or directly to fiction, I think, on the contrary, that as emotional beings we *are* inclined to react to fiction through a belief-of-sorts; that the reality of the fiction, and its entities, extend beyond the television screen and inked pages, and whether these reactions are direct or not is not to be easily dismissed.

The second argument presented by Le Poidevin is that even if we do believe, we only believe for a moment which would mean our emotional response would last only for a moment. I do not think that this is representative of what is going on when we are reading a book or watching a film. We do not, typically, experience 'fleeting emotions' when engaging with fiction. Rather, our emotional response to fiction tends to last longer than the length of the film or the time it takes to read the book. And, if our emotional response is often not 'short-lived' then the suspension of disbelief, which might lead us to (falsely) believing, is also not 'short-lived'. And, since this is the only way we *could* believe (i.e. to momentarily forget we are engaging in fiction), we cannot say that we believe in the existence of fictional entities.

Like the notion that we continue to have beliefs when we are sleeping or when we are not thinking about the subject matter, and that we still have those emotions that are attached to those beliefs, perhaps we could assimilate this to the idea that there does not exist only a 'fleeting moment' in which we can say that we can believe in the existence of fictional entities. Perhaps, after engaging in fiction, when we are asleep or not thinking about the fiction, we still have those emotions that we attach to the fiction. Is it possible that our 'momentary belief' spills over into our world (i.e. not the relevant fictional world)?[46] This is a complex argument, and I am not suggesting that I have successfully refuted the second proposition, and it is not my overall objective to do so, but I am simply exploring an alternative idea. Now I will move on to the next argument.

The nature of general truths

The second argument that Le Poidevin refutes is that fictional emotions are generated by bringing to our attention 'genuine, although quite general truths'.[47] Such as a novel about a troubled family relationship that may cause us to reflect upon our own family relationships and, as a result, evoke guilt, anger or sadness.

This explanation of fictional emotions fails on two accounts, says Le Poidevin. First, it is Le Poidevin's understanding that the nature of fictional emotions may be acute but also short-lived. Whereas, the emotions one feels when contemplating the 'general issues' that fiction may bring to our attention are 'likely to be less acute and last for a longer period of time'.[48] Therefore, there may be an element of truth in the suggestion that it is general truths that generate emotions, but it cannot be the whole story.

The second shortcoming of this account is the suggestion that it is some state of affairs in the world which is described by the fictional situation and *not* the fictional character that is the object of our emotions. This does not correctly describe our experience, says Le Poidevin, for it *is* 'the imaginary characters themselves, not the real situations they symbolise, who have such an immediate call on our feelings'.[49] For instance, Le Poidevin mentions the works of Charles Dickens and the appalling conditions in which the poor lived in Victorian England, and, to a lesser extent, the conditions of the poor today that his novels bring to our attention. Although we might be emotionally connected to the characters in Dickens's novels, it 'may only last as long as the fiction is engaging our immediate consciousness'.[50] Literary figure, Samuel Johnson says a similar thing: 'The delight of tragedy proceeds from our consciousness of fiction; if we thought murders and treasons real, they would please no more.'[51] Let us look at an example of one of Dickens's novels, *The Old Curiosity Shop*.

The events of the book seem to take place around the mid-1820s and tell the story of a young girl, Nell Trent, who is around fourteen years old. Nell is an orphan and has a rather lonely existence with almost no friends her own age. She lives with her maternal grandfather in his shop of odds and ends, and he tries to ensure that she does not die in poverty as her parents did. Of course, we feel a plight for the character of Nell, as Le Poidevin suggests, but my question is, 'How much can we separate Nell from her context?' How can it be said that we certainly feel for Nell (as a character) but that the depiction of poverty of Victorian England in the novel does not emotionally resonate with us once we have read the final page of the book? Yes, we want to say that the object of our emotion is Nell, in this stance, but do we not also want to say that the state of affairs in the novel also plays a significant role in our emotional response and does in fact make the character more *believable*?

A recent article exposes the stories that were told about the people of New York waiting at the pier head for the ship to come in and deliver the final instalment of the book, which would reveal the fate of Nell, with some even calling out 'Is little Nell dead?'[52] The article concluded by saying this:

the 'almost certainly invented story reflects a shift in the myths surrounding Dickens, as well as a broader cultural shift in Anglo-American understandings of fictional characters. The story's rapid cultural transmission demonstrates that twentieth-century readers could easily imagine readers in previous generations treating characters as if they were real people'.[53] My question is, 'Do we not still do this now?' Can we not easily imagine readers in our generation treating characters as if they were real people?[54] I think so. Now I will turn to the third proposition.

(P3) To be moved, we must believe that fictional entities exist

The third proposition of the paradox states that in order to have a genuine emotional response to fiction, one must believe that fictional entities exist, and since we do not believe that fictional entities exist, we are not moved by fictional entities. To demonstrate how this proposition could potentially be overcome, I will mention four thinkers and their theories, those being: Stecker on a cognitivist theory of emotions, Tullman and her argument for a HOT theory of emotions, Gendler's conception of aliefs and Weston's theory on comparing art with *not art*. Each theory will suggest that our ability to genuinely connect to fiction is *not* always and in every way based on 'belief'. And, so, it is possible to be moved by fiction.

Stecker's paper 'Should We Still Care About the Paradox Of Fiction?' states with confidence that, now, 'virtually no one accepts' proposition three of the paradox of fiction.[55] That is, in order to pity someone, for instance, one must believe that they exist. Stecker suggests that the reason why the third proposition is considered a prima facie proposition is because the paradox was formulated during the heyday of the cognitive theory of emotion, otherwise known as the judgement theory, which we looked at earlier on. Moreover, there was a lot of theoretical commitment to proposition three.[56] Therefore, one reason why we might counter (P3) is that we are no longer wholly committed to the judgement theory of emotions. A second reason why the third proposition might be rejected is because it is 'far too strong'.[57] By this Stecker means that it cannot explain how it is that we can feel pity for people who lived in the past, or for someone who no longer exists, or for those who will live in a hypothetical future.[58] In such cases, we do not believe that the object of emotion exists and, yet, we want to say that we are moved.[59]

Tullman and HOT emotions

For Tullman, the paradox of fiction acts as a hurdle for any leading theory of emotions from cognitivists, non-cognitivism and hybrid theories.[60] Two theories in particular that Tullman draws on are Walton's pure-cognitivist theory of make-believe and Noël Carroll's hybrid thought-theory. Similarly to Walton, Carroll argues that it is not the fictional world itself towards which we have an emotional response, rather it is our *thought content* about the fiction. However, in opposition to Walton, Carroll argues that a make-believe theory is not needed in order to justify our emotions because it is possible to have genuine emotions about the contents of our thoughts. Tullman is not convinced that emotions require belief a priori (like Walton), and she draws on recent work in the neuroscience and biology of emotions themselves by Joseph LeDoux to support this, but it is Tullman's elucidation of Carroll's thought-theory that we will look at here.

When engaging in a narrative it is possible to experience a range of emotions from basic to complex. Basic, bodily emotions such as shock and disgust, and complex emotions such as pity, sympathy and pride. To explain how we might experience the latter, Carroll suggests a necessary parallel: the complexity of the emotion reflects the complexity of the thought or judgement. This means that in order to have a complex emotional response to fiction there seems to be some sort of *cognitive appraisal* of the fiction, that is, a thought or a judgement. For example, I pity the character of Anna in cases where I have an evaluative attitude about Anna. This shows why a completely non-cognitivist account like James's is inadequate, but it does not yet require us to regard the cognitive element in emotion to be belief.

However, this theory is supported by recent work on brain systems involved in emotional processing by neuroscientist Joseph LeDoux. To the extent that emotions do appear to necessarily involve cognitive appraisal. If LeDoux's findings are correct, the pure-cognitivist claim that belief constitutes an emotion is undermined, emotions can occur without one first having a belief about one's environment. LeDoux argues that 'feelings do involve conscious content, but we don't necessarily have conscious access to the processes that produce the content'.[61]

It would appear, then, that Carroll's thought-theory of emotions can account for complex emotions, but Tullman believes that the theory needs further elucidation to also account adequately for basic emotions. There are two main reasons for this, the first is that LeDoux's theory suggests that Carroll has the order of the emotional process backwards. Carroll believes that the appraisal causes the bodily change, but research by LeDoux and others has shown that bodily changes are not caused by cognitive appraisals. Rather, it is the other way round: the perceived bodily change takes place *before* the appraisal.[62] Second, we need to get a clearer idea on the extent of our *awareness* of our thoughts concerning fiction. Furthermore, Tullman – who, remember, is also unconvinced by pure-cognitivist theories – seeks to expand Carroll's neo-non-cognitivist theory by devising a *complete* theory of emotions, to explain both basic and complex emotions.

To do this, Tullman utilizes David Rosenthal's philosophy of consciousness. Rosenthal's theory is known as a HOT theory of consciousness. The theory is this: there exists a 'higher-order thought', or 'HOT', which is a thought about a mental state: a sensation, a belief, a thought, an emotion state and so on. Rosenthal's theory is best understood by using the following example.

> Sensing is not . . . the only way we are conscious of things. We are also conscious of something when we have a thought about that thing as being present. I need not see somebody in the audience to be conscious of that person; it's enough just to have a thought that the person is here. There is, moreover, no other way we know about being conscious of things. So, if we are not conscious of our conscious states by sensing them, the only alternative is that we have thoughts about them . . . *higher-order thoughts*.[63]

Tullman uses this theory about consciousness and applies it to fictional emotions, in the hopes of (a) dissolving the paradox of fiction by (b) offering an alternative to the cognitive theory that 'belief' is necessary for a genuine emotional response. She draws on two points from this extract from Rosenthal to demonstrate what the theory of HOTs – in line with Carroll's thought-theory – can tell us about our emotions towards fiction. The first is that it is possible to have HOTs about things 'that are not physically present and that we do not *believe* are physically present'.[64] And, so, according to the HOT theory, we can have HOTs about fictional characters. Moreover, the HOT itself (the thought) can act as the *object of the emotion*.[65]

Recall that, according to Carroll's position, 'an emotion involves an evaluative attitude towards an internal mental state, rather than towards an external object or state of affairs'.[66] I pity the character Anna in cases where I have an evaluative attitude about Anna. The thought that Anna is tremendously sad is the formal object of my emotion, not the state of affairs concerning Anna. Thus, Tullman's HOT theory of emotions maintains Carroll's basic point against the pure-cognitive theory. That is, that emotions do not necessarily involve beliefs. Moreover, then, Tullman is specifically rejecting the third proposition of the paradox because, according to a HOT theory, we need not have a genuine belief about the existence of a situation in order to have an emotion about it.

The second point has to do with our *awareness* of a mental state. That is to ask, 'How aware are we of our mental state when we are engaging in fiction?' Tullman explains that when we are watching a film we are in a conscious state, but 'we are not always *aware* of that state'.[67] Insofar as, basic emotional responses – racing heart and sweaty palms – can take place without one being aware of them. But, as we have said, a complex emotion – pity, sympathy and so on – involves a *cognitive appraisal*. Meaning, we must be conscious of this thought. And this is where the HOT theory comes in again. The HOT itself is not the emotion, but it can *act as the object of the emotion*, 'we need not be conscious of our awareness of a state; the HOT itself need not be conscious'.[68] The theory is a little more complicated than this as it involves a 'higher order awareness' but I think, for our purposes, we can see how Tullman's theory of HOT emotions makes a contemporary attempt to overcome the third proposition of the paradox. She does this by saying that belief is not necessary to explain complex emotions towards fiction, rather developments in philosophy of mind and neuroscience can defend a 'thought' as capable of inducing such a response.[69] We shall now look at Gendler's theory of belief and *alief*.

Gendler: Belief or *alief*?

How should we describe the cognitive state of those who act in ways discordant to their beliefs? That is to say, how should we describe what is going on mentally when a person acts in opposition to their beliefs? For example, when a person is reluctant to eat a delicious piece of fudge that is shaped like dog faeces.[70] Surely they *believe* that the faeces-shaped fudge is indeed regular fudge (unfortunately shaped), but psychologist Paul Rozin has demonstrated, with a study spanning several decades, that well-educated Western adults were reluctant to eat the fudge.[71] Another example from the study showed that subjects were reluctant to drink from a glass of juice that had been stirred by a completely sterilized dead cockroach. It was observed that the subjects were even hesitant to wear a T-shirt that had been worn previously by someone they dislike. And, so, the following question is posed, 'How should we describe the cognitive state of subjects who hesitate to eat fudge shaped like dog feces, or drink from a cup that has been in contact with a sterilised cockroach, or wear a t-shirt that has been previously worn by one's foe?' What is going on here?

Gendler argues that perplexing examples of discordant behaviour, such as these, suggest the existence of another type of cognitive state. A cognitive state that exists alongside or even running against belief, and it's called *alief*. So, when a subject shows real reluctance to eat faeces-shaped fudge, we assume that one *believes* that the fudge has not changed its chemical composition, but perhaps they are also *alieving* something else. Something like this: 'Filthy object! Contaminated! Stay Away!'[72] Alief, then, is an alternative mental state that can explain otherwise perplexing phenomena, that is, discordant behaviour. Alief is a more 'primitive' mental state than belief because it 'directly activates behavioural response patterns' as opposed to 'motivating in conjunction with desire or pretended desire'.[73]

Gendler believes that the mental state of 'alief' can even help to explain what is going on when we engage in fiction. Insofar as, the concept of alief could decipher why it is that we react in ways discordant to our beliefs – that is, I believe, when reading *American Psycho*, that I am not in any real danger of becoming one of Patrick's victims, but I still find myself shrieking and shutting the book out of disgust or terror or both. According to Gendler's argument from alief, the reader *believes* that they are safe, but they also *alieve* that they are in danger.

Furthermore, Gendler applies her theory of alief to the paradox of fiction by way of explaining the belief-discordant nature of fictional emotions. She quotes from Walton's 'Fearing Fictions', namely the passage about Charles watching a horror film, to demonstrate the application of her 'alief theory'. Let us remind ourselves of the passage. While watching the terrible green slime destroy everything in its midst, Charles 'emits a shriek and clutches desperately at his chair' afterwards admitting that he was 'terrified' of the slime.

How should we describe Charles's cognitive state? Surely, Charles does not *believe* that he will be 'slimed' through the television screen (Walton even reiterates that this is not the case, 'Charles knows perfectly well that the slime is not real and that he is in no danger').[74] Would it make sense, then, to say that Charles *believes* that he is safe but he also *alieves* something very different, something along the lines of: 'Dangerous two-eyed creature heading towards me! H-el-p . . .! Activate fight or flight adrenaline now!' (the *voice* of his alief).[75] Thus, the concept of alief can help explain Charles's belief-discordant behaviour. Moreover, aliefs can help to account for *at least basic emotions*, by explaining how and why it is possible to feel fearful towards something you believe not to exist.[76] For alief can explain when 'something is awry' through arguing for the existence of a mental state that runs against one's beliefs, thus explaining a 'belief-behaviour mismatch'.[77]

What is more, Gendler talks in detail about how the concept of alief can explain why one would act in a way that seems to go against what one believes to be the case, something that she dubs *'belief-discordant alief'*. Which means that alief has a 'representational-affective-behavioural content' – that is, the 'visual appearance of the feces-shaped fudge renders occurrent a belief-discordant alief with the content: "dog-shit, disgusting, refuse-to-eat" – an alief that runs counter to the subject's explicit belief that the object before her is composed of a substance that she considers delicious and appealing'.[78] And, the same is true for the case of fictional emotions, says Gendler.

The theory of alief suggests that it is not paradoxical to have an emotional and behavioural response to fiction because our response can be explained through another mental state, that is, not 'belief'. Just for further clarification, what I mean here when I say to respond 'emotionally' and/or 'behaviourally' is only to acknowledge the psychological and physiological elements of emotion, that is, one's 'internal' emotion (perhaps of 'sadness' or 'sorrow') and one's 'external' display of emotion (perhaps a lump in one's throat and eyes welled with tears).

The undetermined order of *'which comes first'*: the 'internal' emotion (cognitive theories, see M. Nussbaum and K. Walton), or the 'external' display (non-cognitivist theories, see W. James, J. Prinz, J. LeDoux), or even to say *which* is the true display of emotion is more complicated than this (hybrid theories, see N. Carroll, R. Solomon), which demonstrates the complexity of emotion theory.[79] I am not looking to enter into this debate; I am, rather, using theories within the debate to explore fictional emotions for the purpose of defending the emotional coherence of fictionalism.

Furthermore, the cognitivist theory, namely the judgement theory of emotions that Radford's paradox is in line with, determines the 'reality' or 'authenticity' of one's emotion by asking, 'Does one believe that the object of their emotions exists?' To put it crudely, if the answer is 'yes', then it is often accepted that the emotional response is genuine. If the answer is 'no', then one's emotional response can be rendered *not* genuine by default. According to the cognitivist, we do not have the 'right kind' of belief about fictions to constitute a real emotion. However, Gendler's theory is important for those who disagree with the cognitivist because their theory does not seem to wholly represent what is going on when we respond to fiction. Our emotions feel genuine to us, and

Gendler's theory of alief can support and explain this without reference to belief as a paradoxical explanation.

The existence of aliefs and their instinctual-like behaviour suggest that 'belief' is not a necessary cognitive component when assessing fictional emotions. Aliefs can explain our 'belief-discordant' response. Interestingly, even when we realize that our aliefs do not reflect reality or what we believe to be true, that they are perfectly 'arational'[80] (for Charles, maybe after the film has ended, revising the fictitious nature of the slime), our aliefs do not just go away. Instead, they stick around and guide much of our behaviour anyway.

> Belief plays an important role in the ultimate regulation of behaviour. But it plays a far smaller role in moment-to-moment management than philosophical tradition has tended to stress.[81]

An alief is a mental state that is '*a*ssociative, *a*ction-generating, *a*ffect-laden, *a*rational, *a*utomatic, [and] *a*gnostic with respect to its content'.[82] So, in the case of Charles watching a horror film, Gendler believes that rather than discrediting Charles's emotion as *not* genuine or irrational; instead we can say that Charles is responding to what he *alieves*: 'Horrible Slime, get away!', and not what he *believes*: 'It's okay, I'm only watching a film.' Why does this happen?

Well, Gendler says that our 'affective processing mechanisms appear to be relatively insensitive to the question of whether the scenario under consideration is real, imagined, supposed or denied'.[83] This happens to the extent that the difference in the intensity of our responses 'can largely be traced to a difference in the intensity of the stimulus'.[84] This, then, can help the fictionalist position that 'belief' is not necessary for a genuine emotional response to religious discourse. But what about other possible explanations? Gendler rules these out too.

By way of further defending the existence of alief, Gendler rules out other possible explanations. Using Charles and the terrible green slime as a specific example: (i) Charles is not trying to fool the film-maker by deliberately deceiving them; (ii) Charles is not trying to deceive himself; (iii) it is not the case that there is any doubt or uncertainty – Charles does not leave the cinema thinking, 'Phew! It's lucky the slime stayed on the screen this time!'; (iv) Charles does not temporarily forget that he is engaging in fiction; and (v) Charles does not *imagine* that he will be attacked by the slime. The concept of 'imagining' lies on a different plane altogether to alief. This is because to imagine, or indeed to believe, is a *propositional attitude*, whereas, alief is not.

And, so, if it is not the case that Charles is deceiving others, or self-deceived, or uncertain, or forgetful, or imagining, then *why* does engaging in fiction cause an emotional response? According to Gendler's theory, the reason is that one's mental state of 'alief' runs against one's 'belief' and reveals an emotional and behavioural response. Can this be extended to the Anna Karenina case? That is to say, can this theory be extended to help explain not only basic emotions but also complex ones too? Can aliefs explain how we feel 'pity' (towards Anna, for example) or really only emotions such as being 'terrified' (as is the case with Charles)? I suggest that the answer to this is that aliefs cannot necessarily explain how it is that we can feel complex emotions when engaging with fiction.

Gendler says that the 'well-functioning aliever' is one 'whose ability to suppress contrary impulse is strong', and she explains this by quoting William James, '[t]o make our nervous system our ally instead of our enemy ... we must make automatic and habitual, as early as possible, as many useful actions as we can'.[85] This suggests that aliefs function more as an impulse (and, thus, impulse control is the 'aim'), remember aliefs are described as '*a*ssociative, *a*utomatic, and *a*rational'; they are therefore 'typically also *a*ffect-laden and *a*ction generating'.[86] To emphasize this point, Gendler even says that these states 'we share with nonhuman animals'.[87] Ergo, it might be argued that although Gendler's theory might provide fresh insight into how we might come to understand 'belief-discordant' behaviour, it might not be able to provide the same insight when it comes to more complex emotions: emotions that are less mechanical, involuntary or habitual in nature, and more conscious, perhaps, sentient in nature.

The discordant response by those engaging in fiction is what Radford is trying to tackle with the paradox: you cannot have a genuine emotional response to something that you do not believe to be true. But this is the wrong conclusion to make, says Gendler.

> [A]ny theory that helps itself to notions like belief ... needs to include a notion like alief in order to make proper sense of a wide range of perplexing phenomena. Without such a notion . . . either such phenomena remain overlooked or misdescribed, or they seem to mandate such a radical reconceptualization of the relation between cognition and behaviour that traditional notions like belief seem quaint and inadequate.[88]

So, we now turn to the question, 'What does this tell us about the emotional coherence of religious fictionalism?' If we are to accept the existence of alief as a mental state, then can we dismantle the paradox or, better yet, argue that there is no paradox at all? On the basis that it is not always the case that when emotionally responding to, say, religious discourse we respond on behalf of our beliefs. Instead, might it be said that we react on behalf of our *aliefs*, and our aliefs are not reflective of our 'sensible beliefs' including what we know to be true or to be the case.

Therefore, we can respond to fiction in a way that is discordant to our beliefs and it does not mean that our emotional response is irrational. Rather, our reaction or, specifically, our fictional emotions go 'all the way down'. By this I mean, that they can be explained through the existence of 'a special sort of physical state – one that occurs in the brain of the conscious subject. And it occurs in her brain as the result of her (or her genetic ancestors) having undergone certain sorts of experience – experiences that result in the creation of clusters of associations with representational affective-behavioural content'.[89] Thus, the fictionalist can use this definition of alief to defend their philosophy that one can have a genuine emotional response or connection to religion insofar as religious discourse is best understood through theological fiction.

However, the theory of alief is limited if it is to be recruited to rescue fictional emotions to theological fiction *alone*. Gendler's theory does not go into detail about more complex emotions, and it is these types of emotions that perhaps the fictionalist might feel, in particular when engaging in religious discourse. What I *do* think Gendler's theory *can do* or promote is to suggest that (1) 'belief' is not the only mental state that can explain one's emotional response to fiction; (2) one's emotional response need not correspond to one's beliefs, in fact they run counter to them; (3) our emotional response (if caused by what one alieves) cannot be 'shaken off', they are powerful and 'around to stay'; and (4) such emotions (if caused by what one alieves) will potentially outlast one's beliefs because aliefs do not change with new evidence, whereas beliefs do. With this in mind, I think that the concept of 'alief' can help argue for fictional emotions towards theological fiction to be 'genuine' insofar as they 'cannot be helped', they are 'here to stay' and they are cognitive. That is, at least for basic emotions evoked by fiction. Now we will turn to Weston's theory of fiction as a work of art.

Weston: Fiction as a work of art

Accompanying Radford's original essay 'How Can We Be Moved by the Fate of Anna Karenina?' ('*I – Colin Radford*') is a counter-response from Michael Weston ('*II – Michael Weston*'). Weston's reply or, rather, critique is centred on the idea that fiction is, and should be treated as, a 'work of art'. Insofar as, the way in which we evaluate the nature of our emotional response to fiction should not be compared to our emotional response to, say, *not* works of art – that is, an event or a story that we know to be true or false, whether the truth or falsity of the event or story is revealed before, during or after the telling of it.

There are ways, Weston proclaims, 'to bring out the coherence of us being moved by fiction' if we come to understand that our response to fiction is a response to works of art, and *this* should be our starting point.[90] Radford begins his investigation on the pretext that *belief* in the factual or probable existence of the object of our emotion is a *necessary condition*, but, says Weston, surely we should begin our investigation with the notion that we *are* moved by fiction and belief in the factual or probable existence of the object *appears not to matter*, so how can we explain this? I will now go through Weston's argument for fiction as a work of art and how this framework can help explain our emotions towards fiction.

It is Weston's understanding that Radford misinterprets fictional emotions as 'incoherent' because he fails to recognize that an object of art is not comparable to an object which is *not* art – that is, we should not compare our response to Mercutio's death in *Romeo and Juliet* to the death of a real young man. As Weston puts it, 'the kinds of response we can have towards dramatis personae are determined by the kind of object works of drama are'.[91] In a real-life context, it is possible to separate a person from their situation, insofar as things might have gone differently for them. That is, it is possible to disconnect the death of the real young man from the man himself, inasmuch as you can imagine things having gone differently for the young man. But, in fiction this is not the case. You cannot separate the event from the person and still feel the same plight. Mercutio must die in the way that he does in *Romeo and Juliet*; otherwise, he is not Mercutio or you are not watching *Romeo and Juliet*.[92] If we are moved by Mercutio's death we are being moved by an episode within the context of the play. Moreover, Weston explains that a fictional account is *not* the same nor comparable to a '*putatively factual* account'.[93] By this he means, that a work of art is not comparable to an account of what we believe to be true or likely.

On this basis, Weston points out that the accounts given by Radford in his paper are paradigmatic, because they are examples of putatively factual accounts and not fictional accounts. Therefore, they fail to tell us anything about the nature of our emotions towards fiction. For example, Radford delivers the following account:

> suppose that you have a drink with a man who proceeds to tell you a harrowing story about his sister and you are harrowed. After enjoying your reaction he then

tells you that he doesn't have a sister, that he has invented the story... once you have been told this you can no longer feel harrowed.⁹⁴

Weston has no qualms with this conclusion, but what he does take issue with is drawing a parallel between this account and a fictional account, and to compare one's emotional response. By extension, the second solution put forward by Radford – *we don't necessary 'forget' but we 'suspend our disbelief' while engaging with the fiction* – is similar to his first solution – *we get 'caught up' in the fiction and 'forget', or are no longer aware, that we are only reading a book or watching a play* – in that, they are both insufficient. They fail to recognize the difference between a 'belief' tout court and a belief that a story may be 'true to life'.⁹⁵ The latter, which is what one may experience when engaging in fiction, does not involve brief delusion, 'I may suspend my disbelief in your story so that I may check it as dispassionately as possible' but, crucially, 'I neither believe nor disbelieve the events'.⁹⁶

Furthermore, Weston indicates that Radford has not yet gotten to the heart of the problem, the problem being this: the failure to seriously consider the ontological state of fictional characters and their role as part of a wider work of art.⁹⁷ Thus, Weston's theory hangs on the notion that we are not only moved by facts but by *ideas*. For instance, if we are moved by Anna's death, according to Weston, 'we are being moved by an episode within the context of a play' or, in this case, a novel.⁹⁸ Moreover, what we are responding to are not facts or beliefs but 'a certain conception of life', and our emotional responses are the 'product of reflection on it'.⁹⁹ A certain amount of epistemic distance, then, is required of the individual. That is, a knowledgeable gap between the emotional demands of one's everyday life and the fiction itself. And, the best way to achieve this distance, says Weston, is to understand fiction as a work of art. That is, to understand our response to fiction as 'part of a conception of what is important in life'.¹⁰⁰

When we say we are moved by the death of Anna, it is necessary, Weston says, to 'go into some interpretive detail' about the novel, because what we are moved by – Anna's death – 'is not independent of the significance we see in the work as a whole', namely as a work of art.¹⁰¹ Without its complex and compelling background, the ending of Part Seven in *Anna Karenina* would be meaningless: Anna's death would appear meaningless. If we are moved by her death it is not recognized through 'temporal, spatial, and physical coordinates, but by the coordinates of the text'.¹⁰² We are moved by the *idea* or by the *thought* that, in this instance, a young woman suffers so greatly that she feels her only escape is suicide. And so, the claim that we cannot respond to the death of a character unless we are 'caught up' in the fiction (a theory that neither Radford nor Weston are convinced by), that is, the claim that we 'can only respond to the beauty and tragedy of the poetry and not to the death of the character',[103] appears inaccurate. We can and do respond to the death of the character because the 'beauty and tragedy' of the fiction is not, says Weston, 'something one can attend to independently of the context in which it occurs, and that context is provided by the structure' of the fiction.[104] The death of Anna, then, and our emotional response to her death can be explained through our 'perception of the significance of her death within that context'; moreover, our response to Anna's death is a response to the sense of the novel of which it is a part, and hence to the conception of life which the novel provides.[105]

Furthermore, understanding fiction as a work of art is one way that this concern for life and its significance appears, and the 'possibility of our being moved by works of art must be made intelligible within the context of such a concern'.[106] Radford's conclusion that our response to fiction is irrational, inconsistent and incoherent does not satisfy our search to answer or comprehend this concern. To drive this final point home, Weston references philosopher Peter Winch, in the following passage.

> Unlike beasts, men do not merely live but also have a conception of life. This is not something that is simply added to their life; rather it changes the very sense which the word 'life' has when applied to men. It is no longer equivalent to 'animate existence'. When we are speaking of the life of man, we can ask questions about what is the right way to live, what things are most important in life, whether life has any significance, and if so what.[107]

Weston refutes Radford's conclusion that our emotional response to fiction is paradoxical and consequently irrational by insisting that Radford fails to differentiate belief tout court from belief in a story to be 'true to life', namely putatively factual accounts from fictional accounts. Therefore, Radford misses the mark on understanding a fictional work as a mirror for how we come to understand life. Fiction, as a work of art, is not a 'self-contained game', but rather 'it has its importance in its connection with what is not art, with our everyday lives'.[108] And it is here that this particular explanation can bring us right back to religious fictionalism. If we agree that Weston has put forward a compelling argument for fiction as a work of art, and if we can insert *theological fiction* as the work of art, might it be argued that religious fictionalism is emotionally coherent? Insofar as, fictional characters and stories bring about an emotional response when we understand the fiction as a whole, that is the story of how everything came to be. And, is religious literature not the ultimate story of life? Surely, then, this fiction, of all fiction, is capable of doing this.

> If we are moved through the significance we see an event possesses within the thematic context of a play, that such significance should matter to us is not itself explained by the play, but must be accounted for by the way our literature can illuminate our lives.[109]

On the one hand, I believe that Weston has provided a theory that encapsulates the 'emotional coherence' of religious fictionalism by demonstrating that fiction is a powerful work of art that helps to make sense of our lives. And, if through religious fictionalism we can consider symbolic religious discourse and, particularly, Scripture as a work of art, it certainly makes sense to say that for millions of people participating in religious discourse and reading Scripture helps uncover the complexity of life. Religion can act not only as a guide for how to make sense of one's life but also for how *life itself* came about and even provides answers for what happens once 'this life' is over.

On the other hand, it would not be appropriate to suggest that Weston has dissolved the paradox, because even if he successfully denies the third proposition, the issue remains that an account of psychological mechanism would need to be provided. That is to say that, if we can use Weston's theory to counter the view that to be moved, we must believe that fictional entities exist, we cannot extend this theory to explain how exactly it is that we find ourselves emotionally involved. We would need to couple Weston's theory with Gendler's theory of aliefs, for example. Which, as we know, would only, then, be able to provide an explanation for basic emotions, and not complex ones.

Suppose further that Weston's theory can offer an explanation for why religious fictionalism might be described as 'emotionally coherent', this is only be the case if the reader/viewer is responding to the conceptions of the 'conceptions of life' (that the world expresses) shown by the work of fiction and *not* fictional characters, because they cannot be the cause of the emotion. Thus, Weston's argument hangs on the thread that our emotions are *only* imbued with the conception of life expressed by *Lord of the Rings* and not Frodo, because this brings us back to the paradox. For even if we are feeling sorry for Frodo-as-a-poor-hobbit-mixed-up-in-some-dark-stuff, the fact remains that this complex object is still fictional. There is no Frodo, hence no Frodo-as-a-poor-hobbit-mixed-up-in-some-dark-stuff. If it is paradoxical to pity Frodo, it is no less paradoxical to pity Frodo-as-a-poor-hobbit-mixed-up-in-some-dark-stuff. Furthermore, Weston's response to the paradox can give us (a limited) reason *why* we might be moved by fiction, but it cannot provide an explanation as to *how*.

Concluding thoughts on the three theories

In light of the three theories that we have just explored, I want to put forward a few concluding points to help round off our investigation into the 'emotional coherence' of fictionalism. When it comes to understanding the difference between 'belief' and 'make-believe', if we agree that 'belief' is generally *in*dependent of will and make-believe is dependent, then Gendler says that it is 'the will dependence of make-believe that explains its difference to the truth of the content'.[110] That is to say, to put it crudely, the 'belief arrow' points to, what is believed to be true. The 'make-believe arrow', however, 'goes the other way around':[111] it comes from what the author is telling you to be true and you deciding whether you are *willing* to imagine cases of moral deviance. And that is, imaginative resistance. I think that Gendler's interpretation illuminates make-believe as a tool that animates themes while allowing (consciously or unconsciously) room for doubt, insofar as what it would mean to lift those themes from fiction to reality, namely to move from make-believing to believing tout court.

Gendler tells us that imagination is distinct from belief. That, as human beings, we have a general capacity to imagine morally deviant situations. And, that we have an unwillingness to do so. It is not only, then, when we believe tout court that which we are invested in, what we believe to be true *and* what we live out and experience as true on a daily basis. When make-believing one is, too, invested in something which we make-believe to be true *and* the lives as we live them out on a daily basis. Furthermore, the fictionalist allows themselves to become emotionally involved to the extent that a religious service, for example, is capable of being an intense experience. And, what remains, as Le Poidevin explains, 'when the game of make-believe is over, is an awareness of our responsibility for ourselves and others, of the need to pursue spiritual goals and so on'.[112] Andrew Eshleman also claims that 'inhabiting the time-tested world of religious narrative and imagery is a valuable means of structuring one's life around a conception of good'.[113] I think Weston, too, articulates this point well.

> The interpretation of a work of art is not a self-contained game, but has its importance in its connection with what is not art, with our everyday lives.

Where we are not concerned primarily with the technical aspects of works, such interpretation consists in articulating the relation the work has to concerns which are important to us independently of art: in establishing its thematic structure, its 'vision of life'.[114]

It might not be make-believing, it might be *alieving* (Gendler), or it might be that '*higher order thought*' – a HOT – of emotion (Tullman) that can explain why we are able to have an emotional response to fiction. It is not only the cognitive state of 'belief' that can explain fictional emotions. It is possible, says Gendler and Tullman, for a cognitive state other than 'belief' to rule one's *willingness* to imagine. As we saw with Rozin's study of those who were reluctant to eat the fudge shaped like dog faeces or drink from a cup that has been in contact with a sterilized cockroach. Perhaps, those people *alieved* the opposite to what they 'believed'. Maybe they alieved: 'Oh, I'm not eating that – that's dog shit!', while believing that it really is just a piece of fudge. Tullman's study taught us that the object of our emotion need not be *believed* in order for the person to have an emotional response to that object.

And does the theory of imaginative resistance not indicate that our 'emotional blinkers' are not caught in a blind spot when make-believing, or alieving or having a 'higher order thought'? But we are, in fact, capable of having an emotional response to fiction *without* believing. Which might be why we feel the 'distance' between ourselves and fiction run between the point of near evaporation all the way to an unwillingness to imagine. That is the power of make-believe, of fiction and of our emotional immersion in it all.

I think that this theme of 'that which is not belief' to explain emotional bonds where the object of emotion is *not* believed to exist ties in with the third type of religious commitment that I listed (III) '*voluntary belief-that and voluntary belief-in*'. That is, when the will chooses to believe that Christianity (for example) is true, and to live according to this truth. The key, tying-in aspect here, I think, is the through-on-through *voluntariness* of this type of faith. In light of what we have just read (on alternative, non-paradoxical approaches to fictional emotions) we might be inclined to interpret the voluntariness of (III) with a dependency on the will; as belonging, perhaps, somewhere between belief tout court (religious realism, (I)) and make-belief/alief/a 'higher order thought' (fictionalism, (IVb)).

We assume, without thinking, that emotions towards that which is considered objectively true or *really real* are genuine. This would be the case, for example, for the religious realist who sheds a tear during a religious service. Those tears are considered genuine because their belief is that of a realist nature. On the other hand, the paradox of fiction has encouraged many thinkers – some of whom we have looked at – to question the conclusion drawn from the previous assumption. That is, fictional emotions are not genuine. Instead, we have looked at those who wish to enter the conversation from the standpoint of, *'but we do cry, let us try to find out why'*, or something along those lines.

If we can say the following about the third type of faith (III) I think that we can defend it as at least emotionally coherent, in that it draws on comparisons to fictionalism and that which is not strictly involuntarily 'belief-that', *and* that its 'in between' stance can be perhaps, in part, defended by the four theories we have looked at. Thus, if we can say that:

- (III) is representative of a faith that may demonstrate the 'the will's willingness' to invest in a way of seeing the world that is different to a way of seeing the world *prior* to adopting (III).
- (III) is different to a purely realist faith (I) – *involuntary belief-that and voluntary belief-in* – in that, emotional responses to (I) are considered genuine.
- We can compare making-believing/alieving/a 'higher order thought' theory to (III) insofar as there is a shared aspect of voluntariness.

Might we say, then, that the identification with this type of religious faith and with the associated emotional response is *not* irrational? It represents a powerful, meaningful and coherent position, as I have concluded about fictional emotions in light of the four theories. Furthermore, if (III) is dependent on the will, then I suggest that this type of religious faith is emotionally coherent at least. It is meaningful. Just as religious fictionalism is meaningful. We will continue now with an investigation into fictionalism as a 'fully coherent' form of (IV). We have asked whether it is 'intellectually coherent' (in Chapter 3), we have just explored fictionalism as an 'emotionally coherent' form of faith and we will turn to ask whether fictionalism is 'spiritually' coherent.

5

Fictionalism and 'the humane turn'

At the end of the previous chapter, we began to question whether (or not) religious fictionalism can provide an 'emotionally coherent' approach to apprehending the reality of God without somehow 'missing the mark'. In this chapter we will continue to challenge the extent to which fictionalism can provide a satisfactory philosophical lens, as we explore a contemporary 'model' for philosophy of religion. This model or 'movement' promotes a connection between the subject and the moral and spiritual sensibilities that shape religious belief. Our question, then, will be this: 'To what extent can fictionalism provide a type of religious commitment that is "spiritually coherent"?' We will be exploring the extent to which fictionalism can be said to support this contemporary 'model' and its mission to utilize the creative and intuitive 'side' of our brains. So, what exactly is this movement?

There is a contemporary movement in philosophy of religion that is encouraging an alternative and more 'humane' philosophical approach to the study of religion.[1] If current ways of thinking can be described as analytical and working in abstraction (i.e. from real life events, testimonies and emotional affiliations), then this movement is reflective of a turn towards more holistic and receptive ways of philosophizing about religion.[2] Blaise Pascal's enigmatic dictum, '*l'homme passe l'homme*', meaning 'man goes beyond himself'; 'humanity transcends itself' is representative here, perhaps, strange *restlessness* of the human spirit which so many philosophers have pondered on. Even those outside of the religious sphere have averted to a space that always seems to recede from view including Wittgenstein's proposal that 'Der Sinn der Welt muß außerhalb ihrer liegen' ('The sense of the world must lie outside of it') and John McDowell who insisted that '[w]e need to recapture the Aristotelian idea that a normal mature human being is a rational animal, but without losing the Kantian idea that rationality operates freely within its own sphere'.[3]

The layout of the chapter is threefold. First, we will explore the humane turn and the philosophers who support the movement, including Stump and Cottingham (this section is called 'The humane turn'). After this, we will investigate the extent to which religious fictionalism uses the epistemic values broadly associated with the movement, including imaginative, holistic, humanistic and personal thinking (this section is titled 'Does fictionalism honour "right-brain" thinking?'). Finally, we will discuss whether associating fictionalism with these 'right-brain' characteristics pushes fictionalism to its edge (in this final section: 'Fictionalism: Pushed to its edge?'). Here I will suggest that the humane turn is intentionally shot through with realism so unless the fictionalist coincides their fictionalist attitude with a kind of minimal realism or agnosticism, they are unlikely to make full use of these epistemic virtues and the humane movement more broadly.

I will conclude the chapter by gesturing towards an ontologically 'thicker' thesis. This type of religious commitment might offer the following: the ability to use the 'best bits' of the humane 'model', namely its attention to intuitive and reflective mode of awareness in our philosophical thinking. This type of commitment might 'go beyond' the parameters of fictionalism, insofar as it is a minimalist realist position. However, it does not take us 'all the way' to traditional religious realism. Therefore, we will go back to the second axis as I emphasize the possibility that we often 'skip over' a texture of reality that might exist somewhere 'in between' fictionalism and traditional realism, that is 'post-traditional' realism.

The humane turn

Two of the most influential forerunners of the humane movement are Eleonore Stump and John Cottingham. They argue that the current reigning style of philosophizing about religion is limited in its scope. It lacks 'down to earth' methods of assessing how it is that religious discourse, language and beliefs truly shape people's lives. Philosophers ought to embrace a whole spectrum of inquiries, they say, including but not exclusively analytical methods. One of the reasons why opening up our rationality to new possibilities is important, they suggest, is because religious beliefs and attachments are often held for reasons more personal and perplexing than conclusions drawn from analytical assessment.[4] Thus, to look for reasons through this line of enquiry alone will most likely not result in any obvious explanation as to why a person holds religious faith. Stump and Cottingham gesture towards recent studies in psychology and neurophysiology on the divided nature of the brain which appear to show the value of the epistemic characteristics that are illuminated by the humane movement and, as we might see, by the fictionalist movement.

The 'right hemisphere'

Twentieth-century psychologist Iain McGilchrist suggests that there are two halves of the brain: the left cerebral hemisphere and the right cerebral hemisphere, and that each hemisphere has its own unique processing mechanisms when it comes to interpreting reality. According to McGilchrist, what this means, in its crudest sense, is that the left hemisphere interprets reality through an analytical lens and exercises our logical and conceptual abilities. While the right hemisphere interprets reality holistically and is associated with more intuitive and imaginative forms of awareness. McGilchrist emphasizes the importance of the right hemisphere and its epistemic qualities.[5]

While appreciating that associating these two modes of awareness (holistic/humane and atomistic/analytic) with the right and left cerebral hemispheres is something of a schematic approximation (something that McGilchrist himself stresses), the epistemic qualities that Cottingham and Stump encourage – creative, imaginative, humane and holistic modes of thinking and awareness – have all been broadly associated with the right hemisphere. Specifically, to be used *in conjunction with* the epistemic characteristics that are, again broadly speaking, associated with the left hemisphere. Those being, analytical modes of assessment upheld by a commitment to clarity and rigour.

It must be made clear that any decent philosopher will subscribe wholeheartedly to these 'left hemisphere' values, but this subscription need not undervalue the right hemisphere and its role in interpreting reality. Moreover, the humane turn, or a turn towards the integration of 'right-brain' thinking, 'keeps alive the traditional grand vision of philosophy' says Cottingham, that is 'the attempt to achieve a comprehensive "synoptic" vision of things; one that endeavours to discern how (or how far) the different areas of our human understanding fit together', that is, both 'left-brain' and 'right-brain' thinking and modes of awareness.[6]

I will suggest that fictionalism might be associated (more, perhaps) with the epistemic characteristics of the right hemisphere. This, in turn, suggests that the humane movement *can* defend religious fictionalism and vice versa.

Insofar as both philosophical views encourage ways of thinking that utilize less analytical and more inventive modes of thinking when interpreting religious texts, while equally aware that we must not allow the imagination to 'carry us away so far that we lose our powers of critical judgement'.[7] But before we get into this, let us gain a better understanding of this contemporary 'turn' in philosophy of religion.

Stump's diagnosis: 'Cognitive *Hemianopia*'

Anglo-American philosophy has been preoccupied with the 'precise definition of terms, fine distinctions among concepts, and complex arguments for philosophical claims', to the extent that its other common name is 'analytic philosophy', Stump tells us.[8] The 'narrowness' for which Anglo-American philosophy is reproached is thus 'a concomitant of the analytical strengths that characterize it'.[9] And all this, she says, is mediated by 'left-brain skills'.[10] As pre-empted above, Stump inserts a crucial caveat in her campaign for the re-examination of philosophical reflection as she emphasizes the importance of carrying out analytical methods when it comes to philosophizing, but she also says that 'the extent to which one prizes rigor, one will eschew or even disdain breadth'.[11]

What Stump means by this is that the 'aridity' of analytic philosophy is 'not altogether unjustified'; she gives examples of Aquinas's analytic analysis of the freedom of the will and Platinga's work of the nature of necessity.[12] However, Stump believes that modern philosophy is suffering from, what she calls, 'cognitive *hemianopia*',[13] which means that the intellectual vision of the right hemisphere is occluded or obscured by the left hemisphere and its detached and rather emotionless worldview. For example,

> [w]hen analytic philosophers need to think about human interactions, they tend not to turn to complex cases drawn from real life or the world's greatest literature; rather they make up short, thin stories of their own, involving the philosophers-crash dummies Smith and Jones.[14]

It follows, then, that philosophers ought not to shy away from the 'messy and complicated issues involved in relations among persons' and that which weighs on our hearts, Stump argues.[15] The faceless characters of 'Smith' and 'Jones' help to perpetuate 'left-brain' patterning processing and its 'tendency to focus more and more on less and less'.[16] Otherwise, in the absolute worst case, philosophy will become 'plodding, pedestrian, sterile, and inadequate to its task', when, in actual fact, the purpose of philosophy, for Stump, is to help understand 'complex, nuanced thought, behaviour, and relations of persons'.[17] Breadth of focus is what is required here, says Stump, and this is a 'right-brain skill'.[18]

Stump's diagnosis of 'cognitive *hemianopia*' indicates that philosophers are limited in their approach to the study of religion, and this is largely because of their current favouring and pursuit of only 'left-brain' thinking. Instead, the philosopher ought to move away from an acute attention to a technicality (an epistemic characteristic of the left hemisphere) and place some emphasis on 'persons and personal relationships'.[19] Stump warns us against the danger of exclusively privileging the left hemisphere and its detached and analytic processing to the point where we become blind (*hemianopia*) to a whole rich range of volitional and affective mental activity that shapes our awareness of reality.

Cottingham and the humane movement

Academic, analytical, Anglo-American philosophizing has been shaped for the most part of the twentieth and the twenty-first century by a 'scientifically inspired model of philosophy' that enforces 'strong links with the notion of "analysis"', Cottingham tells us.[20] But the idea of analysing something, 'to break it up or dissolve it into its component parts', is not, arguably, the job of the philosopher of religion.[21] Instead, the philosopher ought to '*prioritise understanding over verification*', particularly when it comes to understanding a religious worldview and what this might 'look' like.[22] By this Cottingham means that the philosopher needs a new model of understanding, that is, 'a certain *mode* or *manner* of understanding the world'.[23]

Thus, Cottingham explains that moving towards a 'more humane' philosophical approach, compared to the current analytical model, is important because the latter might not be able to truly unpack the processes that take place when a person adopts a religious worldview. For example, an appreciation for the unique *nature of religious truths* and acknowledgement of the *dual transformation* that takes place for the religious believer. I will walk us through both of these processes, as described by Cottingham, before giving his description of the ideal, humane model.

The nature of religious truths

Cottingham suggests that the concept of truth that we often employ on a day-to-day basis tends to imply a straightforward conception of 'truth' based on a scientific model. For example, seeing a glass of water on the table or deciding if it is a sunny day. This means that basic beliefs, such as these, largely form involuntarily, insomuch as the mind almost seems passive in the process. That is to say, 'the data from the senses are processed by the brain, and the belief spontaneously forms itself in the mind, "just like that"'.[24] There is a glass of water, the sun has come out, end of story. But Cottingham explains that we, human beings, are not simply 'passive' observers. Rather, in virtue of our 'unique conceptual powers and sensibilities' we do much more than merely 'encounter' the world, 'we transform it, creating out of the raw data of perception a whole rich "lifeworld"'.[25]

We can better understand this if we compare our human creative skill set to that of a non-human animal that lacks this 'creative dimension'. For them, Cottingham explains, the world is 'given' in a relatively determined and fixed way. That is to say, other animals are not confronted with 'the mystery of being' for instance, because 'they are simply wholly absorbed in dealing with it in ways directly related to their immediate needs'.[26] However, for us, the nature of reality and the idea of what is 'true' are never 'finally packaged up and definitively presented to us'.[27] Which is why, Cottingham says, 'we always reach beyond the given in our human struggle' to understand it. In light of this, Cottingham stresses that our knowledge of the world and coming to know truths, such as the religious kind, come in different forms, those being: detached critical scrutiny (associated with 'the left-brain') and more intuitive and holistic awareness (mediated by the 'right brain'), and that by privileging the former the philosopher risks 'hardening oneself against the porousness and receptivity that is a necessary condition for certain kinds of evidence to become salient'.[28]

For example, when it comes to understanding reported miracles in the Christian Gospels, Cottingham suggests that the philosopher look beyond the kind of truth that might be described as 'bang in front of us', to something that is more ambiguous and less transparent to the responsible observer.[29] In other words, the former is the kind of truth that scientists are interested in, something Cottingham refers to as 'bald truth': unambiguously 'bang in front of us'. But, 'there are many other kinds of truth that are clearly not "bald" in this way', such as the truths contained in the Bible and novels.[30] Thus, Cottingham insists that what the philosopher needs is something closer to

Martin Heidegger's exploration into the Greek conception of truth: *alētheia*, which means 'unconcealment' (in German *Unverborgenheit*).[31] Furthermore, by '[r]eversing the slogan of the positivists, according to whom meaning depends on verification, this more humane model insists that in order to evaluate something you must first understand it properly'.[32] So, how do we come to understand something 'properly'?

When it comes to the discourse of religion, the philosopher is investigating issues in which 'practitioners generally have a *strong personal stake*'.[33] By this Cottingham means that for those holding religious beliefs or a strong religious affiliation, religious discourse will significantly contribute to their 'entire sense of who they are and what kind of a world they inhabit'.[34] Therefore, philosophizing about religion should not be carried out as a detached academic exercise. It must never become a 'lifeless' task. Insomuch as, 'debating the validity of the theistic outlook can never be something about which the believer feels entirely detached'.[35] Therefore, Cottingham is encouraging philosophers to employ ways of thinking that reflect 'right-brain' epistemic values.

> [W]e should be prepared to investigate [complex religious questions] in a humanistic way, that is to say, by opening ourselves to all the resources of human experience that are relevant to the shaping of a philosophically rounded worldview. These will accord logical analysis a central place . . . but in such a way as to allow the insights arrived at to work on our imagination and enrich our understanding. . . . [A] properly enriched philosophy of religion can help us to see more clearly what is at stake.[36]

Aware of McGilchrist's findings, Cottingham argues that the kind of 'left-brain'/'right-brain' distinction between these two distinct but equally vital modes of cognition 'raises complex questions about human awareness that deserve more attention from philosophers generally than they have hitherto received'.[37] Moreover, with the right hemisphere associated with more intuitive, imaginative and holistic forms of awareness, Cottingham calls for a turn towards 'right-brain' thinking when it comes to philosophizing about religious discourse and philosophy in general. Insofar as, 'if McGilchrist is right, there is a danger in always allowing the logical, analytic, detached mode of awareness [typically associated with "left-brain"] to predominate in our philosophical thinking'.[38] Especially since Cottingham tells us that the nature of the subject itself (religion) 'necessarily resists division into hermetically sealed subdisciplines'.[39] Mindful of this, Cottingham says the following:

> [t]he sharp etching tool is required from time to time if philosophical argument is to be more than arbitrary assertion; but the broader brush is also needed to mark out some of the similarities and contrasts between different systems which need to be understood if philosophy is to discharge the task (which no other discipline is equipped to undertake) of placing specialized insights in their wider human context.[40]

Moreover (and resonating with, perhaps, C. S. Lewis),[41] Cottingham embraces the 'hybrid nature' of us, human beings.

> Life might, in a certain sense, be easier for purely intellectual beings, on the one hand, or for unselfconscious life forms, on the other. But we are that strange hybrid, 'half beast, half angel', and the resulting complexity, coloured by the vivid interplay of reason, emotion and bodily response, is what gives human life its special status – generating our fiercest challenges, but the source, too, of our greatest joys.[42]

This 'dualistic' nature of the human person is reflective of Cottingham's second focus of the 'dual transformation'.

Dual transformation

This transformation refers to the process of coming to accept a certain 'picture of reality', theistic belief, for example, 'belief in a personal Being who is the ultimate ground underlying the mystery of being in the universe and the source of its meaning and value, is just such a vision', namely 'a transformative vision that brings into salience features of the world which simply drop out of view in the quantitative printouts of particle interactions'.[43] Therefore, it is a 'vision' that can arise when a person adopts religious faith. The transformation is said to be dualistic in nature because not only does a whole new reality come into view (potentially for the religious believer), but the subjects themselves are also made anew.[44] To explain this Cottingham uses the metaphor of an 'upward spiral' or 'double helix', suggesting that the adoption of a religious belief system, for example, may involve 'successive stages of transformation, both in the subject and in the way the relevant picture of reality takes shape'.[45]

Moreover, this process is not a 'flat' one. Inasmuch as it is not an impersonal or detached process, such as the basic beliefs aforementioned might be. Quite the opposite. Rather, a transformative worldview and access to religious truths require 'personal commitment and even moral change in order for the relevant evidence to come to light'.[46] For it, rather dramatically, replaces an *epistemology of control* for an *epistemology of receptivity*.[47] That is to say, the subject moves from their 'detached' position, from a position where one might 'scrutinize the evidence, retaining [her] power and autonomy in a "left-brain" kind of way' (*epistemology of control*), to a new position.[48] This requires the subject to 'give up the fantasy of being lofty, detached evaluators, surveying the data and pronouncing our verdict'.[49] Whether we like it or not, Cottingham says, we have to be involved, to be receptive, hence why we ought to move to an '*epistemology of receptivity*'.[50] So, what will this model look like?

The new humane model

Cottingham tells us that a 'more humane' model of religious philosophizing is, metaphorically speaking, not like a pair of glasses that can be put on and taken off. It is also not like an object or an item that can be scrutinized or evaluated, like a painting hung in a gallery.[51] The humane model is less like a painting hanging among other paintings in a gallery, but more like this.

> [A] prism, fashioned of stained glass and suspended from a cord high up in the middle of the room. Many visitors ignore it or give it a wide berth, hurrying past to inspect the individual paintings. But others, without perhaps quite knowing why, linger and find themselves moving near it or standing under it. Once the resistance to moving in that direction has been set aside, the room begins, from this position, to look different. Patterns of light and colour in the air and on the walls become visible and begin to glow and shine, in turn bringing about changes in the attitude of the subject. She ceases to be a detached spectator, bent on inspecting and assessing the various objects in the gallery, and starts to be moved: responsive feelings of delight and awe begin to surface. And now she begins to be enthralled, as from this vantage point all manner of objects in the room are illuminated by the prism, bring into focus complex new relationships, which begin to form a wondrous pattern. The meaning of the whole exhibition, before occluded, now comes vividly into view.[52]

Cottingham explains that 'what begins as a mere minimal willingness to pause and look around, becomes, as the transformations take effect, an attentive looking, and then a delighted looking; and at each stage, richer dimensions of reality come into focus'.[53] Thus, not only does the subject themselves undergo an interior change but an external change takes place too. And, it is the epistemic characteristics associated with the right cerebral hemisphere that might be able to 'take the philosopher there', to 'observe the prism' and gaze upon its patterns of light and colour.

> Hence those who insist on casting the 'God question' in a form that is apt for evaluation by 'left brain skills' alone may be missing the core issue that is at stake in the adoption of a religious worldview. The question is not 'Can I, while scrutinizing the data and remaining detached and fully in control, satisfy myself of the rational acceptability of belief in God?'; but rather something like the following: 'How can I embark on a path of moral and spiritual change which might open me to a deeper awareness of something that I now glimpse only faintly'.[54]

And if this question looks a little too steeped in the direction of defending religious realism, then I believe that we can modify the question while retaining its core message. Instead, perhaps the question might read: 'As a philosopher, how might I come to recognise the seriousness of a belief in a deeper sense of awareness in order to grasp a religious subject's path of moral and spiritual change?' Now that we have a better understanding of the humane turn in philosophy of religion, we will turn our attention to religious fictionalism and see whether it can be argued that fictionalism defends this contemporary movement.

Does fictionalism honour 'right-brain' thinking?

In a rather complex way, the humane turn is related to the realist/non-realist debate in philosophy of religion and of course religious fictionalism which, as we know, is a branch of non-realism.

Now on first impression, one might wish to say that religious realism is representative of 'right-brain' thinking and non-realism, 'left-brain' thinking. For creative and imaginative thinking might help to bring into salience a transcendent, divine reality for the realist ('right-brain' skills). While the non-realist strives to show the importance of logic and reason-based thinking ('left-brain' skills). I will argue that if restoring the hemispheric equilibrium – the aim of the 'humane turn' – is important to the reader, then fictionalism might be seen to:

(i) promote the humane movement in philosophy of religion

and

(ii) present itself as a serious and thoughtful alternative to religious realism, as it honours a contemporary movement that arguably protects the intellectual and emotional coherence of religious discourse.

However, this is not the whole story. By this I mean to argue that, ultimately, fictionalism cannot be said to *fully* adhere to the humane model which, if we find this to be the case, could jeopardize the extent to which fictionalism is deemed a serious and thoughtful alternative to religious realism, for those who favour the humane movement and, what we might find, its reliance on an openness to a realist worldview. With that being said, it might be *part* of the story; that is to say, fictionalism might, to a meaningful extent at least, employ the epistemic virtues of the humane turn. Thus, in order to show that fictionalism does (i) and (ii) I will go through each of the characteristics typically assigned to the right hemisphere given in Table 1, and demonstrate how the fictionalist might be said to commend the right half of the brain and its epistemic virtues.[55]

Table 1 Characteristics Typically Assigned to the Right Hemisphere and Left Hemisphere

The Left Hemisphere	The Right Hemisphere
Analytical	Imaginative
Atomistic	Holistic
Lifeless and mechanical	Humanistic and personal

Source: © Jessica Eastwood.

Imaginative

By Le Poidevin's personification of fictionalism, Fiona (whom we met earlier) demonstrates that when practising religious discourse, the fictionalist takes themselves to be engaging in a rather complicated game of make-believe. For them, what religious fiction involves is a 'deeper emotional and imaginative involvement' than one's emotional response to a crime novel, for instance. This will lead not to 'inappropriate attitudes and behaviour, but ones whose value for the self and the religious community vindicates that involvement'.[56]

To give a more specific example, when Fiona, for instance, utters the assertion 'God died for my sins' this is a *pretend* assertion rather than an actual assertion. Thus, Fiona is playing a game in which she 'make-believes' religious statements to be true according to, and only to, the appropriate theological context or, specifically, the theological fiction which she is engaging with. However, Fiona is not trying to cynically deceive anybody. Rather, Le Poidevin explains that 'she wishes to enter into what she takes to be the religious imagination', to the extent that 'she becomes effectively engaged'.[57]

To give another example, when Fiona prays, she does not believe that she is aligning her will with the will of God, because she believes that there is no real will of God because there is no God! Instead, what Fiona is doing is attempting to 'align [her] will with what [she] imagines *would be* the will of God'.[58] This is because a '[f]ictional character though God may be, God represents for Fiona a moral ideal, an expression of perfect love'.[59] Ergo, the fictionist will 'enter more imaginatively into a vision of pure love'.[60] Fiona will engage her imaginative faculties to enter into the fictional, religious world, where she finds community, consolation and comfort.

Le Poidevin's understanding of the fictionalist entering into an imaginative state when engaging in religious discourse might support the case that (i) fictionalism can be seen to encourage creative and imaginative ways of thinking about religious discourse and the nature of God (a 'right-brain' skill), while (ii) not committing to any metaphysical realities and, instead, using imaginative thinking to '*reframe*' the realist conception of God into a fictional reality. By this I mean, the fictionalist might be said to practise religious discourse by engaging in imaginative 'make-believing', without presenting the realist conception of God as existing 'out there' as a necessary belief in order to have a meaningful commitment to religious engagement.

Holistic

The fictionalist idea of '*reframing God*', that is, to 'lift' the traditional conception of God out of its realist context and 'move it' to a theological fictional context or 'frame', might be representative of a 'holistic move' or philosophy. This is because the idea of placing the realist conception of God into a fictional realm does *not* involve 'reconceptualizing' the traditional conception of God. That is to say, it does not involve a process in which the fictionalist atomistically breaks down the realist conception of God in an abstract, detached or decontextualized way. Rather, the fictionalist lifts *the whole conception* of the realist God into a different context. Moreover, this holistic move, as it were, might be said to contribute to the idea that fictionalism is in support of the 'humane turn'. That is, a turn towards more humane and holistic philosophizing about religion, and, thus, a turn away from (what sometimes might be perceived as) wholly analytical and detached ways of thinking about religion.[61]

This holistic method of 'reframing' God into a fictional reality means that if a fictionalist aligns themselves with Christianity (as a set of practices, images and ideals) for instance, they would describe God in exactly the same way as the (realist) Christian would: 'God the Creator', 'God the Sustainer', 'God the supreme moral Judge'. The difference is the context or *frame* in which God exists, with the realist framing God within an objective reality and the fictionalist, a fictional one. I do not wish to underestimate the difference here, I am simply demarcating the similarity of the realist's and the fictionalist's conception of God, if the question of ontology is put aside (as we see on the first axis, a spectrum of conceptions: both the fictionalist and the traditional realist hold the same conception of God from CPT). This makes fictionalism different from other types of non-realism (including Cupitt's) because the realist and the fictionalist share a general semantic schema; that is, 'any given theological statement p is true if and only if it is true in the theological discourse that p',[62] and it's only when it comes to questions of ontology that the basis for the fictionalist's behaviour, that is, their engagement in religious practice, reveals very different philosophical positions.

If this is true, or at least arguable, then it might follow that fictionalism (i) gives voice to a kind of philosophizing about religious discourse which encourages a holistic practice, to treat religious discourse as a whole, and not individual convictions to be assessed independently from that whole. Which is why (ii) fictionalism might be seen as more attractive than other non-realist philosophies. For it protects the fictionalist's emotional connection with religious discourse, a childhood faith perhaps as a 'vision'; a way of life; as something to be adopted wholly, if only as a fictional ideal.

Humanistic and personal

Fictionalism might be recognized as a 'humane' approach to the study of religion because arguably it recognizes and, to an extent, satisfies the importance of a person's religious affiliation to a childhood religion for instance, or a particular religious community, or perhaps to Religion (with a capital 'R') as a general concept. Although fictionalism encourages the abandonment of traditional metaphysical beliefs and rejects the notion of a 'metaphysical God' (i.e. a Creator who exists mind-independently of us), the fictionalist does not outright reject Christianity, for example, as a set of practices, images and ideals.[63]

Rather, fictionalism sees Christianity as 'continuing to have a fundamental role in our spiritual lives'.[64] More than this, religious teachings and language can serve and 'provide a fictional picture which guides us in our moral lives'.[65] Thus, the fictionalist's approach to religious discourse does appeal to the humane turn that Cottingham and Stump promote and does uphold the view that to philosophize and interpret religious language is a personal task. Insofar as (even if God is a fictional character), 'God' still has moral, spiritual, intellectual and emotional influence over our lives.

In another kind of way, fictionalism allows the 'doubting Christian' (who might struggle to adhere to metaphysical claims and commitments perhaps) to continue in their participation and engagement in religious discourse, and to use fictionalism as a philosophical tool in which to map out *their own type faith*; based on their own interpretation of religious language, as either reflective of a reality 'out there' (realism) or an important message contained within a 'make-believe' reality 'down here' (fictionalism). The gap that fictionalism creates here for the doubting Christian is one that might be described as a humane and personal philosophical space.

This is because it allows for a continued presence within one's religious community while figuring out how to navigate their concerns.

In summary, then, I have demonstrated that fictionalism, (i) through its emphasis on participating in religious discourse, promotes a 'down-to-earth' relationship between the believer and their religious beliefs and practices, and therefore (ii) presents itself as an honest and mindful alternative to religious realism, through its commitment to 'right-brain thinking'. We will now move on to the third and final section of this chapter, where we will question the strength of the link we have just drawn between the humane turn and fictionalism.

Fictionalism: Pushed to its edge?

In this chapter I have presented the ways in which fictionalism might be said to commend the epistemic values of the right hemisphere, and thereby promote the current humane movement in philosophy of religion. The paradigm shift that we are talking about here is a turn towards a style of philosophy that is broad in its focus and 'connective' in its approach, to create a 'synoptic' vision of reality. I wish to further promote the humane philosophical approach to the study of religion, with a vision of reforming what appears to be an increasingly fragmented programme which is steered largely towards analytical inquiries. By this I mean,

I wish to promote academic philosophizing that resists hermetically sealed disciplines and, instead, draws on different areas of our human understanding.

As I have stressed, this does not mean inviting irrational or uncritical ways of thinking, and my aim is certainly not to disparage the prevailing model, that is logical analysis. Rather, I wish to say that philosophizing about religion is not just an (abstract) exercise, but something that engages *every part of us*. As Cottingham puts it, 'we should be wary of applying a detached, neutral, quasi-scientific template to all philosophizing about religion. But it should also have emerged that it is possible to move away from strict adherence to the neutral model without thereby sliding into irrationalism or relativism'.[66] It impinges upon who we are and, I think, a deep desire to feel a sense of *coherence* when it comes to our sense of self, how we understand the world and the idea of 'God'. Einstein said this: 'the intuitive mind is a sacred gift and the rational mind is a faithful servant', and, perhaps, we are 'in a world that honours the servant but has forgotten the gift'.[67] I think that this might capture *where we are* historically, culturally and philosophically and *where we might want to be*.

Thus far I have given 'two cheers' to the humane turn in this chapter. The first for its commitment to enriching what might otherwise be a generally quite detached and impersonal approach to apprehend the nature of faith. In other words, the movement utilizes epistemic virtues, such as imaginative, holistic, humanistic and personal ways of philosophizing, that might not otherwise be put into practice. The second is recognition of its potential to defend religious fictionalism as that which encourages 'literary awareness', 'poetic awareness' and 'musical awareness', namely those kinds of outputs that can take us to 'new levels of awareness and understanding'.[68] That is to say, the humane turn might help to demonstrate the fictionalist's use of these same epistemic virtues which might then, in turn, further the notion that fictionalism privileges ways of philosophizing which allow for 'deeper awareness' to be found 'outside of', and not fully grasped by, the reflective, analytic mind. However, I will now explain why I am reluctant to give the humane turn a 'third cheer', insofar as I am hesitant to 'go the whole hog' and say that the humane turn can defend fictionalism and vice versa, by stating three successive concerns.

First concern: Heaney and 'transformative vision'

The question or questions that lie at the heart of Cottingham's book on defending a new model of religious understanding are these: 'What is it to relate to the world religiously?' and 'What is it to understand things in a religious way?'[69] *My* question in relation to Cottingham's appeal is this: 'Is this "humane" conception of philosophizing about religion catered (only) for a realist worldview?' That is to say, can this movement be utilized by the religious fictionalist and their non-realist worldview? If so, to what extent? It will be this final question, on the extent to which fictionalism can embrace this 'humane' *mode* or *manner* of understanding the world, that will demand our attention the most. This is because, arguably, Cottingham's defence of this model that prioritizes understanding over verification does not explicitly reject or embrace fictionalism as a potential type of *vision* or *reality* that encapsulates the kind of religious understanding that Cottingham is promoting. I suggest that fictionalism *cannot* provide a truly 'humane' mode of interpretation.

If the philosopher is to make any kind of 'plausible' account which explains and deepens our 'awareness of ourselves and the reality we inhabit' it 'must make space for' the following forms of understanding: 'imaginative, symbolic, and poetic'.[70] Thus, a plausible account of the human condition should attend to a vision of reality that would lead to 'self-understanding and self-transformation'[71] and 'contributes to the resulting transformations in their moral outlook and their perception of reality'.[72] There are, Cottingham tells us, (at least) two kinds of dimensions to our interaction with the world, there is the empirical processing of data and the creative dimension. The latter is where we use our 'active creative powers of reflecting on and interpreting [our] experience'.[73] He gives the following example of children creating imaginary worlds in their garden.

> A group of children exploring a garden will not simply map it out and find their way round, but will, even from a very young age, transform it creatively into a rich locus of imaginative play, places to hide, scary dark corners to avoid, bushes that are 'monsters' to be confronted, banks that are places of safety and refuge.[74]

The 'sober rationalist', Cottingham says, might regard this kind of 'play' as 'mere imagination', but 'far more is involved than that' Cottingham tells us, because what we are doing is creating 'a whole rich "lifeworld"'.[75] Another way to understand what is going on here, says Cottingham, is to suggest that 'our basic relation to the world', our vision of reality, is 'a kind of poetry, in the strict etymological sense of poēsis, a "making"'.[76] What Cottingham means here by 'poetry' is 'imaginative writing' which impacts the entire 'transformative relation in which human beings stand to the world', and the best way to understand this claim, Cottingham proposes, is to engage with the following passage from Heaney in relation to his own literary activity as a poet.[77]

In order that human beings bring about the most radiant conditions for themselves to inhabit, it is essential that the vision of reality which poetry offers should be transformative, more than just a printout of the given circumstances of its time and place. The poet who would be most the poet has to attempt an act of writing that outstrips the conditions even as it observes them.[78]

When it comes to 'imaginative' forms of writing or poetry we often think of 'fiction' because much literary output is indeed fictional but this is a mistake, says Cottingham.[79] It is 'easy to misunderstand' the point that is being made here by Heaney, it is not that we ought to engage in our human 'capacity to "make things up"', namely works that do not 'record historical occurrences or consist of literal factual propositions' (such as 'fiction') but, rather, Heaney's point about human beings bringing about the most radiant conditions for themselves to inhabit is a 'much more subtle and important one than that'.[80] When thinking about Heaney's idea of a 'transformative vision' there might be four 'transformative' functions, all of which point to a realist, non-fictional account of religious reality.

The first is to say that Heaney's concept of imaginative writing, employed by Cottingham, is not descriptive of a fictional reality in the sense of 'making up things that are literally false'; rather, the key concept here is '*transformation*'.[81] Although it might not be a primary concern of the fictionalist to publicize their view that religious discourse is best understood as theological fiction (albeit a powerfully life-altering one) it is, nevertheless, a non-realist interpretation of religion as, crudely put, a 'made up' divine reality married to a realist ontology that is 'literally false'.

The second is this 'vision of reality' does not 'distort' or 'alter' things, which is to say that it does not change the world as it is, into something that it is not. Poetry has this 'transformative function' because it points to that which is beyond the self and beyond elements of our lifeworld. The third is what Heaney's passage makes clear: the poet, for instance, deals with 'the real world'; she has a 'vision of reality'.[82] What exactly is this vision? What does it do? Cottingham explains that it 'sharply embraces and delineates what is there in view, disclosing its significance'.[83] Moreover, and fourth, poetry is not a 'fiction' but '*truth*', a kind of truth that Heidegger will help us understand.[84]

What kind of 'truth' are we dealing with here? If we cast our minds back to the part in this chapter where we briefly explored one way in which the philosopher could study a Christian interpretation of biblical truth, Cottingham suggests that Heidegger's adoption of the Greek conception of truth: *alētheia*, which means 'unconcealment', might better encapsulate the nature of said truth. That is, compared to scientific, 'bald' truths. Thus, in order to understand the kind of 'truth' that imaginative, literary outputs such as poetry (not 'fiction') present, Cottingham marries Heidegger's promotion of a type of truth that discloses what is (partly) hidden, with Heaney's idea of a 'transformative vision'.[85] Moreover, for Cottingham, the way that the philosopher ought to philosophize about religion is to start from the view that the 'nature of reality is never finally packaged up and definitively presented to us, and we always reach beyond the given in our human struggle to understand it'.[86]

Therefore, it is clear, Cottingham says, that Heaney's idea of a 'transformative vision' 'has application *far beyond the literary domain*'.[87] Furthermore, based on these four elements of what constitute a 'transformative vision' it suggests that that which 'fiction' brings, namely a fictional reality (though it may be emotionally and morally enriching) does not quite match up with the *transformative* nature of what a model of religious understanding might bring, that is: (1) not a 'made up' vision, (2) not a 'distorted' vision, but (3) dealing with 'the real world' and, therefore (4) employs a distinctive kind of 'truth'. Moreover, I suggest that this depicts a realist worldview, or at the very least an openness to a realist worldview, which does not necessarily describe the fictionalist position (but, perhaps closer to an agnostic position).

However, it is worth mentioning a differentiation here, between 'realism' and 'theism', by this I mean that it is important to note that Cottingham recognizes that 'theism' (what we have called CPT) is not the same as to support a 'humane' model of understanding religious discourse that might require (at least an openness to) a realist approach to philosophizing about religion. We are concerned more with a 'framework of *engagement*'.

> [S]omething that must be enacted through involvement and commitment, which offers through openness and listening, a possible way of achieving that state of attunement where we can hope to glimpse, as through a glass darkly, the light meaning and truth that irradiates our world and transforms our human existence.[88]

In this passage we get an insight into Cottingham's answer to his questions on what is it to relate to the world religiously and what is it to understand things in a religious way. To be religious, according to Cottingham, is (in a certain way) 'to embrace the mystery [that is, the existence of the universe], with hope and purpose and joy, but certainly has to regard it as dissolved by an ingenious explanatory hypothesis called theism'.[89] For Cottingham, then, 'classical theism' has 'lost its power to command any allegiance outside of a small and diminishing minority of theologians and philosophers' insofar as belief in the CPT conception of God, as postulated by Swinburne for example, has seen a continued decline (at least in the developed Western world).[90]

More than that, Cottingham acknowledges that revising the prevailing model of religious understanding and religious awareness takes us 'further away' from traditional methods of academic theorizing about religion.[91] Therefore, although there might be grounds to argue that the humane turn is best understood as working within a realist framework, that is not to say that it works better within a classical theistic one. I will now move on to what might be a second reason why fictionalism cannot provide a truly 'humane' mode of interpretation, and that is Cottingham's argument for the 'transcending science'.

Second concern: 'Transcending science'

Part of what it means to truly adopt this 'humane' model of philosophizing about religion is to be willing to 'transcend science', says Cottingham. What does 'transcending science' actually mean? Cottingham explains that, for 'all its magnificent achievements', physics will never be able to demonstrate a 'complete and final explanation of all reality'; this is representative of scientism, rather than science, which does claims that all of reality can be measured.[92] To clarify, this is not a certain sort of religion versus science stand-off; rather, I am simply pointing out that Cottingham opposes not 'science' as such but a reductive naturalism, namely the idea that everything can be reduced to fundamental laws of the natural sciences. Moreover, Cottingham does not suggest, then, that 'theism is equipped to fill the explanatory gap', but rather he suggests that we ought to think clearly about how we wish to understand the world religiously and proceed from the following position: '*not* an attempt to dissect and analyze and explain it in the manner of modern science . . . but rather a mode of engagement, or connection, with reality as whole'.[93] Moreover, Cottingham says,

> the kind of connection it searches for cannot be achieved by the critical scrutiny of the intellect alone, but requires a process of attunement . . . a moral and spiritual opening of the self to the presence of the divine.[94]

In sum,

> the 'religious understanding' we are seeking cannot come about by abstract theorizing, but only through more direct and imaginative forms of involvement and engagement.[95]

In light of this wanting to 'transcend science', my question is this: 'If the fictionalist is to exercise "imaginative forms of involvement and engagement" when it comes to philosophizing religiously about the world, is the fictionalist happy with the idea of "transcending science"?' My instinct is to say, not necessarily. This is because to suggest that the fictionalist is open to modes of thinking and deeper levels of awareness in which to interpret reality and the nature of religious truths, may make the fictionalist reader a little anxious. For it is one thing to say that the fictionalist will engage their imaginative faculties in order to enter into their theological game of 'make-believe' but it is quite another to imply that the fictionalist encourages philosophers of religion to 'go beyond' analytical forms of enquiry and use their imagination when interpreting reality. The best way to explain why this might be is to ask this follow-up question: 'What is the purpose of "transcending science"?'

If the purpose is *to ease the cognitive tension between science and religion* then I posit that the fictionalist might be on board with Cottingham's appeal to 'transcending science', and I point here to Lipton and Le Poidevin's 'immersion solution'. Put briefly, Lipton explains that one's religious commitment 'flows from the contents of the texts of one's religion literally construed', and thus describes 'a fairly full-blooded fictionalism about religion', that is compared to Le Poidevin's description: 'I shall take religious fictionalism to be the view that to immerse oneself in the religion, to employ its discourse to express that immersion, and to allow it to influence (in part via the emotional responses it evokes) is to engage in a game of make-believe.'[96] Both Lipton and Le Poidevin put forward the immersion position or 'solution' to the apparent incompatibility of 'religion and science'; Le Poidevin gives the following clear summary of Lipton's aim and explains why the immersion position can be adopted by the fictionalist.

> The constructive empiricist uses scientific theories to generate observational predictions, and to these predictions the appropriate attitude is truth-normed. Moreover the warrant to believe in the truth of the predictions is that they follow from theories which have passed empirical tests. Religious texts do not provide warrant for believing anything, but they do, as Braithwaite argued, induce attitudes which are warranted on other, non-religious, grounds. (Lipton's aim, incidentally, is to reconcile religious attitudes with trust in the deliverances of science, a reconciliation which is achieved by combining scientific realism with religious fictionalism, though Lipton does not employ the word 'fictionalist'. He labels his view the 'immersion solution.')[97]

Moreover, if the purpose for Cottingham wanting to 'transcend science' is to reconcile the tension between 'religion and science', through something like the 'immersion' solution (defended by fictionalists Le Poidevin and Lipton), then we might say that the religious fictionalist may sympathize with Cottingham's appeal and thus, potentially, adopt a more 'humane' model of philosophizing about religion. However, I suggest that if the (at least sole) purpose of 'transcending science' is not to (only) present a possible solution to the 'religion and science' conflict, but to *show that religious belief gestures towards that which 'lies beyond' and points to some kind of divine reality*, then the fictionalist will be less inclined to indulge Cottingham and his mission to 'transcend science'. This is because it is one thing to be a realist about science and non-realist (fictionalist) about religion, but it is quite another to support a philosophical approach to religion that requires a realistic vision of science that goes even 'beyond' that which science teaches us.

Now, undoubtedly this is a somewhat complex situation and it could amount to a number of responses based on numerous nuanced versions of each position (be it, Le Poidevin's fictionalist position, Lipton's 'stronger' fictionalist positions or Cottingham's approach to 'transcending science' and how 'fiction' falls into this, and his wider take on the 'humane' model), therefore I tentatively make the claim that if the purpose of Cottingham's wanting to 'transcend science' as part of defending the benefits of the humane turn is to, perhaps subtly, promote the existence of some kind of mind-independent, divine reality, then the fictionalist might not be keen to adopt this model of philosophizing.

Another way to understand why I make this claim is to 'plug in' a formula used by Lipton. Originally, Lipton's formula is used in the former context, namely, that if one wants to reconcile the tension between religion and science then the philosopher must choose between two strategies. To remind us, those strategies are '*adjusting content*' (which means 'giving up some claims') and '*adjusting attitude*' (which means 'keepings the claims but changing one's epistemic attitude toward at least some of them').[98] As we saw before,, Lipton favours the *adjusting attitude* and the fictionalist approach to apprehending religious texts and concludes that this approach can sit with constructive empiricism (which stands in contrast to the type of scientific realism that claims the following: science aims to give us, in its theories, a literally true story of what the world is like; and acceptance of a scientific theory involves the belief that it is true). However, I am going to use this 'choice of two strategies' and plug it into the following example: a cognitive tension between 'analytic philosophizing about religion' and more 'humane philosophizing about religion'.

I think it might be up to each fictionalist (as it is up to each philosopher in Lipton's original scenario) to choose. Yes, the fictionalist is inclined to 'adjust their attitude' when it comes to trying to 'preserve as much as possible from both religion and science without ignoring the tensions between them'; however, I suggest that we cannot assume that the same 'strategy' ('*adjusting attitude*') will be chosen when it comes to choosing between 'analytic' and 'humane' models of philosophizing. That is to say, it cannot be assumed that the fictionalist will be willing to 'adjust their attitude' when it comes to 'humane' epistemic virtues and modes of thinking that require, for example, 'going beyond' that which science tells us for certain. Moreover, it might require the fictionalist to broaden their philosophical horizon and their worldview so that it may include that which science cannot explain, namely an openness to mind-independent, divine reality.

I am *not* suggesting that the fictionalist will be inclined to 'adjust the content' of their claims, nor am I suggesting that the fictionalist can only favour analytical modes philosophizing about religion. Instead, what I am tentatively suggesting is that the happiness of the fictionalist to 'adjust their attitude' when it comes to finding a route which preserves the intellectual integrity of both religion (qua fictionalism) and science (namely, constructive empiricism) cannot necessarily be replicated when it comes to marrying religious fictionalism and the possibility of a reality which science does explicitly make a case for or point to.

To support this claim, I argue that it is in fact the *agnostic*, not the fictionalist, who is more inclined to fully embrace the humane turn and its call to 'transcend science'. That is to say, we are more likely, perhaps, to see a marriage between religious agnosticism and 'transcending science' (and, thus, use of the 'humane' model), rather than religious fictionalism and 'transcending science' (and acceptance of the 'humane' model). This is because the agnostic has a more 'open-minded attitude, and a willingness to look at new evidence and arguments' and is 'part of the wider phenomenon of uncertainty, and uncertainty is positive insofar as it promotes creativity, theoretical progress'.[99]

Moreover, all we can really say with confidence, and any kind of 'sweeping statement' we can make about fictionalists 'in general', is that we ought not to assume that the fictionalist will be open (nor closed off) to Cottingham's appeal to 'transcending science'. We may be able to say that the fictionalist might not be initially or immediately inclined to want to 'transcend science' because the roots to their type of philosophizing about religion are in non-realism and not realism. Which might suggest that their philosophical horizon does not expand to those parts which science cannot confirm or be said to allude to, namely a divine, mind-independent reality. Importantly, that is not to say that the realist is any less in favour of rigorous scientific theorizing; rather, I suggest that they are perhaps more inclined to be accepting of this openness to 'going beyond' because of their realist religious worldview. Finally, as I present my final concern, I want to further my instinct that what we are talking about here with the humane turn goes beyond levels of exploration and commitment than that which the fictionalist might be comfortable with.

Third concern: Cottingham's conception of the soul

In light of Cottingham's latest publication, *In Search of the Soul: A Philosophical Essay* (2020), there are good grounds, I will briefly argue here, to suggest that there is a realist (not necessarily classical theistic) aspect running through Cottingham's book: an aspect that is brought into salience when he talks about his concept of the 'soul', as interconnected with the kind of worldview one needs if we are to take seriously a 'humane' model of philosophizing about religion.

> all the properties and capacities that we group under the heading of 'soul', and which we rightly value as indispensable to our humanity – our powers of thought and feeling, our imaginative and emotional powers, our capacity for profound and transformative spiritual experience. . . . Humans, we can say, do have souls in this attributive sense: our worldview needs to make room for the soul.[100]

What exactly is the 'soul' according to Cottingham? Thomas Nagel's conception of consciousness is referenced here as Cottingham describes consciousness as 'an instrument of transcendence that can grasp objective reality and objective value',[101] so perhaps we are tapping into the Nagelian idea of a 'great cognitive expansion' from the particular, individual 'perspectival form' to an 'objective, world-encompassing form' that exists 'intersubjectively'.[102] And this idea is potentially expanded upon by Cottingham, as he says:

> when the individual subject reaches out and encounters a world of meaning and value, then sooner or later it is drawn to reflect on the second of the two dimensions of the transcendent . . . the *objective* dimension. Our world picture needs not just to make room for us humans, and the 'soul qualities' that give us individual conscious awareness as subjects of experience, but also to make room for the *reality of what we apprehend* when we exercise qualities.[103]

Without wanting to dive much deeper into Cottingham's concept of the soul, I hope that this small insight might lend itself to my tentative claim that the religious fictionalist might be less inclined to practice this 'humane' style of philosophizing, that is certainly compared to traditional realist, the agnostic and I would suggest the post-traditional realist; as they are certainly open to the vision of reality that 'transcends science' and opens up the possibility of some kind of divine, mind-independent reality.

Where do we go from here?

The threefold nature of this chapter has, first, explored the humane turn and the philosophers who support the movement, including Stump and Cottingham. Second, we looked at the ways in which the fictionalist might be said to honour the epistemic virtues often associated with the type of philosophizing exercised by proponents of the humane movement. And last, I offered counter-arguments for reasons why the fictionalist *might not be* compatible with this type of philosophizing. In doing so, I gave 'two cheers' to fictionalism and its compatibility with the humane turn, but remain hesitant to give a 'third cheer' in light of this final section and my tentative claim that the humane turn really requires some kind of realist worldview in order to fully embrace its aims.

And, so, my next question is this: Can we 'go beyond' fictionalism by thinking about the importance of 'right-brain' thinking and the space that it creates for thinking about one's emotional affiliation with 'God?' Do the epistemic values associated with the right cerebral hemisphere reveal the philosophical limitations of fictionalism? Does fictionalism truly and freely allow for imaginative modes of thinking and awareness when it comes to contemplating the reality in which 'God' might exist? Is fictionalism too 'flat' in this sense? In relation to the second axis, I argue that we have potentially 'skipped over' a texture of reality that might exist somewhere 'in between' fictionalism and traditional realism, that is 'post-traditional' realism. If this is the case, our next chapter will explore a realist type of commitment that might satisfy these virtues, without insisting a commitment to traditional realism not the God of CPT. Namely, the 'post-traditional' reality.

6

God and numbers
A minimal realism

In this chapter we will be talking about both axes, first of all the question of how we *conceptualize* objects which are considered abstract (in relation to axis one), and, second, the kind of *reality* we ought to ascribe to such objects (in relation to axis two). The main focus will be on the latter as the purpose of this chapter is to help soften any major opposition to the possibility of 'post-traditional' religious realism as a genuine conceptual space that might exist somewhere 'between' religious fictionalism and traditional religious realism. However, in order to do this, we will need to draw an analogy between the nature of abstract objects that we might find in the world of mathematics and the nature of what might be considered '*the* abstract object' in theology.

With that being said, I will draw two analogies which will bring realism in theology (and philosophy of religion) into conversation with realism in philosophy of mathematics.[1] The first will be in relation to the first axis. I will draw an analogy between the distinctive, 'minimalist' conception of God and abstract mathematical objects (such as numbers, sets and functions). The second will be in relation to the second axis. I will draw an analogy between 'post-traditional' religious realism and object realism in mathematics.

There are (at least) two different forms of mathematical realism that we need to separate out before we can draw any kind of useful analogy with a 'post-traditional' form of religious realism. However, before we explore these different kinds of realism within philosophy of mathematics it will be helpful, first, to get a better understanding of the *nature* of these abstract mathematical objects. Therefore, we will begin by looking at the first axis, and how these abstract objects are generally conceptualized. I will present what might be three characteristics that are typically used when conceptualizing abstract mathematical objects, in relation to the first axis (this section will be titled, 'Conceptualizing the objects of mathematics').

Then, I will give four different philosophical approaches to interpreting the kind of reality that ought to be ascribed to such objects (titled, 'Different commitments to the mathematical objects'),[2] with a particular focus on that which separates 'object realism' from 'mathematical platonism' (the ontologically most robust realist position) (this subsection is titled, 'Object realism versus mathematical platonism').[3] After which, I will ask the question, 'What exactly is it that the theologian (or philosopher of religion) can take away from this general conception of abstract mathematical objects, and the kind of reality that mathematical realists ascribe to these objects?' The second part of the chapter will answer these questions and suggest the following.

In regard to the first part of the question – the general conception of abstract mathematical objects – I suggest that the distinctive, 'minimalist' conception of God might share these same three characteristics. That is to say, there might be good theological reasons for holding that this conception of God shares the three principal characteristics of abstract objects that are evident in the case of mathematical objects (according to the realist) (section titled, 'Conceptualizing the object of theology'). And, if such an analogy can be drawn, then I will suggest – in regard to the kind of reality that mathematical realists ascribe to these objects – that we can meaningfully draw an analogy between religious post-traditional realism and mathematical realism. On the grounds that both kinds of conceptual space ascribe a reality (to their respective mathematical or theological 'object') that is *conditionally necessary* and *semi-independent* (section titled, 'Different commitments to the theological object').

The language of 'supervenience' will be used to help unpack these terms: *conditionally necessary* and *semi-independent*. Supervenience is a notion in analytical philosophy that refers to a type of dependence relation between properties, discourse or facts of one type, and properties, discourse facts of another. Therefore the theory is drawn on to distinguish various kinds of internalism and externalism and to test claims of reducibility and conceptual analysis. It gained quick currency with the mind-body problem, for instance, and, more broadly, it has been claimed that aesthetic, moral and mental properties supervene upon physical properties. Thus, the core idea of supervenience can be captured by the following slogan, 'there cannot be an *A*-difference without a *B*-difference'. By exploring different variants of supervenience and utilizing the well-established apparatus, I hope to defend the legitimacy of the post-traditional minimalist proposal. My aim is to use the notion of supervenience to help to unpack the terms *conditionally necessary* and *semi-independent* when it comes to the unique, asymmetrical relation of ontological dependence between God (via a suitably qualified version of Anselm's formula) and us, human persons, existing in this universe, as explored in this book.

I will conclude the chapter by arguing that *mathematical realism and its ontology about abstract mathematical objects might help the theologian (and philosopher of religion) think about broadening the scope of religious realism and the potential adequacy of a conceptual reality such as that posited by 'post-traditional' religious realists to ascribe to a 'post-traditional' conception of God.*

Before we begin, I have a number of caveats I need to insert. The first is to say that when I refer to 'God' in this chapter I will be referring to the distinctive, 'minimalist' conception of God, unless stated otherwise. I will also refer to God as 'the object of theology' and abstract mathematical objects as 'objects of mathematics'.[4] The second caveat is to clarify that what I will be doing in this chapter is to *draw analogies* between (a) the object of theology and the objects of mathematics, and (b) the kind of ontology ascribed to the object of theology and the kind of ontology ascribed to the objects of mathematics. I am *not* suggesting that 'God is like the number three' in the sense that numbers have no theological significance and ought only to be thought about in ways that are 'non-spiritual' and 'non-emotive'. Rather, I will suggest that the kind of ontology that the realist mathematician ascribes to the number three, for example, might be of a similar kind of distinct ontology that the 'post-traditional' religious believer ascribes to their distinctive, 'minimalist' conception of God. How and why this comparison might be made and appear useful will unfold and hopefully become clear as we make our way through the chapter.

A third caveat that I want to insert is to say that I will *not* be making any serious claims in regard to whether the mathematician ought to have a realist or non-realist attitude when it comes to mathematical discourse. The point is that it might help to reduce any scepticism surrounding the possibility of this kind of ontology by demonstrating that a similar kind of ontology is proposed by some realist mathematicians.

My final caveat is that I will *not* be piggybacking mathematical fictionalism; that is to say, I will not be using fictionalism in mathematics as a helpful springboard to leap us into a 'thicker' kind of (realist) reality, as we have done previously in other chapters with religious fictionalism. There are two reasons for this: the first is because I will argue that (a particular strand of) mathematical realism, instead, can provide a closer model of 'post-traditional' religious realism. That is, compared to the kind of ontology that mathematical fictionalism can offer the post-traditional religious realist. The second reason is that mathematical fictionalism does not offer an imaginatively and emotionally rich kind of (non-realist) ontology that can be built on in a meaningful way in the same way that a religious fictionalist ontology can. Thus, I will draw an analogy between the kind of reality that some realist mathematicians ascribe to abstract mathematical objects and the kind of reality that the post-traditional religious realist ascribes to their conception of God.

Conceptualizing the objects of mathematics

Since the purpose of this chapter is to draw an analogy between mathematical objects conceptualized as 'abstract' (and not only existing in language or not at all), I will be working with the mathematical realist construal of mathematical objects as posited by Stewart Shapiro and used by Victoria Harrison. That is, the objects of mathematics hold three characteristics: '*inaccessible to the senses, acausal, and non-spatio-temporal*'.[5] Granted, Harrison acknowledges Bob Hale's (1987) concern that these characteristics 'cannot serve as criteria', which enables one to differentiate between abstract and concrete objects but, it is nevertheless 'beyond serious question' that they are typical characteristics of abstract objects and 'few would be prepared to doubt' that they can be ascribed to abstract *mathematical* objects.[6] Thus, as we go forward, we will be using the realist construal of mathematical objects as possessing the following characteristics:

- Inaccessible to the senses
- Non-spatio-temporal
- Abstract[7]

Different commitments to the mathematical objects

What I will do here is present four different philosophical approaches to interpreting the kind of reality that ought to be ascribed to mathematical objects. After which I will go into more detail about that which separates the two types of mathematical realism, before highlighting why it is important for our project to point out the distinction. Roughly speaking there are realist and non-realist approaches to how we ought to interpret mathematical discourse (as we find in theology/philosophy of religion). There might be two types of mathematical realism that can be individually assessed, that is, *object realism* and *mathematical platonism*.

Object realism 'is the view that there exist mathematical objects'.[8] It is, thus, the 'conjunction of **Existence** and **Abstractness**'.[9] In other words, object realism is a realist 'philosophical position that mathematical statements such as "there are infinitely many prime numbers" are true and that these statements are true by virtue of the existence of mathematical objects – prime numbers, in this case'.[10] Moreover, object realists agree with the three characteristics mentioned above, namely that mathematical objects are (i) inaccessible to the senses, (ii) non-spatio-temporal and (iii) acausal. What separates object realism from mathematical platonism is the condition of **Independence**. That is the view that mathematical ontology is wholly independent of all rational activities, that is, the activities of all rational beings. As M. C. Escher puts it, 'The laws of mathematics are not merely human inventions or creations. They simply "are"; they exist quite independently of the human intellect.'[11]

Therefore, platonism is the 'stronger' philosophical position, in the sense that it is the 'more committed' position compared to object realism precisely because of this additional characteristic of 'independence'. So, what exactly does 'independence' mean in this context? The additional characteristics of 'independence' to the existence of abstract mathematical objects refer to the platonist view that 'mathematical objects are independent of intelligent agents and their language, thought, and practices'.[12] What this means is that 'independence' is the 'counterfactual conditional that, had there not been any intelligent agents, or had their language, thought, or practices been suitably different, there would still have been mathematical objects'.[13] So, what are the consequences of this addition and why does it leave object realism as the 'weaker' position?

'Independence' is meant to 'substantiate an analogy between mathematical objects and ordinary physical objects'.[14] One way to understand this is to compare the platonist's interpretation of a mathematical statement to a non-mathematical statement. For example, the statement 'the moon orbits the earth' is made true by the existence of the moon and the earth and their perfectly objective properties. For the platonists, the same is true for mathematical statements, that is, in the sense that the statement '4 + 4 = 8' is true by virtue of the existence of the numbers '4' and '8'.[15] In short, mathematical objects are just as 'real' as ordinary physical objects.

Thus, platonism about mathematics is the metaphysical view. Moreover, the platonist conception of mathematics does not similarly make the claim that there exist abstract mathematical objects but 'adds a claim' commenting on the 'robust reality' of said objects, namely that mathematical objects 'are at least as real as ordinary physical objects'.[16] We will go into more detail about that which distinguishes object realism and platonism (including the addition of another characteristic alongside 'independence', namely 'necessity'), but before then I will briefly define *mathematical fictionalism* and *mathematical non-realism*.

Mathematical non-realism (or nominalism) is the view that there are no such abstract mathematical entities. Therefore, non-realist mathematicians also deny the existence of a realm of abstract mathematical entities. In other words, this approach denies that mathematical entities are among the entities we need to be ontologically committed to. One of the major assumptions made by the nominalist which sets them apart from the realist is that mathematical objects were '*invented*' rather than discovered (Wigner, Hersh, Azouni, Yablo).[17]

Now, although fictionalism about mathematics is said to share the 'virtue of ontological parsimony' with other nominalist accounts of mathematics, which is to say that mathematical fictionalists deny the existence of a realm of abstract mathematical entities, it is, however, distinct in its approach to interpreting mathematical statements, namely as true but no longer about mathematical entities.[18] Therefore, mathematical fictionalism suggests that when we take mathematical discourse at face value, and take its statements to be true, we are doing so in error. Hence, fictionalism in this respect is known as 'error theory'.[19]

However, where fictionalism notably differs from 'standard' non-realism is this. Although the fictionalist insists that we are in error if we take mathematical statements at face value, they do insist that said statements are true in the story of mathematics.[20] The idea here is, as we might suspect, borrowed from literary fiction, where statements like 'Harry Potter is a wizard' are, strictly speaking, false (because wizards do not exist), but it is a true statement in J. K. Rowling's fictional, wizarding world. Thus, fictionalism in the philosophy of mathematics is the view that mathematical statements (such as '1 + 1 = 2' and 'π is irrational') *are* to be interpreted at face value and thus interpreted as false.[21] Typically, mathematical fictionalists are driven to reject the truth of such statements because they imply the existence of mathematical entities and, according to fictionalists, there are no such entities. Hartry Field, for instance, takes mathematical language at face value as he holds that mathematical objects do not exist, and mathematical propositions have 'objective but vacuous truth-values'.[22] Moreover, Field believes that the idea is to think of mathematical objects as being like characters in fiction, where '[t]he number three and the empty set have the same status as Oliver Twist', for example.[23]

In this next section we are going to revisit the two strands of mathematical realism that I mentioned (object realism and mathematical platonism) and go into more detail about what it is that sets these realist theories apart, as it is important for our overall investigation into what it is that the theologian (and the philosopher of religion) can learn from realism in mathematics.

Object realism versus mathematical platonism

There is a menagerie of realisms in the philosophy of mathematics, and there are different ways to focus points which will highlight the distinctions. One way to mark the difference is to compare 'the objectivity of mathematics' and 'the existence of mathematical objects'. For some mathematical realists, mathematical statements are true independently of our beliefs and attitudes towards them, this is mathematical objectivity. For some realists, 'this is all it takes to be a realist about mathematics'; what is important to notice here is that there is 'nothing in this about there being any mathematical objects'.[24] Whereas, others take the mathematical realist thesis to be that mathematical statements are 'objectively true *and that they are made true by the existence of mathematical objects*'.[25] What does this mean? Well, take the statement 'there is an even prime', for the latter group of realists this statement is not about objectivity because, for them, mathematical realism is *not* a matter of defending the belief that mathematical statements are true, and they are true independently of our attitudes and beliefs towards them. Rather, they take mathematical realism to be the thesis that some mathematical statements are objectively true and they are made true by the existence of mathematical objects.[26]

Another way to draw a divide among the realists is this: 'mathematical objects are abstract' and 'mathematical objects are physical'. The former is the realist view that we have adopted in this chapter which says that mathematical objects are 'abstract entities – objects without causal powers and lacking space-time locations'.[27] However (often driven by epistemological concerns), some realists claim that mathematical entities *are* physical, with one mathematician even claiming that you can *see* them! Penelope Maddy once argued that 'every time you look in the refrigerator and see a dozen eggs you are seeing the set of 12 eggs. You are thus face to face with a mathematical object, namely a set'.[28] However, I wish to draw on a different distinction to those that we have just looked at, one which focuses more on ontology (rather than semantics or epistemology):

> mathematical objects are i) inaccessible to the senses, ii) non-spatiotemporal, and iii) acausal and mathematical objects are i) inaccessible to the senses, ii) non-spatiotemporal, iii) acausal, *iv) independent and v) necessary.*

The 'inflated ontology' demonstrated by the latter realist position adds the characteristics of 'independence' (as we spoke about before) and (as we briefly mentioned) 'necessity'. To clarify, when we talk about the platonists' claim that mathematical objects have 'independence' we are talking about a 'very rich ontology indeed'.[29] What is more, this 'traditional' branch of mathematical realism suggests that not only do the objects of mathematics exist independently from intelligent agents and their language, thought and practices but, crucially, 'had there been no intelligent life, 2 + 2 would still have been 4'.[30] This explains the traditional platonistic conception of mathematics (namely, Platonism with a capital 'P') that 'truth is not accidental – as it is accidental that you are currently reading this book – but that 2 + 2 = 4 is necessarily true, that is, true not only as things actually are, but true no matter how things might have been'.[31] Moreover, the characteristic of 'necessity' is considered part of the abstract nature of mathematical objects by the platonists (it is part of the traditional Platonistic conception of mathematics).[32] This means that these objects are necessary insofar as 'things could not have been otherwise', to the extent that it is 'safe to appeal to these [mathematical] truths when reasoning not only about how the world actually is but also when reasoning about how it would have been had things been otherwise'.[33] Thus, 'part of the cash value of the claim that the truths of pure mathematics are necessary is that such truths can freely be appealed throughout our reasoning about counterfactual scenarios'.[34] As I said, 'had you not been reading this book, or had some girders been twice as thick, 2 + 2 would still have been 4'.[35] That is to say, big claims such as the following can be made on this platonistic/Platonistic mathematical thesis: 'the truths of pure mathematics can be trusted even in an investigation of how things would have been in scenarios where the laws of nature are different'.[36]

To reiterate the importance of these additional characteristics,[37] remember that object realism (realism in ontology) 'does not, by itself, have any ramifications concerning the nature of the postulated mathematical objects (or properties or concepts), *beyond the bare thesis that they exist objectively*'.[38] Those realists that develop or hold lightweight forms of object realism that stop short of full-fledged platonism (and, certainly, Platonism with a capital 'P') do not, then, account for or commit themselves to the 'necessity' of mathematics to the extent that 'the truths of mathematics are independent of anything contingent about the physical universe and anything contingent about the human mind, the community of mathematicians, and so on'.[39] Thus, the existence of the abstract and detached mathematical realism might exist for the realist but it is not necessarily a realm that is absolutely distinct from us human beings, to the extent that had we not existed mathematical objects would be there waiting to be discovered, as the platonist might claim.[40] However, this ought not to be compared with J. S. Mill's approach, this being that the objects of mathematics are 'necessary' entities but only insofar as 'we cannot imagine things to be otherwise'.[41]

So, what exactly is it that the theologian (or philosopher of religion) can take away from this general conception of abstract mathematical objects, and the kind of reality that mathematical realists ascribe to these objects? We will now address this question as we move into the second part of the chapter, as we bring the focus back to theology. The first thing I will do is draw an analogy between how the mathematical object realist conceptualizes the objects of mathematics, and how the 'post-traditional' realist conceptualizes the object of theology (their distinct, 'minimalist' conception of God). Might I ask the reader at this point to recall the second caveat that I inserted at the beginning of the chapter: that I will not suggest that (the 'post-traditionalist's' conception or God, nor the CPT's, nor Cupitt's for that matter) God shares anything in common with mathematical objects (such as numbers, sets and functions) *besides*, potentially, the three characteristics used by some realist mathematicians to describe the abstract nature of *their* objects. Let us begin, then, by exploring the appropriateness of ascribing to the theological object the same three characteristics typically ascribed to mathematical objects by the realist.

Conceptualizing the object of theology

In this section I will begin by presenting Harrison's argument that 'there are good theological reasons for holding that the theological object shares the three principal characteristics of abstract objects',[42] before explaining how I will nuance this idea in such a way as to perhaps (a) minimize any uncertainty when it comes to the appropriateness of the analogy by (b) fleshing out her very brief suggestion that this analogy can only really be applied to a 'minimalist' conception of God (and not the God of CPT). A conception that is similar, I will argue, to the post-traditional, distinct, 'minimalist' conception of God.

Thus, I will be using Harrison's argument as a foundation on which to build the twofold argument of this book. That is, (1) to argue for the plausibility of a texture of reality that might exist somewhere 'between' fictionalism and traditional realism and (2) to argue for a conception of 'God' that falls somewhat 'below' the traditional realist's conception of God, in reference to the first axis, without abandoning, what might be considered, a fundamental component of what the concept of (a) 'God' (at least) ought to amount to.

To begin, it might be helpful to quote Harrison's proposal, after which we can discuss the way she went about fulfilling her proposal and any questions we might have by the end of it.

> I argue [,Harrison says,] that mathematical objects and the central object of Western theological traditions – God – can be usefully thought of as having a number of key features in common, namely those features typically ascribed to abstract objects: lack of spatio-temporal location; inaccessibility to the senses; and acausality.[43]

The purpose of Harrison's work on mathematical realism and theological realism is, at least partly, to explain why we might think of God – as *the* theological object – as also possessing those characteristics ascribed by the realist mathematicians to what they consider to be 'abstract' mathematical objects. And, if there are good theological reasons for holding that the theological object shares the three principles (lack of spatio-temporal location, inaccessibility to the senses and acausality) it might be useful to investigate whether the (philosophical, realist) theologian is able to make 'new' and insightful epistemological and ontological claims in light of the types of claims that the realist mathematician might make about *their* objects. Harrison thinks that by drawing on a realist account on the nature of mathematical objects, it may be possible to make similar epistemological and ontological claims about the object of theology. Namely, an epistemological claim about how we might come to 'know' the abstract, theological object, in the same way that some realist mathematicians claim to 'know' abstract, mathematical objects.[44] I am, however, more interested in Harrison's ontological claim. Harrison suggests that it is not hugely contestable that 'the central object of Western theological traditions', that is, God of CPT, also holds these same characteristics.[45] She argues this by going through each of the three principles and explains the possibility that 'not all abstract objects belong to the mathematical realm, [and] we should not be surprised to find that these arguments can be deployed elsewhere'.[46] Thus, she considers the proposal that 'the object of theology shares some of the key features of abstract mathematical objects'.[47]

And so, Harrison attempts to 'clarify certain important issues concerning the characterization of the object of theology'.[48] To do this, she takes each characteristic of a mathematical abstract object and demonstrates how these same characteristics might also be applicable to *the* theological abstract object.

I will not go through each of her arguments in detail, but here is a quick review of each. For 'inaccessibility to the senses' (which is really more relevant within the domain of theological epistemology, which is not our focus here), Harrison argues that it is generally agreed upon in theology that 'God cannot be known through the senses' and that according to this theological tradition, knowledge of God 'is not knowledge of an empirical object. Consequently, the source of such knowledge cannot be the senses'.[49] Harrison draws on Christian theology, and the writings of Edith Stein on John of the Cross's teaching on the night of faith, as an example of this tradition; that it is possible to arrive at 'perfect certainty' about God which, as Harrison points out, 'seems to align it more with mathematical knowledge than with knowledge of the empirical realm'.[50]

We next need to consider the category of 'acausality', which is highly relevant within the domain of theological ontology. The inability of mathematical objects to enter into causal relations (at least, physical causal relations) begs the question, 'How do acausal abstract objects relate to the physical world?' And, more specifically for theology, 'Is it necessary that God (as Creator) is involved in physical causal relations?' Harrison answers this question with the following response, 'what it means for God to create is not well understood.... Our experience of causation comes from the spatio-temporal realm of physical objects.... So the theological claim that God is the Creator does not entail, as far as we can judge, that it is necessary that God is involved in physical causal relations'.[51] Thus, Harrison assumes that God as Creator can possess the abstract characteristic of 'acausality' without potentially jeopardizing the essence of God.

Finally, Harrison asks, 'What might be theologically problematic about the claim that God is not an object with spatial or temporal location?'[52] It seems that this is a tricky question, as Harrison goes back and forth, wrestling with potentially conflicting statements, which leads her to questions like this, If '[t]heists typically hold that God is a personal being who can enter into relations with us, then how could a God construed as lacking spatial or temporal properties fit this description? Wouldn't such a God be irrelevant to beings such as ourselves who are firmly embedded in the sensory world of space-time?' Or, might we say that, 'God without a particular spatial or temporal position could – like the number 3 – be simultaneously accessible at all times and places (which would seem to be an obvious theological desideratum)'?[53] What these worries and sense of confusion show us is that theological issues can arise when one tries to draw an analogy between the abstract nature of mathematical objects and the abstract nature of the theological object. However, I would like to emphasize that this may be true, but might we overcome this predicament if we insert an 'if' at the end and extend the statement so that it reads something more like this:

Theological issues can arise when one tries to draw an analogy between the abstract nature of mathematical objects and the abstract nature of the theological object, *if* the working object of theology is the God of CPT.

Harrison recognizes that the traditional realist who holds a classical conception of God might not appreciate the analogy between the God of CPT and abstract mathematical objects for the following reason.

> [T]he comparison between abstract mathematical objects and the object of theology is illegitimate because the latter possesses a host of other, non-abstract, properties that it would be unthinkable to ascribe to mathematical objects. God is, for example, as acknowledged above, typically referred to as personal.[54]

I am sure that the reader can also think of other reasons why the traditional realist would not necessarily be inclined to draw on this analogy. It looks as though this potentially useful analogy, then, between mathematical realism and theological realism can only apply to a non-CPT conception of God, if we want to avoid a whole host of conflicting statements and maximize any benefit of bringing these two disciplines into conversation. With that being said, the statement of intention might now be read as the following question,

'Do theological issues arise when one tries to draw an analogy between the abstract nature of mathematical objects and the abstract nature of the theological object, *if* the working object of theology is *not* the God of CPT but, instead, some kind of 'minimalist' conception?

Acknowledging that this might indeed be the case, Harrison suggests that the theological object that she outlines – the object of theology conceived as inaccessible to the senses, acausal and non-spatio-temporal – is certainly 'self-consciously minimalistic'.[55] In only a couple of sentences within a concluding paragraph, Harrison expands on this idea of a 'self-consciously minimalist' conception of God only to say that this is a 'bare theological object' that could only be used as 'conceptual scaffolding' upon which 'more elaborate theological systems can be built'. Lastly, she compares this bare and self-consciously minimalistic conception to a suitably qualified version of Anselm's 'that-than-which-a-greater-cannot-be-conceived',[56] and it is this idea that I really want to build on.

As I say, Harrison does not go into detail about what this 'bare theological object' really amounts to, therefore what I propose to do is to insert the distinctive, 'minimalist' conception of God defended in this book into Harrison's analogy. That way, the statement of intention will read as follows.

Perhaps theological issues that arise when one tries to draw an analogy between the abstract nature of mathematical objects and the abstract nature of the theological object can be mitigated if the theological object is understood to be a distinct 'minimalist' conception of God rather than the God of CTP.

In light of this latest 'statement of intention', we will revisit the three characteristics assigned to abstract objects by the realist, but this time insert the object of theology now conceived as distinctively 'minimalist' in nature into the analogy, and see whether the analogy works better.

With the category of 'inaccessibility to the senses' we previously suggested that knowledge of the CPT conception of God cannot be reached through the senses, I suggest that the post-traditional realist will say something similar. That is, the view that knowledge of 'God' (however construed) is not knowledge of an empirical object, thus, the source of such knowledge cannot be the senses. However, unlike the traditional realist, the post-traditional realist is not *as* concerned with the idea of 'inaccessibility' as the traditional realist might be. The traditional realist might insist that the term 'inaccessible' is problematic because it implies an 'impossibility'; that it is impossible for God to reveal himself to us through the senses if and when He so chooses. Whereas, the 'post-traditionalist' is not committed to a conception of God that would necessarily 'reveal' Godself in this way. Therefore, if we insert the post-traditional conception of God here, that is, a distinctive 'minimalist' conception of God, then to say (for the purposes of this analogy) that this God is 'inaccessible to the senses' is, arguably, highly less problematic than to suggest that the God of CPT cannot be 'accessed' via sensory experience.

As you might recall with the next category of 'acausality', the inability of mathematical objects to enter into physical causal relations begged the question as to how such objects can relate to the physical world, which then led us to ask, 'How is it that God, if also construed as "acausal", can be involved in physical causal relations?' Now, in a similar way to the previous characteristic, the post-traditional realist does not share the same concern with the traditional realist when it comes to explaining how God 'can relate to the physical world'[57] if God cannot enter into causal relation. This is because the post-traditionalist's distinctive, 'minimalist' conception of God is not necessarily a Creator God, whereas the God of CPT 'must be capable of involvement in physical causal relations because God is the Creator of everything that exists and creation is a causal process'.[58]

Thus, the issue of whether it is necessary that God as Creator is involved in physical causal relations is not an issue for the post-traditional believer because their conception of God does not rest on, nor include, God's ability to create and connect with the world and us, human beings. Or, at least, not so intensely, in the sense that the traditional realist will feel that it is possible to connect with the God who created the world and us, as his love is written about in the Scriptures, for example, and it is a spiritual aim to grow closer to this personal and powerful God.

The post-traditional believer will feel some type of connection to *their* 'minimalist' conception of God in two ways. The first is that God as 'that-than-which-a-greater-cannot-be-conceived' is tethered to us in some way and, on this understanding, God is always 'connected' to us. The supervenience thesis explored in the upcoming sections ('Realism as "Mind-Independent"' and 'Necessity') will help to unpack this claim. The second is that we can (learn to) 'tap into' this divine conceptual space ascribed to this God, and thus feel (more) 'connected' to God. These two ways of feeling 'connected' to the distinctive, 'minimalist' conception of God are not expressing the same kind of 'connectivity' that the traditional believer will claim to experience or believe is possible to experience with their God (of CPT). For them, God being described as abstract, in the sense that God is 'acausal', might contradict their unwavering belief that God is personal and able to enter into causal relations. Furthermore, if we insert the post-traditional conception of God here then (again, for the purposes of this analogy) to suggest that this God is 'acausal', it is considerably less problematic than to suggest that the God of CPT is acausal.

Finally, when it comes to drawing an analogy between the objects of mathematics and the object of theology (from CPT) on the basis that both objects lack spatio-temporal location, Harrison predicts that this might unsettle the traditional religious realist. The reason is that if the God of CPT is non-physical (in a similar way, perhaps, to the objects of mathematics), how can God be relevant to our (His creatures') lives if we are spatio-temporal beings? Moreover, the traditional realist is concerned with how the God of CPT can be a 'personal being who can enter into relations with us' and wants to avoid inadequate consequences, such that the God of CPT becomes 'irrelevant to beings such as ourselves who are firmly embedded in the sensory world of space-time'.[59] The 'post-traditionalist' is not necessarily concerned about whether (their) God can enter into 'relations' with us because (their) God is not a 'personal being' in the same way that the God of CPT is thought to be a 'personal being'.

That is to say, the God of CPT is a personal God understood to be omnibenevolent, to love His creatures (as their Creator) and to continue to watch over them. Whereas, the post-traditional realist might understand (their) God to be 'personal' insofar as God is 'semi-dependent' on human beings to exist. That is to say, as I said before, this conception of God is in some distinct way tethered to human persons, which is *not* to say that this God was 'invented' by us humans but, rather, that this God is at least dependent on our existence for God's own existence. Or, using the language of supervenience, God (qua a suitably qualified version of Anselm's formula) irreducibly supervenes on a whole possible world (which contains human minds). That God (divine facts/properties/discourse) arises out of a whole range of relational properties (including human epistemic practices) means that we cannot give a full account, because of our epistemic limitations. Therefore, importantly, God as 'semi-independent' remains open to further thought because of the intrinsic mystery of the subject matter.

It is worth noting again, as I said in Chapter 1, that I have purposely chosen to qualify the independent nature of post-traditional realism as '*semi*' independent rather than '*quasi*' independent. The reason for this is because 'quasi' means 'as if' that is, an 'as if' reality and this does not capture divine reality as conceived by the post-traditional realist. The independence of a post-traditional realist conceptual space, insofar as it exists, is genuine. It is dependent on the human mind ('spirit'), but once the human mind is in place, it is not something optional/ornamental/chosen/made-up or voluntaristically constructed. Thus, this is what is at stake here, therefore 'quasi' is not necessarily appropriate. For example, Simon Blackburn spoke about 'quasi realism', and this is not reflective of the space offered by post-traditional realism.[60]

If the distinctive, 'minimalist' conception of God is described as lacking spatio-temporal location, the post-traditional believer does not necessarily worry about how their God can *also be* a God that is personal and relevant, because they are less likely to refer back to Scripture, for example, and question whether it really makes sense (even for the purposes of an analogy) to describe this dominant and dynamic God as abstract and, thus lacking spatio-temporal location. Instead, their conception of God as purely 'that-than-which-a-greater-cannot-be-conceived' does not implicitly have to tackle this paradox that being, how a specifically personal God (in accordance with the Scriptures, for instance) can lack spatiotemporal location?[61] Furthermore, if we insert the post-traditional conception of God into the analogy and suggest that this God exists outside the spatio-temporal domain, perhaps this statement is significantly less problematic than the idea that the God of CPT might be non-physically related to the spatio-temporal realm.

At this point, I want us to go back to the first part of the question that was posited for this section: 'What exactly is it that the theologian (or philosopher of religion) can take away from this general conception of abstract mathematical objects?' I have suggested that it can be suitably argued that the distinctive, 'minimalist' conception of God might share the three characteristics typically ascribed to abstract objects (at least, less problematically than the God of CPT). Now, if such an analogy can be drawn between abstract mathematical objects and the distinctive, 'minimalist' conception of God offered in this book, then I will now suggest that we can meaningfully draw an analogy between religious post-traditional realism and mathematical realism (object realism). On the view that both ascribe a reality (to their respective mathematical or theological 'object') that is *conditionally necessary* and *semi-independent*. Now we will move on to answer the second part of the question: 'What exactly is it that the theologian (or philosopher of religion) can take away from the kind of reality that mathematical realists ascribe to these objects?'

Different commitments to the theological object

In the previous section we focused on the conceptualization of abstract objects. Specifically mathematical objects according to the mathematical realist (namely the three characteristics), and asked whether it is appropriate to ascribe these same characteristics to the God of CPT and/or the distinctive, 'minimalist' conception of God. Thus, we were working with the first axis (a spectrum of conceptions of God). What we will do now is jump to the second axis (a spectrum of commitment) by 'examining theological ontology through the lens of philosophy of mathematics'.[62] The aim of this section is twofold. First, we will bring the additional characteristics which describe the kind of reality ascribed to the object(s), namely 'independence' and 'necessity', back into the fold. I will suggest that these (platonistic) characteristics are not necessarily compatible with post-traditional realism, but instead are more compatible with traditional realism.

Second, and based on what we find with this proposal in the first section, I will draw what might be the most suitable analogy between mathematical realism and theological realism. That is to say, we will make our way through what might be rather weak analogies between mathematical platonism and traditional religious realism toward a hopefully more fruitful analogy between object realism and post-traditional realism. This is the analogy that Harrison hinted at, and what I want to draw our attention to in this chapter, and argue that the theologian (or philosopher of religion) can use a particular strand of mathematical realism, namely object realism, to help ease any major resistance towards the plausibility or possibility of the kind of (divine) reality posited by the religious post-traditional realist. With that being said, I will now present Harrison's ontological claim, before offering my nuanced take on it, which will develop Harrison's working conception of God.

Realism as 'mind-independent'

Here is a quote from Harrison describing her account of realism and non-realism in mathematics:

> Realism about ontology in mathematics is a position about the possibility of the objective, mind-independent existence of mathematical objects. Conversely, non-realism about ontology denies the possibility of the objective, mind-independent existence of mathematical objects and seeks to provide an alternative – reductive or eliminativist – characterization of them.[63]

She presents the same account of realism and non-realism in theology (and philosophy of religion) by simply replacing 'mathematical objects' with 'the theological object'.[64] Although nothing too controversial is being stated, it is interesting that Harrison consciously chooses to use similar language when describing the realism/non-realismdebate in both disciplines. We know that Harrison refers to 'God' as 'the theological object' and numbers, sets and functions, and so on as 'mathematical objects', but now we hear how *both* the theological object and the mathematical objects can be described as having an 'objective, mind-independent' existence according to the (mathematical and theological) realist. In the same manner, we also see how both the mathematical and the theological non-realist will deny the existence of objective, mind-independent object(s).

Similarly, again, both the mathematical and the theological non-realist may seek to 'provide an alternative – reductive or eliminativist – characterization of it'. Reductionist non-realism, for example, proposes that it is possible to reduce objects as fictional objects. We find this in religious fictionalism and mathematical fictionalism, where the objects of each discipline might be considered objective and mind-independent but only insofar as these objects are objective and mind-independent in accordance with the relevant (mathematical or theological) fictional world.

However, I believe that in order for Harrison's analogy (between mathematical realism and theological realism) to maximize its potential and provide a useful analogy – one which will invite insightful conversation on how we ought to understand different textures of reality – a qualification needs to be made. Specifically, when it comes to the 'mind-independent' existence of the theological/mathematical object(s). If we start with mathematical discourse, the possibility of mathematical objects having a mind-independent existence invites a platonistic approach to interpreting the kind of reality that these objects hold. In the previous section where we looked at how one might define mathematical platonism ('Different commitments to the mathematical objects') we said that it might include the following three theses: **Existence** (there are mathematical objects), **Abstractness** (mathematical objects are abstract) and **Independence** (mathematical objects are independent of intelligent agents and their language, thought and practices).[65]

The first two characteristics – **Existence** and **Abstractness** – are also true of object realism (the less ontologically ambitious branch of mathematical realism), but it is the characteristic of '**Independence**' that suggests something 'extra'. Might it be the case that Harrison has (unknowingly perhaps) included this 'extra' thesis in her 'general' concept of mathematical realism? If so, this could potentially conflict with her brief gesture towards the kind of religious realism from which the analogy can be drawn, namely one that can be ascribed to a bare, 'minimalist' conception of God. In that case, Harrison's claim that realism about ontology in theology and mathematics 'is a position about the possibility of the objective, mind-independent existence of the theological object' is problematic.

The mathematical platonist might use the characteristic of 'mind-independence' to justify their claim that abstract mathematical objects have an 'independent' existence. This, as we remember, refers to the view that mathematical objects exist independently of intelligent agents and their language, thought and practices. This might correlate to the traditional religious realists' view about *their* object insofar as God (of CPT) is certainly conceived by the traditional realist to exist independent of intelligent agents and their language, thought and practices.

However, the traditional realist is less likely to draw an analogy with mathematical realism in the first place. This is because, as we saw earlier, an analogy cannot be easily drawn between mathematical objects and the object of theology (from CPT). For this reason, and because a particular strand of mathematical realism – namely, object realism – might help to open up a conceptual space that might exist 'between' fictionalism and full-blown traditional realism, I suggest that we qualify Harrison's realist view of 'mind-independence', and instead state '*semi*-independence'. By doing this, we could also draw out the distinction between the object realist's view that mathematical objects have some kind of mind-independent quality, without committing to the mathematical platonist's view that these objects exist *wholly* independently from us, human beings to the extent that had there not been any intelligent agents, or had their language, thought or practices been suitably different, there would still have been mathematical objects.

Much in the same way, the post-traditional religious realist will want to say that their (distinctive, 'minimalist' conception of) God exists somewhat independently from the individual ('semi-independently') insofar as they will deny the view that God was simply 'invented', but this is quite different from suggesting that God has a *wholly* independent existence and would, therefore, have existed whether or not humanity existed. To further unpack this nuanced term of 'semi-independence', it might be helpful to draw on the concept of supervenience by articulating a distinctive type of dependency relation, which permits a degree of autonomy (this will be explained), and appeals to epistemic humility. Supervenience, as was previously and briefly explained, is a type of dependence relation between properties or facts of one type, and properties or facts of another; or it can be a type of dependence between one type of discourse and another.[66] Thus, supervenience can help the philosopher to think about different ways to represent how objects, properties, facts, events and the like enter into dependency relationships with one another, 'creating a system of interconnections that give structure to the world and our experience of it'.[67] The idea comes to this: A-properties are supervenient on B-properties, thus the term 'supervene' characterizes a relation that emergent properties bear to their base properties. So, we are talking about the correlations between supervenient properties and their base properties. For example, 'moral properties, in particular, the rightness or wrongness of an action, are supervenient on their nonmoral properties (which could provide reasons for rightness or wrongness)'.[68]

There are at least three distinctions between types of supervenience. We will explore each type and, in doing so, I will build up the kind of supervenience that might best represent, first of all, the 'semi-independent' nature of the conceptual space that I am looking to defend in this book and, later, in the following section, the concept of 'conditionally necessity'. The first distinction is 'reductive' and 'non-reductive' (otherwise written as 'reducible' and 'irreducible').[69]

If a type of supervenience has a reductive relation it means that properties/facts/objects/discourse of type x can be reduced to properties/facts/objects/discourse of type y, without any loss of context. For example, 'the average man is 160 cm tall' is reducible to facts about individual instances. However, the reducibility thesis has been largely abandoned (Moore, Hare and Davidson) with a non-reductive relation preferred, which says that supervenient dependence does not entail the reducibility of the supervenient to its subvenient base.[70] In other words, properties/facts/objects/discourse of type x cannot be reduced to properties/facts/objects/discourse of type y. Examples in the literature of a non-reductive relation include consciousness in relation to neurobiological properties and moral value in relation to natural properties.

The idea of non-reducibility might help to explain what is meant by 'semi-independent' here. This is because the conceptual space that I am gesturing towards could be characterized as irreducible. A space illustrative, I hope to have shown, of a weak type of (object) realism found in the philosophy of mathematics. In this context, mathematical divine discourse/facts/properties cannot be reduced to naturalistic discourse/facts/properties about human epistemic practices (including consciousness). In our philosophy of religion context, this book is arguing that *divine* discourse/facts/properties cannot be reduced to naturalistic discourse/facts/properties about human epistemic practices (including consciousness).

The second distinction is between 'strong' and 'weak' supervenience. According to Kim, there are two types of individual supervenience: weak and strong, and they are defined by means of quantification over possible worlds. 'Strong' supervenience, as you would imagine, is stronger than weak supervenience because it entails that one knows that there is an 'if and only if' relation here, whereby properties of type y can only ever arise in possible worlds where there are properties of type x. In the literature it is often depicted in the following way:

> A-properties *strongly supervene* on B-properties if and only if for any possible worlds w_1 and w_2 and any individuals x in w_1 and y in w_2, if x in w_1 is B-indiscernible from y in w_2, then x in w_1 is A-indiscernible from y in w_2.[71]

What this means is that x and y are A-indiscernible if and only if they are exactly alike with respect to every A-property, and the same can be said for B-indiscernibility. Strong supervenience entails that there are no possible individuals that are B-indiscernible but A-discernible, *whether they are in the same world or different worlds.*[72] Indiscernibility in A or B can be 'cross-world' as well as within a single world, thus, and in accordance with Brian McLaughlin, we might put the definition like this: 'A *strongly supervenes* on B just in case *cross-world indiscernibility in B entails cross-world indiscernibility in A.*'[73] 'Weak' supervenience, as the name indicates, can be described as the following weaker position: if one is not claiming that properties of type *y* only ever arise in possible worlds where there are properties of type *x*. Or, it can otherwise be written like this:

> A-properties *weakly supervene* on B-properties if and only if for any possible world *w* and any individuals *x* and *y* in *w*, if *x* and *y* are B-indiscernible in *w*, then they are A-indiscernible in *w*.

Weak supervenience says that there is no possible world that contains individuals that are B-indiscernible but A-discernible. What this means is that weak supervenience does not commit to the stronger thesis that 'if in another world an object has the same B-properties that it has in this world, it must also have the same A-properties It has in this one'.[74] That is to say, the particular associations between A-properties and B-properties in a given world 'cannot be counted to carry over into other worlds'.[75] Therefore, weak supervenience only requires that '*within* any possible world there not be two things agreeing in B but diverging in A'.[76] Moreover, this weaker thesis offers an 'interesting and significant' relation of, what Kim Jaegwon calls, '*partial* dependence'.[77] Partial dependence describes a supervenience that 'cannot in general be relied on to be stable from world to world' because a 'full sense of dependency cannot be captured by weak supervenience'.[78] However, Kim argues that weak supervenience can be 'entirely consistent' with autonomy, in terms of what supervenes in relation to its base, and this might be one of its 'chief attractions': the base does not wholly determine the supervening properties.[79] There are two reasons why the conceptual space pointed to in this book and the post-traditional conception of God as 'semi-independent' might be clarified by drawing on *weak* supervenience language. The first is that weak supervenience states that, for example, particular associations between A-properties and B-properties in *this world* cannot be assumed to carry out into all or any other possible world. Whereas, strong supervenience can guarantee world-to-world stability for the correlations between A-properties and B-properties, for instance. Therefore, weak supervenience exercises or requires epistemic humility, by this I mean that if one does not *know* that properties of type A can arise or not in a possible world without properties of type B. This is my position if I remain agnostic, say, about panpsychism, or the continuation of consciousness and identity after death. In contrast, then, strong supervenience is epistemically confident, in the sense that those who appeal to this strong thesis will claim to *know* that properties of type A can indeed arise in worlds without properties of type B. For example, this would be the case if one knew that molluscs/planets had a type of consciousness, independently of neurobiological brain processes. There can be good principled reasons for finding it rational to say that one does not know something, given human limitations and/or the complexity of the subject matter. To be epistemically humble allows one to do some thinking alongside acknowledging a degree of 'unknowing'. In a way, then, this is the point of 'supervenience' language in the wider philosophical literature, especially in philosophy of mind: consciousness ('whatever that is') *somehow* depends on ('how?') neurobiological processes ('although we are only beginning to understand these'), because it enables philosophers to say that one sort of thing 'depends' ('somehow') on another type of thing, without having to offer psychophysical laws or causal accounts.

So how does this relate to my book? The position I am suggesting, namely the post-traditional minimalist proposal with relation to facts/discourse/properties about God, is 'weak' and epistemically humble. By this I wish to argue that naturalistic discourse/facts/properties about human epistemic practices (including consciousness) are sufficient to give rise to divine discourse/facts/properties, but I do not claim to know that divine discourse/facts/properties can arise or *not* in a possible world *without* the human epistemic practices.

The second reason why drawing on the language of weak supervenience might help to convey what is meant by 'semi-independence' (when describing the post-traditional minimalist proposal) is that although strong supervenience may not satisfy all the forms of reduction, it does at least conform to the standard conception of reduction as it is articulated by Thomas Nagel and is, thus, sufficiently reductive to be unsuitable for the conceptual space that I am defending. When it comes to consciousness, Nagel would occupy a weak supervenience position about consciousness as he says: yes, our consciousness is supervenient on neurobiology, but perhaps, for all we know, galaxies and molluscs, and everything in between, might participate in a type of consciousness (together and/or individually).[80] Arguably, Aristotle's concept seems to be supervenience in the weak sense too when discussing the relationship between human bodies and consciousness. He says, if you lived in a world where all triangles were golden, you might think this was essential for triangles, but it is not. In our experience, consciousness needs bodies, but this might not be the case (for all we know).[81] In relation to this book then, I am arguing that divine discourse/facts/properties cannot be reduced to this naturalistic discourse/facts/properties about human epistemic practices (including consciousness).

The third distinction is 'regional' supervenience and 'global' supervenience. Regional (or 'local') supervenience restricts the supervenience relation to a space–time region within a world. Terence Horgan sets out the concept in the following way: A-properties supervene on B-properties whenever two spatio-temporal regions are exactly alike concerning all qualitative intrinsic B-properties, and exactly alike concerning all A-properties which are also intrinsic to them.[82] In simpler terms, regional supervenience narrows the field that this type of property A arises from precisely this type of property B. For instance, 'the property of *being taller than one's own father* is an extrinsic feature of the individual *x* instantiating it, but intrinsic to a spatiotemporal region containing *x* as well as *x*'s father'.[83] We can then compare this to global supervenience, which can be described as the thesis employed to help capture the indiscernibility considerations globally to 'worlds' (or 'entire possible worlds') taken as units of comparison. In other words, '[w]orlds that are indiscernible in respect of subvenient properties are indiscernible in respect of supervenient properties'.[84] Formulated in the same way as the previous two types ('strong' and 'weak') it reads as follows:

> A-properties *globally supervene* on B-properties if and only if for any worlds w_1 and w_2, if w_1 and w_2 have exactly the same world-wide pattern of distribution of B-properties, then they have exactly the same worldwide pattern of distribution of A-properties.

It was once assumed (Kim, 1984) that strong supervenience entailed global supervenience but this was later rejected (Kim, 1987), and it has even since been suggested (Kim, 1990) that 'global supervenience, along with weak supervenience, can qualify as a nonreductive relation'.[85] This is good for this project, as I wish to suggest that, in light of what I have said thus far, a type of supervenience that is *irreducible*, *weak* and *global* can help to unpack what I mean when I describe the post-traditional divine conceptual space as 'semi-independent'. There are two reasons why global supervenience (rather than regional supervenience) best captures what is meant by 'semi-independent'.

The first is because it leans into that epistemic humility that I suggest the post-traditional believer will exercise, because it recognizes our human epistemic limitations but virtue of its holistic character. By 'holistic' I mean that extrinsic (or broadly relational) properties are considered important when formulating a supervenience thesis. For instance, if one were to say that A and B share the same physical properties, what is to count as a physical property? Naturally, we want to include intrinsic physical properties like molecular structure, but we might also want to include broadly relational, or extrinsic, physical properties, like being 200 miles from the centre of mass of the solar system at time t.

Examples from the literature would include,[86] how some aestheticians (Walton, 1970) insist that even if two paintings are alike in their intrinsic physical properties (so that there could be no physical tests one could carry out to determine which is which) they may still not be alike in their aesthetic properties. The reason is that the aesthetic properties of the work depend partly on its history, and two apparently identical paintings can have different histories. In order to include the history of the work we would have to build in broadly relational properties when we consider the requisite notion of sameness.

Similarly, when we turn to the alleged supervenience of the mental on the physical (Putnam, 1975), there is reason to think that the thesis is plausible only if we include, in the condition of physical sameness, relational properties. Putnam argues that a person's psychological state is not a matter simply of what is going on 'in their head' but also of what external objects one is causally related to. Another (social) example might include becoming prime minister, to become PM is not just a matter of what one thinks and does, it depends upon what others think and do as well. So, one's social characteristics are clearly not determined by one's own individual characteristics alone. If individual facts determine the social facts, they do so in a global rather than a local way. Therefore, global supervenience recognizes that there is an undeniable sense in which such facts are holistically constituted. Moreover, global supervenience merely demands that, if there is to be a social (for example) difference between worlds u and w (at time t) there must be some difference between them concerning the thought or behaviour of at least some individual (up to t).

In addition to global supervenience displaying epistemic humility, the second reason why global supervenience (rather than regional supervenience) better characterizes post-traditionalism is because of its intrinsic mystery. By this I mean, the complexity and difficulty of the properties/facts/discourse. Because although it states that certain patterns of property covariation hold, it does not claim to know *why* those patterns hold nor the precise nature of the dependency involved. This claim can be leveraged against *all* forms of supervenience (including both 'weak' and 'strong'); however, one could argue that global supervenience resists the temptation to assume knowledge of the deep truth about why a certain pattern holds in order to guarantee us a coherent pattern. Rather, the thesis is 'global' if it generalizes over all the relevant worlds and over whole worlds to boot. This means, then, that when one asserts that properties of type A in a world with properties of type B, but over the 'whole possible world', so one does not claim to know, or to be able to give a full account, which parts of the 'supervenience base' give rise to the supervening properties.

In regard to my thesis then, when describing the nature of the semi-independent divine conceptual space, using the language of global supervenience, I wish to argue the following: that divine facts/properties/discourse arise out of a whole range of relational properties (including human epistemic practices) which we cannot give a full account of because of our epistemic limitations. Partly because of this epistemic limitation, I remain open to the further thought that this is because of the intrinsic mystery of the subject matter. This orientation to unknowing relation to intrinsic mystery has 'apophatic' theological resonances, perhaps, although this is not a load-bearing beam in the argument.

And, so, with this range of options (those being: reductive/non-reductive, weak/strong and regional/global), the position that I am proposing, namely a 'semi-independent' divine conceptual space with relation to facts/properties/discourse about God is *irreducible*, *weak* (and epistemically humble) and *global* (certainly motivated by epistemic humility, but open to considerations about intrinsic mystery). Thus, the language of supervenience can help deliver the post-traditional minimalist proposal: it is a sui generis conceptual space that goes beyond fictionalism, but without affirming a conceptual space beyond a richly conceived naturalism (namely, 'minimalist theologies' as explored by Adorno, and more recently de Vries, Ellis, Wiggins and McDowell),[87] somewhere that exists 'beyond' (the 'as if' space depicted by) fictionalism but not beyond naturalism. I am not claiming, then, that we know God (even the minimalist conception of God presented in this book) to be exhausted by the naturalistic but, rather, will not claim, in principle, that naturalism sets the limits of what could be real.

In light of what supervenience language can offer in terms of helping to legitimize the possibility and plausibility of this kind of 'semi-independent' relation between God (qua a suitably qualified version of Anselm's formula) and a naturalistic state of affairs (naturalistic discourse/facts/properties about human epistemic practices), if we add this qualification ('semi') to Harrison's description of mathematical realism, it might read something like this:

> Realism about ontology in mathematics is a position about the possibility of the objective, *semi*-independent existence of mathematical objects.

And, if we mirror this same qualification onto Harrison's description of religious realism, it will read something like this:

> Realism about ontology in theology is a position about the possibility of the objective, *semi*-independent existence of the theological object.

To clarify, what I have done here is argue that if we nuance Harrison's claim that the type of realist reality ascribed to abstract objects is 'semi-independent', rather than wholly mind-dependent then we might be able to (a) avoid an unnecessary and unhelpful overlap between the ontological thesis held by the object realist, and the richer ontological thesis held by the mathematical platonist. And (b) ensure that Harrison's suggestion that 'the object of theology conceived as inaccessible to the senses, acausal, and non-spatiotemporal – is self-consciously minimalistic' is represented in the analogy (rather than the God of CPT).[88] Furthermore, we are then able to insert the distinctive, 'minimalist' conception of God offered in this book to 'flesh out' Harrison's suggestion and strengthen the potential value of this analogy. So, what does this mean for religious post-traditional realism and its appropriateness?

In the introductory chapter, where I presented an ontological construal of the realism/non-realism distinction, I said that the central question here is whether x (the abstract object) exists independently of mind or not. The non-realist will say that x depends on the mind for its existence, and the realist will say that x exists *in*dependently of mind. The difference between the traditional religious realist about x (the God of CPT) and the post-traditional realist about x (a distinctive 'minimalist' conception of God) is that the former will suggest that x has a *wholly independent* existence, whereas the latter says that x has a *semi-*independent existence.

That is to say, the reality ascribed to 'God' as construed by the traditional realist does not depend in any way upon the existence of us, human beings. By contrast, the post-traditionalist ascribes a reality to x that is semi-dependent on the existence of us, in the sense that we are distinctly tethered to God.

In light of this distinction, might we now say that based on Harrison's original description of realism about ontology – as 'a position about the possibility of the objective, mind-independent existence' of a theological/mathematical object – this position is more reflective of the traditional realist's ontological thesis (wholly independent). And that the nuanced version of realism about ontology that I offer – as a position about the possibility of the objective, *semi-*independent existence of the theological object – is more reflective of the post-traditionalist's ontological thesis (semi-independent). Thus, if it is agreed that in order for an analogy between religious realism and mathematical realism to prove beneficial, we ought to nuance Harrison's take on realism in toto. As well as perhaps inserting the distinctive, 'minimalist' conception of God (which was argued in the previous section, 'Conceptualizing the object of theology').

Moreover, what I have tried to do here is to suggest that we need to qualify Harrison's understanding of realism, first when it comes to claiming 'mind-independence'. This is because it invites a platonistic thesis and therefore alters the kind of reality that is being ascribed to the abstract object. The reality is too rich; it is ontologically richer than the post-traditionalist will want to commit to. And since the post-traditionalist is most likely to draw on this analogy, Harrison's realism ought to be qualified. The qualification might also, importantly, help to ease any major resistance towards the legitimacy of a 'post-traditional' type of realist commitment.

What we will do now is to look at another claim made by Harrison which, again, might invite a platonistic ontological thesis. Namely, a richer ontology which is not the same as what the object realist claims. This is important, and ought not to be ignored because, as we remember object realism is not concerned with the nature of abstract mathematical objects beyond the basic thesis that they exist objectively.

Necessity

In addition to the three characteristics typically ascribed to abstract objects, namely: inaccessibility to the senses, acausality and lack of spatial or temporal location, Harrison suggests that there are a number of 'related characteristics' that 'for obvious reasons' would be 'highly relevant to a more detailed argument'.[89] Such characteristics include, for Harrison, 'necessity'.[90] Here I will argue that 'necessity' cannot be seamlessly added to these three theses.

I want to begin by suggesting two things. The first is that the idea that 'necessity' might be better understood as describing the kind of 'reality' that is ascribed to an abstract object, rather than a 'characteristic' of said object (at least for the purposes of this project). The second is to argue for a qualification to be added to Harrison's use of the concept of 'necessity', at least in the context of this analogy between religious realism and mathematical realism. I suggest that we qualify Harrison's concept of 'necessity' so that it reads 'conditionally necessary'. This is because to simply assert 'necessity' postulates a platonist approach. That is, abstract objects have an '*un*conditionally necessary' kind of reality. What does the concept of 'conditionally necessary' amount to? What is the difference here, between a 'conditionally necessary' type of existence and an 'unconditionally necessary' type of existence? To answer the former, I will draw, again, on supervenience language, and in response to the latter we will look at each in turn in relation to different types of realism found in the philosophy of mathematics and the philosophy of religion.

The language of supervenience can also help to clarify the meaning of this nuanced term of 'conditionally necessary'. As we saw with the concept of 'semi-independent', the variant of weak supervenience, compared to strong supervenience, can help to clarify its meaning by demonstrating epistemic humility. Another aspect of weak supervenience is that it entails a *coextension*: each supervenient property is coextensive with some base property. Put another way: If A *weakly* supervenes on B, each A-property has a *coextension* in B. I suggest that there is a parallel between weak supervenience entailing coextension and post-traditional realism entailing a type of necessity that is 'conditional'. Both weak supervenience and post-traditional realism describe a type of dependence relationship between properties/facts/discourse of one type and properties/facts/discourse of another type *without* determining the strength of the coextension and thus avoiding the possibility of reducibility by exercising epistemic humility. Moreover, it is this weaker variant of supervenience that can best help clarify this post-traditional conceptual space.

Another benefit of drawing on the language of supervenience when it comes to clarifying the concept of 'conditionally necessary' is that it helps to legitimize the seeming vagueness of this nuanced term, by demonstrating that this epistemic humility is recognized and practiced in other areas of philosophy. Philosophers typically do not feel embarrassed about making these types of claims, without complete (or even very much partial) knowledge. In some areas such 'unknowing' may seem inappropriate but not with consciousness for instance. I think one could run a similar intuition in the case of talking about God insofar as exploring the complex relationship/type of dependency between a whole possible world and God because it is so mysterious. Particularly, when one refines the strand of supervenience as irreducibility, weak and global then the humility and unknowing increase further.

Moreover, the motivation for drawing on supervenience is as follows. It is a mystery why we believe and do the things we do, but I think there is a cogent story here: someone moved to *have-to-speak-of-and-believe-in-God*, who cannot (by choice or conviction) go beyond a rich naturalism, but who is also allergic to an epistemic arrogance about naturalism. The same type of arrogance which, ironically, mirrors the purported absolutism that some atheists accuse religious believers of.

To strengthen this claim, it is also said in the literature that strong supervenience is committed to the existence of *necessary coextension* in the base family for each supervenient property, which can otherwise be written as: if A *strongly* supervenes on B, every A-property has a *necessary coextension* in B. I suggest, then, that strong supervenience entailing necessary coextension parallels 'strong' (or 'thick') realism entailing a type of necessity that is *un*conditional. By this I mean that both strong supervenience and the traditional realist's ascription of an 'unconditionally necessary' divine conceptual space exercise epistemic confidence (one would claim to *know* that properties of type A can indeed arise in worlds without properties of type B).[91] Thus, strong supervenience demonstrates how this type of full dependence 'can lead to, and in turn be supported by, the expectation that one domain can be understood – reduced, defined, explained etc. – in terms of the other through the discovery of necessary equivalences'.[92]

Now we will turn to that second question, what is the difference between a 'conditionally necessary' type of existence? and an 'unconditionally necessary' type of existence? To answer this, let us look at different types of realism found in the philosophy of mathematics and the philosophy of religion:

- Object realism in mathematics: abstract objects are ascribed a conceptual space that is 'conditionally necessary' in the sense that these objects exist objectively 'out there' and have a necessary existence *insofar as the world is the way that it is*, but had things had been otherwise we cannot know for certain the ontological nature of said objects.
- Platonism in mathematics: abstract objects are ascribed a conceptual space that is '*un*conditionally necessary' in the sense that these objects exist objectively 'out there' and have a necessary existence *not only in the sense of how the world actually is but also when reasoning about how it would have been had things been otherwise.*
- Post-traditional realism in theology: the abstract object is ascribed a conceptual space that is 'conditionally necessary' in the sense that the object exists objectively 'out there' and has a necessary existence *insofar as the world is the way that it is*, had things had been otherwise we cannot know for certain the ontological nature of said object.
- Traditional realism in theology: the abstract object is ascribed a conceptual space that is '*un*conditionally necessary' in the sense that the object exists objectively 'out there' and has a necessary existence *not only in the sense of*

how the world actually is but also when reasoning about how it would have been had things been otherwise.

What we can understand from this is that, for the mathematical realist (namely, the object realist), numbers, sets, functions and so on exist objectively 'out there' but they are not ascribed a 'necessary' existence. Which is to say that had things been otherwise, their ontological status cannot be predicted. Whereas, the mathematical platonist is prepared to say that had things been otherwise (where the laws of nature are different, for instance) the ontological status of natural numbers, for example, would absolutely remain the same.

Similarly, for the traditional religious realist, had the world been different, God (of CPT) would exist just as God does now. That is to say, God's existence is not conditioned by the way that the world actually is. Whereas, the post-traditional realist does not commit themselves to this richer ontological thesis; rather their ontology is more reflective of the mathematical object realist, which is to say that the necessity of God (their distinctive, 'minimalist' conception) might in some way be distinctly or conditionally dependent on the way that the world actually is.

Moreover, what we see here, then, is that the object realist's view of 'necessity' (i.e. 'conditionally necessary') is closer to the post-traditionalist's view of 'necessity' when it comes to the nature of the reality that they ascribe to their abstract object. And, the platonistic (and Platonistic) view of 'necessity' (i.e. '*un*conditionally necessary') is more reflective of a traditional realist view of 'necessity'. However, if we agree that the post-traditionalist is more likely to use this analogy (compared to the traditional realist, given the paradoxes and complications that might arise, as we saw in the previous section) then we might wish to emphasize the significance of this qualification, namely the addition of 'conditionally' when it comes to ascribing a 'necessary' realist reality to abstract objects. Thus, I suggest the following. This stronger assumption of '*un*conditionally necessary' is a characteristic of a platonistic form of realism and traditional religious form of realism. It is *not* necessarily shared with the object realist, nor with the post-traditional religious realist. Thus, I suggest that Harrison might be mistaken when she suggests that the concept of 'necessity' can be listed as a fourth characteristic (in addition to inaccessibility to the senses, acausality and lack of spatial or temporal location) ascribed to abstract objects. This is because, if we agree (at least in regard to this project) that the concept of 'necessity' might best be conceived as describing a kind of realism, rather than the object itself, then the three characteristics that we have focused on conform to object realism, and not mathematical platonism. 'Necessity' is a characteristic of a platonistic construal of mathematical realism and a characteristic of a traditional construct of religious realism. Therefore, it cannot also be applicable to what a 'necessary' kind of realism might mean to the object realist, nor the post-traditional religious realist.

Furthermore, if we are to insert object realism and post-traditional realism into the analogy, then we will need to qualify Harrison's assumption that 'necessity' can be used to further the description. Thus, the characteristic of 'necessity' ought to be qualified so that it reads 'conditionally necessary'. Moreover, in light of this qualification, I will now move on to the second part of this section, where I will nuance what might be Harrison's original analogy so that it better reflects her aim of opening up an insightful conversation between the (most suitable) mathematical realist and the (most suitable) theological realist.

Finding the right analogy

An analogy between mathematical realism and theological realism can be drawn, suggests Harrison, on the assumption that both types of realism describe a conceptual reality that is 'mind-independent' and 'necessary' in nature. Without qualifying these concepts, and if we try to insert traditional realism (and the God of CPT), then the analogy might read something like this:

- Mathematical platonism and traditional religious realism.

Now although these types of realism might suitably mirror one another, in regard to being both 'mind-independent' and 'necessary' in nature, their object(s) cannot be suitably compared. This is because although the platonist is happy to describe their abstract mathematical objects as inaccessible to the senses, acausal and lacking spatial or temporal location, the traditional religious realist is not necessarily eager to describe *their* theological object (the God of CPT) as holding these characteristics. Thus, if we insert what might represent Harrison's brief suggestion that the object ought to be conceptualized as 'minimalist' in nature, the analogy will change, and might read something like this instead:

- Mathematical platonism and non-traditional religious realism.

This, perhaps, is a more accurate representation of Harrison's attempt to draw an analogy between mathematical realism and religious realism. As we know, this analogy is potentially problematic for a number of reasons, including the fact that the ontological thesis provided by mathematical platonism is richer than the type of ontology that a non-traditionalist religious realist is likely to commit to. I suggest that we can do at least two things to improve the usefulness of the analogy. The first is to insert a specific type of non-traditional religious realism, one which is 'religiously serious' but not 'traditionally realist'; a reality that is both non-traditionally realist by nature and serious by disposition. In doing so, the analogy will read something like this:

- Mathematical platonism and 'post-traditional' realism (as presented in this book).

Second, if we agree that the ontological thesis offered in post-traditional realism is more reflective of a less ontologically 'weighted' thesis, such as that offered by the mathematical platonists, and instead, closer to that of object realism, then perhaps we ought to insert this branch of mathematical realism instead. We can do this by qualifying Harrison's concept of 'necessity' to signify a type of reality that is 'conditionally necessary'. And so, the analogy can be presented in a different way, but before I present what I think might be the most suitable analogy between a distinctive type of realism in mathematics and a distinctive type of realism in theology, I wish to attend to a query that the reader might have at this point.

And the query might be this: Could the post-traditionalist be 'agnostic' about 'unconditional necessity'? Or could one even be a post-traditionalist and accept unconditional necessity or would this make you a traditionalist? In other words, is belief in conditional necessity the 'minimum' for post-traditional realism or, also, a maximum? I suggest that the post-traditionalist need not commit to the idea that God has a conditionally necessary existence however, I argue that this does not draw a similarity between the post-traditionalist and the agnostic in this respect, because post-traditionalism and its set of beliefs *amount to more than* agnosticism and its claims, and here is why.

The attitude that the post-traditionalist has towards the traditional realist's 'unconditionally necessary' stance is that it *could* be true, but they do not necessarily wish to commit themselves to this position. One reason why the post-traditionalist might consider the possibility of their God having an unconditionally necessary existence might be, for instance, because it could help to actualize the 'objectivity' of God (understood to be 'that-than-which-a-greater-cannot-be-conceived'). However, arguably, the primary reason why the traditional realist will insist on the unconditionally necessary nature of God is because God needs to exist 'before' humanity in order to create the cosmos (and us!). However, the post-traditionalist does not necessarily need a non-scientific explanation for the existence of the cosmos, therefore they do not need to posit the unconditionally necessary existence of God in this (primary) case. Furthermore, although I would not impose that the post-traditional believer *can only or must only* insist that God (understood to be 'that-than-which-a-greater-cannot-be-conceived') has a conditionally necessary existence, it might be the type of necessity (between 'conditionally' necessary and 'unconditionally' necessary) that suits their commitment the best.

Furthermore, it is in principle parsimony, because the post-traditionalist does not deny the possibility of an unconditionally necessary existence, they are just not committing themselves to that claim. Rather, they are saying that God believed to have a conditionally necessary existence is enough: that which I do know (God has a conditionally necessary existence) is enough to confirm this. Therefore, it is not agnosticism because this is an affirmation. So, in other words, belief in conditional necessity might be described as the 'minimum' for post-traditional realism, insofar as the 'maximum' might be belief in the 'unconditionally necessary' existence. It is important perhaps to 'keep the door open', for it is not my intention to pigeonhole the post-traditionalist and insist that they believe in certain claims, and no more or no less than those claims.

Rather, the point of the second axis (a spectrum of commitments) is to indicate different spaces, to highlight what might be different and latent textures of reality. It is *not* to suggest four 'pillars of commitment' with no 'space' or flexibility between each type of commitment. Thus, you might find that there are different construals of post-traditionalism: some that are further 'left' on the spectrum, thus closer to fictionalism (this believer would be less open-minded to the possibility of an unconditionally necessary existence), or you could have a post-traditionalist who is further 'right' of the spectrum, thus closer to traditional realism (therefore they would be a lot more open to the idea of God, still their distinctive, minimalist conception, as having an unconditionally necessary existence). Again, the interesting question might be why they feel that they are or want to be open to this possibility.

Going back to our search for the 'right' analogy, if we agree that the post-traditionalist's ontology is a less weighty thesis, such as that offered by the mathematical platonists, but closer to that offered in object realism, I suggest that we plug this branch of mathematical realism into the analogy instead. To do this, we can qualify Harrison's concept of 'necessity' with the prefix 'conditionally'. Therefore, the analogy can be presented in the following way.

- Object realism and 'post-traditional' realism (as presented in this book).

This, we might find, is the best 'version' of the analogy between mathematical realism and religious realism.

Conclusion

We are now in a position to conclude a drawing of an analogy between 'mathematical realism' and 'theological realism'. By nuancing and qualifying Harrison's exploration into the possibility that realism about mathematical objects can provide a model for thinking about realism within theology, here I have attempted to defend the feasibility of the distinct kind of conceptual space ascribed to God, as conceived by the post-traditional realist. In the first half of the chapter, I focused on the first axis (a spectrum of conceptions) and I suggested that the best way to draw an analogy between the nature of mathematical objects and the object of theology might be to insert the distinctive, 'minimalist' conception of God. Therefore, we might be able to argue that this conception of God *and* mathematical objects hold the same three characteristics that are often ascribed to that which is considered abstract.

In the second half of the chapter, we focused on the second axis (a spectrum of commitment) and I suggested that in order to draw a useful analogy between the kind of reality ascribed to mathematical objects and that ascribed to the theological object we might want to clarify which type of mathematical realism we are using in the analogy. This is because there are (at least) two types: one which is a lot richer (namely, platonism) and requires a 'greater' commitment, one that the post-traditional believer will not necessarily wish to make, thus rendering the analogy useless. However, if we are to insert the 'lesser' ontological commitment (namely, object realism) the analogy might work better, as I suggest that this type of realism is a greater reflection of post-traditional religious realism.

Moreover, the purpose of this chapter has been to argue that object realism in philosophy of mathematics and its ontology about abstract mathematical objects might help the theologian (and the philosopher of religion) think about broadening the scope of religious realism and the potential adequacy of a conceptual space such as that posited by 'post-traditional' religious realism. This is a type of realism that might resonate with those who believe that 'that -than-which-a-greater-cannot-be-conceived' exists objectively 'out there', without wanting to necessarily commit themselves to the belief that God conceived in this way exists *wholly independently* (that is not to say that God does not depend in any way on the existence of us, human beings), and has an *unconditionally necessary* existence (which means that God's existence is not in any way conditioned by the way that the world actually is). Instead, post-traditional realism posits a reality that is *semi-independent* (that is to say that God is in some distinct way tethered to our existence) and has a *conditionally necessary* existence (which means that God's existence might in some way be conditioned by the way that the world actually is). Furthermore, I suggest that the analogy, if construed in this way, can instigate a fruitful conversation on the different types of textural realities that might exist under the umbrella of religious realism.

Conclusion

Post-traditional realism and a distinctive 'minimalist' conception of God

In many ways this book might look to be less an attack on non-realism and more a defence of realism, more specifically a kind of *post*-traditional realism and its interpretation of involuntary 'belief-that'. In other words, I have recommended a contemporary approach to philosophical theology that might be considered to distil the 'best bits' of traditional realist approaches, those that preserve God's *realness*, and non-realist approaches, those that are committed to an intellectually coherent and meaningful worldview. Thus, insofar as I have made non-realism plausible (giving 'two cheers' to fictionalism) I have been casting a favourable light on minimal realism by ascribing an ontologically weaker texture of reality to a suitably qualified version of Anselm's 'that-than-which-a-greater-cannot-be-conceived'.

Moreover, I have attempted to locate post-traditional realism as a variant of faith classically conceived, through defending a conditional mind-independent ontology and a theologically rooted albeit 'minimalist' conception of God. In doing so I hope to have revealed what might be a missing texture of 'reality' in the contemporary realist/non-realist debate. This reveals a 'gap' in the current philosophical landscape somewhere 'between' fictionalism and traditional realism. Furthermore, the purpose of this book has been to offer a 'stripped-back' conception of God, and to argue for the plausibility and possibility of a divine conceptual space (a way of 'being real') that does not commit those with 'involuntary belief-that' to classical philosophical theism if a minimalist understanding of God resonates better with their 'cannot help but' belief.

This framework is set out in the Introduction in the form of two axes. On the first axis, I set out *a spectrum of conceptions of God* (from CPT to minimalist conceptions). On the second axis, I set out *a spectrum of commitments* (from standard non-realism to traditional realism). Besides providing what might be a helpful illustration of the realism/non-realism debate, the axes have shown how the conception of God offered in this book differs from other minimalist conceptions of God, thereby establishing the 'location' of post-traditional realism as somewhere 'between' fictionalism and traditional realism. I suggested that if we broaden what it means to have a 'realist' approach to God then perhaps we can find a way to overcome the current polarizing 'theological realism' versus 'religious seriousness' impasse. It also helps to navigate *all the ways* that one might feel an affiliation with a 'cannot help but' belief-that and an emotional pull towards that which is considered greater than oneself: towards God.

In Chapter 1 we explored the different ways that philosophers have preserved a distinct space for God as we looked at what might be considered four types of 'faith' composed of two belief components: 'belief-that' and 'belief-in'. We focused our attention on the nature of these beliefs, namely whether they are 'voluntary' or 'involuntary', and whether *both* belief components feature in each particular type of faith. Therefore, the purpose of this chapter was to cement further 'post-traditional' realism as a variant of faith classically conceived by showing how it shares the same 'type' of faith with traditional realism, that is, something along the lines of *'involuntary "belief-that" and voluntary "belief-in"'*. This displayed how it differed from the non-realist 'type' of faith, which might be characterized as *'voluntary "belief-in" without involuntary "belief-that"'*.

In the following chapters we made our way along the second axis, beginning with 'standard non-realism' in Chapter 2. The former Anglican priest, Don Cupitt, radically disavowed the traditional conception of God as a transcendent being. We looked at his body of work from the late 1970s to the late 2000s and how it contributes to the debate. Although my own position is not aligned with non-realism and is, therefore, not reflective of Cupitt's (later) conception of God (namely God as synonymous with 'life'), nor the mind-dependent reality that he ascribes to 'God', post-traditional realism *is* reflective of the 'non-conforming' attitude that Cupitt encourages religious believers to embrace. However, there is an important difference between our positions. Cupitt insists that *all religious believers* ought *not* to conform to traditional realism, whereas this book merely seeks to offer an alternative (realist) approach for religious believers who are uncertain about how or where to direct their 'involuntary belief-that'. Therefore, I am sympathetic to Cupitt's mission: to renew what it might mean to be a person of 'faith' if the traditional 'way' no longer embodies, witnesses and conserves, one's values. My approach does not give such a committed reading of the cultural and industrial shifts as that given by Cupitt, but I am interested in exploring alternative textures of 'reality' that we might ascribe to a minimalist conception of God.

This leads to a question: 'What if you do not have an 'involuntary belief-that'?' Chapter 3 investigated contemporary approaches to faith *without 'belief'(-that)*. They included replacing 'belief' with different components such as 'beliefless assuming' (Howard-Snyder, McKaughan and Zamulinski), 'rational steadfastness' (Jackson) and 'acquiesce' (Buchak). It was here that I gave my first 'cheer' to fictionalism. I 'cheered' its dedication to the intellect and one's desire for faith that 'fits' coherently with *everything* one knows, while believing *in* the benefits of engaging in religious discourse, even if only as a powerful and meaningful theological *fiction*. However, I inserted the following caution: it might be the case that the religious believer has conflated their loss of belief-that the God of CPT exists 'out there' in the classical sense, *with* losing 'involuntary belief-that' altogether. I suggested that losing faith in the objective existence of an omni-God *does not necessarily indicate a consequential loss of involuntary 'belief-that' tout court*. It is possible, then, I suggest, to reconfigure one's 'cannot help but' belief in such a way that one's belief is acknowledged and taken seriously without committing oneself to a full-blown traditional realism.

The 'second cheer' for fictionalism was given in Chapter 4 as I attempted to dismantle the paradox of fiction and defend the significance of emotions, as evoked by fiction, even if these emotions can only be described as not irrational and not disingenuous. After defending fictionalism as an intellectually coherent account of faith, and arguing that fictionalists are not simply confused if they allow religious narratives to shape their emotional lives, we then continued to test the boundaries of fictionalism. I achieved this by investigating the extent to which fictionalism can support another contemporary movement that also encourages more imaginative and holistic approaches to religious discourse, a movement known as the 'humane turn'.

In Chapter 5 we explored the roots of the 'humane turn', by engaging with the works of Cottingham and Stump, and carefully assessed, first of all, the degree to which fictionalism might be said to 'use' the same epistemic virtues that the humane turn defends (including imaginative, holistic, humanistic and personal modes of thinking) and, second, evaluating whether fictionalism can coherently be said to 'work alongside' this contemporary approach to philosophy of religion. In response to the first inquiry, I suggested that to a considerable degree fictionalism can be said to utilize the same 'right-brain' epistemic values, and, in relation to the second inquiry, fictionalism cannot be said to take full advantage of the 'turn' and the 'humane' values often associated with it because of its non-realist footing.

Rather, I argued that the humane turn is in synergy with traditional realism, the reason being that the humane turn employs these modes of awareness arguably to contribute to a greater cause, namely to preserve something like traditional realism and CPT. Thus, I concluded that having now explored the similarities and the important differences that separate fictionalism from traditional realism, there might be a texture of reality that exists somewhere 'between' traditional realism and fictionalism, since the current 'gap' requires a 'leap of faith' that is too large for many believers and, thus, leaves many with an incoherent account of faith, unless there does exist a latent but live conceptual space that can fill this gap, something like a 'post-traditional' realism.

By bringing realism in theology (and philosophy of religion) into conversation with realism in philosophy of mathematics I attempted, in Chapter 6, to soften any major opposition to the possibility of 'post-traditional' religious realism as a genuine conceptual space. In order to do this, I drew two analogies, the first between the post-traditionalist's distinctive, 'minimalist' conception of God and abstract mathematical objects such as numbers, sets and functions. The second drew an analogy between 'post-traditional' religious realism and object realism in mathematics. In the light of our investigations here, I argued that mathematical realism and its ontology about abstract mathematical objects might help the theologian (and philosopher of religion) think about two things, those being: to broaden the scope of religious realism, and the plausibility of ascribing a kind of minimal realism to God.

'All creatures', as Meister Eckhart puts it, 'are gladly doing the best they can to express God',[1] and this was the aim of the book: to answer that which might weigh on our hearts: that is, how to characterize and accommodate 'cannot help but' beliefs about the transcendent, by offering a 'post-traditional' pathway that takes seriously both the realness of God and the sincere intellectual concerns of some contemporary people.

Notes

Introduction

1. Cupitt, Don, *The Sea of Faith*, Second edition, London: SCM Press Ltd, 1994, 59.
2. Hölderlin, Friedrich, 'Was Is Gott?', from *Hymische Entwüfe* (Sketches for Hymns), 1800–1905, in *Selected Poems*, London: Penguin, 1998, 270.
3. Swinburne, Richard, *The Coherence of Theism*, Oxford: Oxford University, 2016, 247 and Plantinga, Alvin, *God and Other Minds*, Ithaca and London: Cornell University Press, 1990, 1.
4. Swinburne, Richard, *The Existence of God*, Oxford: Clarendon Press, 2004, 7.
5. For a defence of the contrary, namely that the fictionalist need not be as committed to the traditional conception as the traditional realist; which is to say that the fictionalist could appeal to a being which does not exhibit *all* of the 'omni' properties, see Nagasawa's *Maximal God: A New Defence of Perfect Being Theism*, Oxford: Oxford University Press, 2017: a presentation and defence of an alternative perfect being theism in terms of a God who has the highest levels of power, knowledge, and so on that are consistent with each other.
6. Fictionalism has been defended for a number of different domains of philosophical interest, including ethics (Joyce, Richard, 'Moral Fictionalism', in *Fictionalism in Metaphysics*, ed. Kalderon, Mark Eli, Oxford: Oxford University Press, 2005), mathematics (Field, Hartry, *Science without Numbers*, Princeton: Princeton University Press, 1980), modality (Rosen, Gideon, 'Modal Fictionalism', *Mind*, 99, 1990, 327–54) and science (Van Fraassen, Bas, *The Scientific Image*, Oxford: Clarendon Press, 1980).
7. Le Poidevin, Robin, *Religious Fictionalism*, Cambridge: Cambridge University Press 2019, 2.
8. Le Poidevin, Robin, 'Playing the God Game: The Perils of Religious Fictionalism', in *Alternative Conceptions of God*, ed. Yujin Nagasawa and Andrei Buckareff, Oxford: Oxford University Press, 2016, 1.
9. Le Poidevin, *Religious Fictionalism*, 51.
10. We will explore this idea further in Chapter 3.
11. Cupitt, *The Sea of Faith*, 59.
12. Cupitt, Don, *Taking Leave of God*, London: SCM Press, 1980, 9–10.
13. Ibid., 13.
14. Cupitt, *The Sea of Faith*, 277.

15 Nihilism is a common theme that runs throughout Cupitt's non-realist works, see *Emptiness and Brightness*, Santa Rosa, CA: Polebridge Press, 2001, 57–71; *Above Us Only Sky*, Santa Rosa, CA: Polebridge Press, 2008, 59–63; *The Sea of Faith*, 201–20 (section on Nietzsche); and almost any of his other books.
16 Sachs, Carl, 'The Acknowledgement of Transcendence: Anti-theodicy in Adorno and Levinas', *Philosophy and Social Criticism*, 37(3), March 2011, 273–94, 287.
17 Levinas, Emmanuel, *Difficult Freedom*, Baltimore, MD: The John Hopkins University Press, 1990, 159.
18 Ibid., 195. For more on Levinas and a potentially minimalist conception of God, see Hilario, Gerald, 'The Notions of God by Emmanuel Levinas' (October 10, 2019). Available at SSRN: https://ssrn.com/abstract=3467746 or http://dx.doi.org/10.2139/ssrn.3467746.
19 Ellis, Fiona, *God, Value and Nature*, Oxford: Oxford University Press, 2014, 99.
20 Sachs, 'The Acknowledgement of Transcendence', 284.
21 Adorno, Theodor, *Minima Moralia: Reflections on a Damaged Life*, tran. E. F. N. Jephcott, London and New York: Verso, 2005, 247.
22 De Vries, Hent and Geoffrey Hale, *Minimal Theologies: Critiques of Secular Reason in Adorno and Levinas*, Baltimore, MD: Johns Hopkins University Press, 2019, 109.
23 Adorno thought that 'acts of overcoming – even of nihilism – are always worse than what they overcome' (Insole, Christopher, 'A Trace on the Wind', *The Times Literary Supplement*, 30, 2006. The Times Literary Supplement Historical Archive, 1902–2013, https://link.gale.com/apps/doc/EX1200542248/TLSH?u=duruni&sid=TLSH&xid=b790f12c). Philosophers such as Timo Jütten argue that Adorno's philosophy articulates a radical conception of hope, see Jütten, Timo, 'Adorno on Hope', *Philosophy & Social Criticism*, 45(3), 2019, 284–306.
24 De Vries and Hale, *Minimal Theologies*, 5. Other philosophers whose minimalist approach to theology that might be of similar ilk to de Vries are Jerome Stone and his empirical, naturalistic viewpoint on 'realities and ideals which are *relatively transcendent* to our situations within nature' and that experience tells us that that which is considered sacred in the world and its ability to come to us as transforming grace does not come from beyond the world, but rather from creative relationships and interconnectedness within the world (*The Minimalist Vision of Transcendence: A Naturalist Philosophy of Religion*, Albany: State University of New York Press, 1992); Shailer Mathews and his 'minimalist' conception of God, 'For God is our conception, born of social experience, of the personally responsive elements of our cosmic environment with which we are organically related' (*The Growth of The Idea of God*, New York: Macmillan Co., 1930); and Bernard Meland, who focuses on the tentativeness of all human formulations of our apprehension of the divine. Calling for an openness towards the provisional nature of our thinking and language about the world, especially to the ultimate reaches of thought and experience. Thus, Meland's contribution to the minimalist theological approach is his recognition of

the provisional character of all models, theories and concepts of the divine (*Realities of Faith*, Oxford: Oxford University Press, 1962).
25 Ellis also refers to this as the 'traditional naturalism versus theism debate' (*God, Value and Nature*, 3).
26 Ellis, *God, Value and Nature*, 117.
27 Ellis, Fiona, 'Between Orthodox Theism and Materialist Atheism', in *Current Controversies in Philosophy of Religion*, ed. Paul Draper, New York and Abingdon, Oxon: Routledge, 2019, 152.
28 Ibid., 153.
29 Ellis, *God, Value and Nature*, 175.
30 Ibid., 98.
31 Ibid., 98. The original quote from is Rahner's *Foundations of Christian Faith: An Introduction to the Idea of Christianity*, trans. William V. Dych, London: Darton, Longman and Todd, 1978, 63.
32 Importantly, this is not to conflate 'that-than-which-a-greater-cannot-be-conceived' with 'the greatest conceivable being'. The point for Anselm is that God is greater than even that which *can* be conceived. Arguably, Ellis's use of Rahner's description of God places more emphasis on the radical otherness of God rather than placing an emphasis on omni-characteristics more typically associated with the CPT conception of God. And so, in this sense, Ellis's approach to apprehending God might resonate more with the 'minimalist' conception of God (qua this book) than the perfect God of CPT. For more on Ellis, see my article, Eastwood, Jessica, 'Theistic Expansive Naturalism: Which God?', *Religious Studies*, 2023, 1–15. doi:10.1017/S0034412523000112.
33 For more on this notion of separating out perfect being theism from the omni-God book, see Yujin Nagasawa ('A New Defence of Perfect Being Theism', *Philosophical Quarterly*, 58, 2008, 577–96; 'Anselmian Theism', *Philosophy Compass*, 6, 2011, 564–71; *Maximal God: A New Defence of Perfect Being Theism*, Oxford University Press, 2017).
34 Insole, Christopher. J., 'Realism and Non-realism', in *The Oxford Handbook of the Epistemology of Theology*, ed. William James Abraham, Frederick D. Aquino, Oxford: Oxford University Press, 2017.
35 Ibid., 275.
36 Different motivations behind choosing to embrace a realist or non-realist position here varies. To see more on this, see pages 275–7.
37 Ibid., 284.
38 Ibid., 279.
39 Ibid.
40 Ibid.
41 Ibid., 230.
42 Le Poidevin, *Religious Fictionalism*, 11.

43   Insole, 'Realism and Non-realism', 286–9.
44   Ibid., 286.
45   Ibid., 287.
46   Ibid.
47   Ibid.
48   Ibid., 278.
49   Le Poidevin, *Religious Fictionalism*, 60.
50   Ibid., 58–60.
51   Whether or not we are able to label religious non-realism as a type of 'faith' is debatable, I will not contribute directly to this debate; instead I simply state that it is convenient to refer to each of these religious commitments as different accounts of 'faith'. Thus, I use the term 'faith' here to mean a kind of belief commitment to (either) God and/or religious discourse. For more on the aforementioned debate, see Cupitt, Don, *Long-Legged Fly: A Theology of Language and Desire*, London: SCM Press, 1987, Howard-Snyder, Daniel, 'Can Fictionalists Have Faith? It All Depends', *Religious Studies*, 55(4), 2019, 447–68 for a defence, and Malcolm, Finlay and Michael Scott, 'Faith, Belief and Fictionalism', *Pacific Philosophical Quarterly*, 98, 2017, 257–74 and Malcolm, Finlay, 'Can Fictionalists Have Faith?', *Religious Studies*, 54(2), 2018, 215–32 opposing the notion that non-realist's hold a kind of faith.
52   See Insole, Christopher J., *The Intolerable God*, Michigan and Cambridge: Wm. B. Eerdmans Publishing Co., 2016.
53   Singer, Peter, 'Dialogue 9: Hegel and Marx', in *The Great Philosophers: An Introduction to Western Philosophy*, ed. Bryan Magee, Oxford and New York: Oxford University Press, 1987, reprinted 2009, 194.
54   Kilby, Karen, *Karl Rahner: Theology and Philosophy*, London and New York: Routledge, 2004, 21.
55   Tillich, Paul, *The Courage to Be*, Second edition, New Haven and London: Yale University Press, 2000, 186.

Chapter 1

1   I tentatively place agnosticism into this type of commitment because if there is a 'spectrum' of agnosticism, then some agnostics might be more open to the possibility of God (of CPT or not) existing therefore, depending on where the agnostic positions themselves on this spectrum, it will dictate whether or not '*voluntary "belief-in" without involuntary "belief-that"*' is viewed as an adequate description of their type of 'religious commitment'. When it comes to the first part, '*voluntary "belief-in"*', those agnostics who lean more towards realism and the possibility of there existing an objective God (of CPT or not) might allow this

possibility (i.e. the objective existence of a good God) to play a role in their decision making and the way that they live their life. Whereas, those who lean the other way, that is, closer to the standard non-realist position (and maybe even atheism), might rarely think on the existence (or non-existence) of God, and would not necessarily say, then, that they 'choose to actively and positively engage with religious discourse and God'. Equally, when it comes to '*without involuntary "belief-that*"', the former type of agnostic might say that this misrepresents their open-minded attitude to the possibility of an objective God (of CPT or not) existing objectively 'out there'. Whereas, on the other end of the spectrum, you might have an agnostic who is almost certain that God (again of CPT or not) does not exist mind-independently and might feel more comfortable with this 'labelling'. Le Poidevin suggests that agnosticism might be a variant of (IV) as he gives the following definition of agnosticism: someone who suggests that the agnostic 'accepts the realist construal of theological statements: they are intended as being (more or less) literally descriptive of reality. But the agnostic does not know whether they are in fact true or not' (Le Poidevin, *Agnosticism: A Very Short Introduction*, New York: Oxford University Press, 2010, Online publication 2013, doi:10.1093/actrade/9780199575 268.001.0001. I will be using the online version. p. 12). We will refer back to agnosticism again in the thesis, usually in comparison with the fictionalist position.

2 On the whole, religious fictionalism is presented from a non-realist standpoint; however, there are cases in which fictionalism is used to defend a realist account of faith, see Jay, Christopher, 'Testimony, Belief, and Nondoxastic Faith: The Humean Argument for Religious Fictionalism', *Religious Studies*, 52(2), 2016, 247–61.

3 Some philosophers have attempted to argue that Hume's account of belief can be understood from the position of the opposing Dispositional Analysis, see D. G. C. MacNabb, *David Hume: His Theory of Knowledge and Morality*, Oxford: Basil Blackwell, 1951; H. H. Price, *Belief*, New York: Humanities Press, London: George Allen & Unwin, 1969; D. M. Armstrong, *Belief, Truth and Knowledge*, Cambridge: Cambridge University Press, 1973; B. Stroud, *Hume*, London: Routledge, 1977 and J. S. Marušić, 'Does Hume Hold a Dispositional Account of Belief?', *Canadian Journal of Philosophy*, 40(2), 2010, 155–83.

4 In *An Enquiry Concerning Human Understanding* Hume says this on belief: 'Were we to attempt a definition of this sentiment we should, perhaps, find it a very difficult, if not impossible, task; in the same manner as if we should endeavour to define the feeling of cold or passion of anger, to a creature who never had any experience of these sentiments. Belief is the true and proper name of this feeling' (New York: Library of Liberal Arts, 1955), 62. Across Hume's works we find a baffling list of different terminologies. He speaks of belief as (1) a manner of conception (*A Treatise of Human Nature*, Selby-Bigge, Oxford: University Press, 1941, 9, 629, *Appendix*; *Enquiry*, 63; (2) an act of the mind (*Treatise*, 29 and footnote on 96–7; 3), an operation of the mind (*Treatise*, 628; 4), a feeling (*Treatise*,

629, *Appendix*, 621; *Enquiry*, 62; 5), a sentiment (*Appendix*, 624; *Enquiry*, 61), found in above ed. of *Enquiry*, see Selby-Bigge, Oxford: University Press, 1941 ed. of *Treatise*. This version will continue to be used.

5   See list given in Edward Craig's 'Hume on Thought and Belief', *Royal Institute of Philosophy Lecture Series*, 20, 1986, 93–110, 93.
6   Dorsch, Fabian, 'Hume', in *Routledge Handbook of Philosophy of Imagination*, ed. Amy Kind, New York: Routledge, 2016, 40.
7   Ibid.
8   Ibid., 42.
9   Gorman, Michael. M., 'Hume's Theory of Belief', *Hume Studies*, 19(1), 1993, 89–101, 97.
10 See list given in Edward Craig's 'Hume on Thought and Belief'.
11 Hume, *Treatise*, 183. We might want to replace 'in any sense' in the third bullet point to: 'in some sense'.
12 Craig, 'Hume on Thought and Belief', 108.
13 Ibid., 109.
14 Hume, *Treatise*, 121.
15 Townsend, Dabney, *Hume's Aesthetic Theory: Taste and Sentiment*, New York: Routledge, 2001, 126.
16 Hume, *Enquiry* (1955) Section 5, Part II.
17 Ibid.
18 Swinburne, Richard, *Epistemic Justification*, Oxford: Oxford University Press, 2001. Oxford Scholarship Online, 2003. doi: 10.1093/0199243794.001.0001, 35.
19 Swinburne, Richard, *Faith and Reason*, Second edition, Oxford: Oxford University Press, 2005. Oxford Scholarship Online, 2007. doi: 10.1093/acprof:oso/978019 9283927.001.0001., 5. I will be using the online version from here on out unless stated otherwise.
20 'S' is used as a universal symbol of a human person.
21 Swinburne, *Faith and Reason* (2007), 28.
22 Alston, William, 'Swinburne on Faith and Belief', in *Reason and the Christian Religion: Essays in Honour of Richard Swinburne*, ed. Alan Padgett, Oxford: Clarendon, 1994, 21, ProQuest Ebook Central, https://ebookcentral.proquest.com/lib/durham/detail.action?docID=4962807.
23 Alston identifies two key issues within Swinburne's concept of belief. The first, that his definition excludes from its application all types of believers because of its restrictive attentiveness to the case of probability. Young children, persons with diminished mental capacity and complex non-human animals. Although it is undeniable that these persons and intelligent animals are, as Alston says, capable at the most basic rudimentary cognitive level to 'have beliefs about things they encounter in their environment', what they cannot do is to 'weigh-up' probabilities. That is to say, this category of subjects is not capable of evaluating probabilities

to the extent to which various propositions are rendered more or less probable by evidence. Despite the fact that the probability element does not constitute, necessarily, especially for non-basic beliefs, numerical probability, Alston insists that comparative probability judgements are still too sophisticated for many believers (ibid.).
24 Swinburne, *Faith and Reason* (1984), 1–11.
25 Ibid., (2007), 6.
26 Swinburne, *Epistemic Justification*, 35.
27 Swinburne, *Faith and Reason* (2007), 25.
28 Ibid.
29 Ibid.
30 Swinburne, Richard, 'Science and Religion: Exploring the Spectrum', *Life Story Interviews*, Interviewed by Paul Merchant, The British Library, Ref. no. C1672/15, 2015–2016, 53–4.
31 See Swinburne's *Faith and Reason* (2007).
32 Ibid., 226.
33 Ibid., 227.
34 Ibid.
35 Plantinga, Alvin, 'Reason and Belief in God', in *Faith and Rationality*, ed. Alvin Plantinga and Nicholas Wolterstorff, Notre Dame: University of Notre Dame Press, 1983, 18.
36 Ibid.
37 See, Plantinga's *Knowledge and Christian Belief*, Cambridge: Wm. B. Eerdmans, 2015.
38 Ibid., 58.
39 Ibid., 59.
40 Ibid., 58.
41 Ibid., x.
42 It is worthwhile mentioning that Ryle's account of dispositional belief is rather distinct, insofar as it does not wholly align to traditional dispositional attitude. I am referring here to the 'baggage' that comes with Ryle's particular stance; thinkers such as Goodman, Nelson, *Fact, fiction, and Forecast*, Cambridge, MA: Harvard University Press, 1955 have criticized Ryle's 'inference ticket' conception of dispositional claims, and his claim to philosophical behaviourism. Moreover, with the 'baggage' put aside, as it were, what was left was 'functionalism'. This is a view that has been said to save the 'reality' of the mental from the 'eliminativist' or 'fictionalist' tendencies of behaviourism while acknowledging the insight (often attributed to Ryle) that the mental is importantly related to behavioural output or response (as well as to stimulus or input). For more on this, see Goodman, *Fact, fiction, and Forecast*. That is to say, we do not, of course, have to buy all of Ryle's account of the mind to accept a dispositional analysis of belief. Indeed, we might

view functionalism as a dispositionalist analysis which avoids some of the problems of the Rylean view.

43 Alston, William P., 'Dispositions and Occurrences', *Canadian Journal of Philosophy*, 1(2), 1971, 125–54, 125.
44 Ryle, Gilbert, *The Concept of the Mind*, Watford, Hurts: William Brendon and Son, 1949, 116.
45 Ibid., 119.
46 Ibid., 120.
47 Ibid., 135.
48 In comparison, the word 'know' is a 'capacity verb' and in the same family as 'skill words', ibid., 133–4.
49 Ibid., 40.
50 Tejedor, Chon, 'The Early Wittgenstein on Ethical Religiousness as a Dispositional Attitude', in *Wittgenstein, Religion and Ethics: New Perspectives from Philosophy and Theology*, ed. Mikel Burley, New York: Bloomsbury Publishing, 2018.
51 Moyal-Sharrock, Danièle, 'Certainty as Trust: Belief as a Nonpropositional Attitude', in *Understanding Wittgenstein's on Certainty*, Houndmills, Basingstoke, Hampshire and New York: Palgrave Macmillan, 2004. For more, see Dallas M. High, 'On Thinking More Crazily than Philosophers: Wittgenstein, Knowledge and Religious Beliefs', *International Journal for Philosophy of Religion*, 19(3), 1986, 161–75.
52 Phillips, D. Z., 'On Really Believing', in *Is God Real?* ed. J. Runzo, Basingstoke: Macmillan, 1993, 94.
53 Burley, Mikel, 'Phillips and Realists on Religious Beliefs and the Fruits', *International Journal for Philosophy of Religion*, 64(3), 2008, 141–53. For more on their relationship, see, D. Z. Phillips, 'Philosophy, Theology and the Reality of God', in *Wittgenstein and Religion*, ed. D. Z. Phillips, New York: St Martin's Press, 1993. For more on a general insight into Wittgenstein's account of belief and his idea that 'it is a mistake to attempt to reduce religious faith to assent to propositional doctrines', see High, 'On Thinking More Crazily than Philosophers'.
54 For more on this, see Parfit, Derek, *On What Matters*, Vols. 3, Oxford: Oxford University Press, 2017b.
55 To absolutely clarify, this is not Aquinas's own understanding of faith. Rather his account is 'voluntary "belief-in"', insofar as it is the act of the will to believe in all sorts of Christian elements, such as grace, the trinity and original sin. But, if you were to ask Aquinas: Do you know that there is a God? Aquinas would say 'yes', in the sense that he finds it totally impossible *not* to have 'belief-that' God exists. In other words, he has a minimalist belief in the 'first cause'. Thus, Aquinas's account also has, arguably, an 'involuntary "belief-that"' element. Moreover, Aquinas's own account of faith is a hybrid account, in that it is between (I) classically conceived and in relation to 'involuntary "belief-that"', and (III) in relation to 'voluntary "belief-in"'.

56 Swinburne, *Faith and Reason* (2007), 140.
57 Aquinas, like others, quotes the definition given by Hugh of St Victor that 'faith (fides) is a form of mental certitude about absent realities that is greater than opinion (opinio) and less than scientific knowledge (scientia)' (De Sacramentis 1.10.2.); see Swinburne's *Faith and Reason* (2007), 139.
58 James 2:19.
59 Swinburne, *Faith and Reason* (2007), 141 (in reference to Aquinas's *Summa Theologiae 2a. 2ae. 5. 2 ad.3.*).
60 That which x, y or z might represent is important, but it is not important that we specify and assess what some of the reasons might be, because it is not essential to this particular book and its aim to ease many major resistance towards the feasibility of a distinctive conceptual space that might exist between realism and non-realism. Therefore, I wish for the reader to insert for themselves any reasons they may be aware of as to why a person may feel that they can no longer hold a traditional, realist conception of God. For literature on the rise of the non-realist movement, see Cupitt, Don, *The Sea of Faith*, Second edition, London: SCM Press Ltd, 1994 and *Taking Leave of God*, London: SCM Press, 1980.
61 Clifford, William K., 'The Ethics of Belief', in *The ethics of belief and other essays*, ed. T. Madigan, Amherst, MA: Prometheus, 1999 (originally published in 1877), 70–96.
62 On the whole, religious fictionalism is presented from a non-realist standpoint; however, there are cases in which fictionalism is used to defend a realist account of faith, see Jay, 'Testimony, Belief, and Non-Doxastic Faith'.
63 Bultmann, Rudolf, 'What Sense Is There to Speak of God?', *The Christian Scholar*, 43(3), 1960, 213–22.
64 Ibid., 219.
65 Ibid., 218–15.
66 Ibid., 218.
67 For more recent articles on the philosophy of language and expressivism in this context, see Pendlebury, Michael, 'How to Be a Normative Expressivist', *Philosophy and Phenomenology Research*, 80, 2010, 182–207 on the understanding of expressivism as expressing pro or con attitudes rather than factual beliefs; Price, H. H., *Thinking and Experience*, Cambridge, MA: Harvard University Press, 2013 for its useful comparison of expressivism and fictionalism; Mabrito, Robert, 'Are Expressivists Guilty of Wishful Thinking?', *Philosophical Studies*, 165, 2013, 1069–81 against the claim that expressivists can be charged with 'wishful thinking' according to Silk, Alex, 'How to Be an Ethical Expressivist', *Philosophical Phenomenological Research*, 91, 2015, 47–81, Dorr, Cian, 'Non-cognitivism and Wishful Thinking', *Noûs*, 36(1), 2002, 97–103 and his development of *ordering expressivism*; Kappel, Klemens and Emil F. L. Moeller, 'Epistemic Expressivism and the Argument from Motivation', *Synthese*, 191(7), 2014, 1–19 an argument for epistemic expression known as the *Argument from Motivation*; Baker, Derek

and Jack Woods, 'How Expressivists Can and Should Explain Inconsistency', *Ethics*, 125(2), 2015, 391–424 with the aim of showing that expressivists have sufficiently more theoretical resource than is often thought and van Roojen, Mark, 'Expressivism', in *Routledge Encyclopedia of Philosophy*, Taylor and Francis, 2015 demonstrating how expressivism has developed from emotivism. For our purpose, Braithwaite gives us the full weight of what I want to say here on expressivism.
68 Braithwaite, Richard, 'An Empiricist's View of the Nature of Religious Belief', in *The Philosophy of Religion*, ed. Basil Mitchell, Oxford: Oxford University Press, 1971.
69 Ibid., 77.
70 Ibid., 78.
71 Ibid., 80 (my own *italics*).
72 Ibid., 81–2.
73 Ibid., 84.
74 Ibid., 84 (my own *italics*).
75 Ibid., 85–6.
76 Ibid., 89.
77 He notes that the most influential literature in a Christians life, after the Bible, has historically been Bunyan's *Pilgrim's Progress* and novels by Dostoevsky (ibid., 86).

Chapter 2

1 Le Poidevin, Robin, *Religious Fictionalism*, Cambridge: Cambridge University Press, 2019, 1.
2 Ibid., 20.
3 Philips, D. Z., *Wittgenstein and Religion*, New York: St Martin's Press, 1993, 2,1.
4 Cupitt, Don, *The Sea of Faith*, London: SCM Press, 1994, 15.
5 Cupitt, Don, *The Leap of Reason*, London: Sheldon Press, 1976 (second edition 1985, US edition 1976, I am using the first edition); and Cupitt, Don, *Life, Life*, Santa Rosa, CA: Polebridge Press, 2003. We will not focus on Cupitt's later publications – with his last being, *Ethics in the Last Days of Humanity*, Salem: Polebridge, 2016 – important as they are.
Although we did explore the continuation of his philosophy in the 2010s in the introductory chapter, including *Above Us Only Sky*, Santa Rosa, CA: Polebridge Press, 2008, *The Meaning of the West: An Apologia for Secular Christianity*, London: SCM Press, 2008, *Turns of Phrase: Radical theology from A to Z*, London: SCM Press, 2011 and 'A Secular Christian', *Sofia*, 110 Christmas 2013, the reason for this narrower investigation here in Chapter 2 is because, arguably, the most significant shift in Cupitt's conception of God and his attitude towards metaphysical

approaches to philosophizing about God (and religion) took place between the 1970s and the early 2000s. See also Cupitt, *The Sea of Faith* (paperback edition 1985, US edition 1988, Chinese 2015, second edition, revised, 1994, 'Classics' reprint 2003).

6 Cupitt, *Leap of Reason*, 93.
7 Ibid., 111.
8 Ibid., 105.
9 Ibid., 117, my own use of italics.
10 Ibid., 112.
11 Ibid., 114, my own use of italics.
12 Ibid., 114.
13 Ibid., 118.
14 Cupitt, Don, *The Meaning of It All in Everyday Speech*, London: SCM Press, 1999, 94.
15 Cupitt, Don, *What Is a Story?* London: SCM Press, 1991 ('Xpress' reprint 1995), 76, 38.
16 Ibid., 155.
17 Ibid., 129.
18 Cupitt, Don, *Creation out of Nothing*, London: SCM Press; Philadelphia: Trinity Press International, 1990, 148.
19 Ibid., X.
20 The first part appeared earlier that year (1999) called *The New Religion of Life in Everyday Speech*, London: SCM Press. It argues that the word 'life' is displacing the symbol 'God' in current. The third instalment was published the following year, called *Kingdom Come in Everyday Speech*, London: SCM Press, 2000 which extended this approach more broadly.
21 Cupitt, *The Meaning of It All*, 13.
22 Biernot, Daniel and Christoffel Lombaard, 'The Prayers, Tears and Joys of Don Cupitt: Non-realist, post-Christian Spirituality Under Scrutiny', *HTS Teologiese Studies/Theological Studies*, 74(3), a4971, 2018. Cupitt, *Life, Life*, 7.
23 Cupitt, *Life, Life*, 7.
24 Ibid., X.
25 See list in *Life, Life* in the Appendix, 143–6.
26 Ibid., X.
27 Wittgenstein quote from *Tractatus Logico-Philosophicus*, 1921, trans. Pears, D. F. and B. F. McGuinness, London: Routledge, 1961, quoted on page 3 of *Life, Life*.
28 Cupitt, *Life, Life*, 1.
29 Ibid., 6.
30 Ibid., 6, my own use of italics.
31 Ibid., 6.
32 Ibid.

33 Ibid.
34 This brief insight into Cupitt's personal/academic journey and how it intersects with his non-realist philosophy is taken from Hyman, Gavin, 'Don Cupitt', in *The Palgrave Handbook of Radical Theology*, ed. Christopher D. Rodkey and Jordan E. Miller, London: Palgrave Macmillan, 2018, 136 - 139.
35 Cupitt, *The Leap of Reason*, 112.
36 Ibid.
37 Ibid.
38 Cupitt, *Life, Life*, 12.
39 Cupitt's official website: https://doncupitt.chi.ac.uk.
40 Cupitt, *The Sea of Faith*, 59.
41 The contrast between Descartes and Pascal that Cupitt draws is, arguably, more to do with 'rationalist versus pragmatic' justification than with 'realism versus non-realism', for both Pascal and Descartes are clearly realists: Descartes the rationalist and Pascal the pragmatist (ibid., 54).
42 Ibid., 54.
43 Ibid.
44 Ibid.
45 Ibid., 55.
46 Ibid., 53, 55.
47 Ibid., 55.
48 Ibid., 56.
49 Ibid.
50 Ibid., 58.
51 Ibid.
52 Ibid.
53 Ibid., 59.
54 Ibid.
55 Ibid., 54.
56 Ibid., 59.
57 Ibid.
58 Ibid.
59 Biernot and Lombaard, 'The Prayers, Tears and Joys of Don Cupitt', 7.
60 Ibid., 7–8.
61 Cupitt, Don, *The Time Being*, London: SCM Press, 1992, 35.
62 Cupitt, Don, 'Face to Faith: Learning to Live with One Foot in the Grave', Sofia website: https://sofia.org.nz/cupgrave.html (first appeared in the Guardian's 'Face to Faith' column in December 1993).
63 Ibid., 35.
64 Ibid.. See also page 26.
65 Cupitt, *The Time Being*, 120–4.

66 Cupitt, Don, *After All: Religion Without Alienation*, London: SCM Press, 1994, 103.
67 Ibid.
68 Ibid.
69 Cupitt, 'A Secular Christian', 4–7, 5.
70 Eastwood, Jessica, *New Directions in Philosophical Theology: Essays in Honour of Don Cupitt*, ed. Gavin Hyman, Aldershot, Hants: Ashgate Publishing Company, 2004.

Chapter 3

1 Palmqvist, Carl-Johan, 'Desiderata for Rational, Non-doxastic Faith', *SOPHIA*, 61, 2022, 499–519, 499. https://doi.org/10.1007/s11841-021-00862-4.
2 Abrams, Nancy Ellen, *A God that Could be Real: Spirituality, Science, and the Future of Our Planet*, Massachusetts: Beacon Press, 2015, xix.
3 Howard-Snyder, Daniel and Daniel J. McKaughan, 'Faith', in *The Encyclopaedia of Philosophy of Religion*, ed. Stewart Goetz and Charles Taliaferro, Wiley-Blackwell, forthcoming, 10, with Daniel McKaughan, forthcoming (2020) available here: http://faculty.wwu.edu/~howardd/FaithWBEPRSubmitted.pdf.
4 Ibid., 9.
5 Ibid.
6 Ibid.
7 Ibid.
8 Ibid.
9 Ibid.
10 Ibid., 10.
11 Ibid., 3.
12 Ibid., 4.
13 Ibid.
14 Ibid.
15 For more on different non-doxastic, positive cognitive attitudes that can replace 'involuntary belief-that', see Bratman, Michael, *Faces of Intention: Selected Essays on Intention and Agency*, Cambridge: Cambridge University Press, 1999; Cohen, L. Jonathan, *An Essay on Belief and Acceptance*, Oxford: Oxford University Press, 1992; Alston, William, 'Belief, Acceptance and Religious Faith', in *Faith, Freedom and Rationality*, ed. Jeff Jordan and Daniel Howard-Synder, Lanham, MD: Rowman and Littlefield Publishers, 1996 and Howard-Snyder, Daniel, 'The Skeptical Christian', in *Oxford Studies in Philosophy of Religion*, ed. Jonathan Kvanvig, Oxford: Oxford University Press, 2017. on 'propositional acceptance'; Audi, Robert, *Rationality and Religious Commitment: An Inquiry into Faith and Reason*, New York: Oxford University Press, 2011. and McKaughan, Daniel,

'Authentic Faith and Acknowledged Risk: Dissolving the Problem of Faith and Reason', *Religious Studies*, 49(1), 2013, 101–24 on 'propositional trust' and Alonso, F. M., 'What Is Reliance?', *Canadian Journal of Philosophy*, 44(2), 2014, 163–83 and Rath, Beth, 'Christ's Faith, Doubt, and the Cry of Dereliction', *Approaches to Faith*, 2017, 161–9 on 'propositional reliance'.

16 'Faith', forthcoming (2020), 4.
17 Ibid., 4.
18 For example, '[t]he captain assumes that the quarterback called a fullback plunge; as a result, he puts six 5 men on the line, in order to stop the offense. The general assumes that the enemy is situated thus-and-so; consequently, she disperses her troops for a pincer movement, in order to thwart the enemy' (ibid., 4–5).
19 Ibid., 4–5.
20 Ibid., 5.
21 Ibid., 7.
22 Other ways include: believing that the relevant propositions are likely, or more likely than not, or more likely than any credible contrary, through other positive non-doxastic cognitive attitudes such as acceptance (ibid., 7).
23 Kolodiejchuk, Brian, *Mother Teresa: Come Be My light: The Private Writings of the Saint of Calcutta*, New York: Doubleday, 2007.
24 Howard-Synder AND McKaughan, 'Faith', forthcoming (2020), 7.
25 Ibid., 10.
26 Ibid.
27 Ibid.
28 Howard-Snyder, Daniel, 'Can Fictionalists Have Faith? It All Depends', *Religious Studies*, 55, 2019, 447–68. For more on Howard-Snyder's account of 'faith without belief', see Howard-Synder, 'Does Faith Entail Belief?', *Faith and Philosophy: Journal of the Society of Christian Philosophers*, 33(2), 2016, 142–62; Howard-Snyder, 'Faith', in *The Cambridge Dictionary of Philosophy*, Third edition, ed. Robert Audi, New York: Cambridge University Press, 2015 and Howard-Snyder, 'Propositional Faith: What It Is and What It Is Not', *American Philosophical Quarterly*, 50(4), 2013, reprinted in *Philosophy of Religion: An Anthology*, ed. Pojman, Louis and Michael Rea, Cengage 2013, 6th edition, with an additional section entitled, 'Reasons for the Common View'.
29 Zamulinski acknowledges that it is, '[o]f course', 'customary to use the term, 'belief, as a synonym for "faith"'; however, the argument that he puts forward here, he thinks, 'would be charitable to conclude that Christians have used 'belief ambiguously and to regard what I have done as a clarification' (ibid., 343). But, more than this, if this is *not* the case, then Zamulinski says he would argue that 'Christians ought to reform their understanding of faith' (ibid., 343).
30 Ibid., 340.
31 Ibid., 341.

32 Ibid., 333.
33 Ibid., 339.
34 Ibid.
35 Ibid. My own use of *italics*.
36 Ibid., 340.
37 Ibid.
38 Ibid., 341.
39 Ibid., 340. See, Cohen, *An Essay on Belief and Acceptance*, 4.
40 Ibid., 340.
41 Ibid.
42 Ibid., 341.
43 Peels, Rik, 'The Ethics of Belief and Christian faith as Commitment to Assumptions', *Religious Studies*, 46, 2010, 97–107.
44 Zamulinski, Brian, 'Reconciling Reason and Religion: A Response to Peels', *Religious Studies*, 46, 2010, 109–13.
45 Zamulinski, Brian, 'Christianity and the Ethics of Belief', *Religious Studies*, 44(3), 2008, 333–46, 342.
46 Ibid., 342–3.
47 Zamulinski, 'Reconciling Reason and Religion', 111.
48 Ibid.
49 Ibid.
50 Ibid.
51 Ibid., 111–12.
52 Ibid., 112.
53 Ibid.
54 Ibid.
55 Jackson, Elizabeth, 'Belief, Credence, and Faith', *Religious Studies*, 55(2), 2019, 153–68, 155.
56 Ibid.
57 For more on this, see Jackson, Elizabeth, 'The Relationship Between Belief and Credence', *Philosophy Compass*, 15(6), 2020, 1–13.
58 See Jackson, Elizabeth and Andrew Rogers, 'Salvaging Pascal's Wager', *Philosophia Christi*, 21(1), 2019, 59–84.
59 Jackson, 'Belief, Credence, and Faith', 164.
60 Ibid., 163.
61 Ibid.
62 Jackson recognized that this might be considered and responds, ibid. 167n30.
63 Ibid., 167n30.
64 For more on Jackson's work on this topic, see her following articles: 'Belief and Credence: Why the Attitude-Type Matters', *Philosophical Studies*, 176(9), 2019, 2477–96; 'How Belief-Credence Dualism Explains Away Pragmatic

Encroachment', *The Philosophical Quarterly*, 69(276), 2019, 511–33 and 'Wagering Against Divine Hiddenness', *The European Journal for Philosophy of Religion*. 8(4), 2016, 85–105.

65 Jackson, 'Belief, Credence, and Faith', 163.
66 Of course, it is possible for there to exist a scale within non-realism, with those who may lean closer to realism, or atheism, but on average I would suggest that we would not describe the non-realist 'confidence level' as low but, rather, confident (as one can be) that God does not have an objective existence.
67 Buchak, Lara, 'Can It Be Rational to Have Faith?', in *Probability in the Philosophy of Religion*, ed. Chandler, Jake and Victoria S. Harrison, Oxford: Oxford University Press, 2012, 225.
68 Ibid.
69 Ibid., 226.
70 Ibid., 226n1.
71 Ibid.
72 Ibid.
73 Ibid., 257.
74 Ibid., 259.
75 Ibid.
76 Ibid., 257.
77 Ibid., 271; Malcolm, Finlay and Michael Scott, 'Faith, Belief and Fictionalism', *Pacific Philosophical Quarterly*, 98, 2017, 257–74.
78 For Howard-Snyder and McKaughan's thoughts on Buchak's theory, see their 2022 paper 'Theorizing about faith with Lara Buchak', *Religious Studies*, 58, 2022, 297–326.
79 Scott, Michael and Finlay Malcolm, 'Religious Fictionalism', *Philosophy Compass*, 13(3), 2018, 1–11, 8.
80 Palmqvist, Carl-Johan, 'Forms of Belief-less Religion: Why Non-doxasticism Makes Fictionalism Redundant for the Pro-religious Agnostic', *Religious Studies*, 2019, 1–17, 1.
81 Le Poidevin in *Arguing for Atheism*, London and New York: Routledge, 2003 provides a negative definition of fictionalism before attempting to demonstrate why this is an inaccurate definition, 107.
82 Le Poidevin, *Religious Fictionalism*, Cambridge: Cambridge University Press, 2019, 49.
83 Ibid.
84 Ibid., 52.
85 Ibid.
86 Ibid., 48.
87 Deng, Natalja, 'Religion for Naturalists', *International Journal for Philosophy of Religion*, 78(2), 2015, 195–214, 196.

88 Le Poidevin, Robin, 'Playing the God game: The Perils of Religious Fictionalism', in *Alternative Concepts of God: Essays on the Metaphysics of the Divine*, ed. Andrei Buckareff and Yujin Nagasawa, Oxford: Oxford University Press, 2016, 178.
89 Ibid.
90 Le Poidevin, 'Playing the God Game'.
91 Ibid., 178.
92 Ibid..
93 Ibid.
94 For a positive approach to this issue, see Lipton, Peter, 'Science and Religion: The Immersion Solution', in *Realism and Religion, Philosophical and Theological Perspectives*, ed. Andrew Moore and Michael Scott, Aldershot: Ashgate, 2007.
95 I use the phrase 'pseudo non-realist' here; as Le Poidevin states, fictionalism is just one strand of a non-realist approach to interpreting Christianity and not all non-realist would endorse this philosophy.
96 Lipton, 'Science and Religion', 32.
97 Ibid., 32.
98 Ibid., 34–5.
99 Scientific fictionalism is invoked simply as an analogue for the position on religion Lipton wants to adopt.
100 Ibid., 45.
101 Blackburn, Simon, 'Religion and Ontology', in *Realism and Religion, Philosophical and Theological Perspectives*, ed. Moore, Andrew and Michael Scott, Aldershot: Ashgate, 2007, 54.
102 Ibid., 56.
103 Ibid., 58.
104 Le Poidevin, 'Playing the God Game', 179–80.
105 Ibid., 180.
106 Ibid.
107 Cognitivists mainly use the ideas of the later Wittgenstein, in particular his *Philosophical Investigations*, Third edition, ed. G. E. M. Anscombe, R. Rhees and G. H. von Wright, Oxford: Blackwell, 1968. For more on this, see Loobuyck, Partrick, 'Wittgenstein and the Shift from Noncognitivism to Cognivisim in Ethics', *Metaphilosophy*, 36(3), 2005, 381–99.
108 Ibid., 178.
109 Ibid., 179, 189–90.
110 Ibid., 190.
111 Ibid., 189. Le Poidevin tells us that Andy 'has read and been inspired by the writings of Tillich and Bultmann'.
112 Ibid.
113 See Wittgenstein's *Philosophical Investigations* (1953). It should also be noted that Wittgenstein did not write a treatise or even exclusively on the subject of

religion and, thus, his influence on religion is, as John Hyman put it, 'due to scattered remarks, marginalia and students' notes', Nielsen, Kai, 'Wittgenstein and Wittgensteinians on Religion', in *Wittgenstein and The Philosophy of Religion*, ed. Robert L. Arrington and Mark Addis, London: Routledge, 2001.
114 Nielsen, 'Wittgenstein and Wittgensteinians on Religion', 140.
115 Ibid., 140-1.
116 Ibid., 141.
117 Ibid., 141-2.
118 Ibid., 147.
119 Ibid.
120 Wittgenstein, Ludwig, *Culture and Value*, ed. G. H. Von Wright, Trans. Peter Winch, Oxford: Basil Blackwell, 1980, 64e.
121 Ibid.

Chapter 4

1 Adapted from Colin Radford's 'How Can We Be Moved by the Fate of Anna Karenina?', *Proceedings of the Aristotelian Society, Supplementary Volumes*, 49, 1975, 67-93.
2 The character of Anna Karenina was originally used by Radford, 'How Can We Be Moved by the Fate of Anna Karenina?', and this particular formulation features in Robert Stecker's 'Should We Still Care About the Paradox of Fiction?', *The British Journal of Aesthetics*, 51(3), 2011, 295-308. I will often refer back to the character of Anna for explanatory purposes, so wherever I say 'Anna' I am referring to the character of Anna Karenina.
3 Radford, 'How Can We Be Moved by the Fate of Anna Karenina?', 71-8. Radford does not include these connections to the propositions.
4 Ibid., 74.
5 Ibid.
6 Ibid., 75.
7 Ibid., 78.
8 Ibid.
9 Stecker, Robert, 'Should We Still Care About the Paradox of Fiction?', *British Journal of Aesthetics*, 51(3), 2001, 295-308, 295.
10 Robinson, Jenefer, *Deeper than Reason: Emotion and Its Role in Literature, Music, and Art*, Print publication date: 2005, Print ISBN-13: 9780199263653, Published to Oxford Scholarship Online: February 2006, 6-8, doi:10.1093/0199263655.001.0001.
11 Stecker, 'Should We Still Care About the Paradox of Fiction?', 303.

12 An extensive list is given in LeDoux's 'Rethinking the Emotional Brain', *Neuron*, 73(4), (2012), 653–76.
13 I will not be focusing here on possible neurological, or psychological solutions, or reports concerning our emotions and fiction, but see these articles for if you are interested in further reading: Vrana, S. R., B. N. Cuthbert, and P. J. Lang, 'Processing Fearful and Neutral Sentences: Memory and Heart Rate Change', *Cognition and Emotion*, 3, 1989; Harris, Paul L., *The Work of the Imagination*, Oxford: Blackwell, 2000, 70; Gerrig, Richard J., *Experiencing Narrative Worlds: On the Psychological Activities of Reading*, New Haven: Yale University Press, 1993, 81; Jose, Paul and William Brewer, 'Development of Story-Liking: Character Identification, Suspense, and Outcome Resolution', *Developmental Psychology*, 20, 1984; Roberts, Robert C., *Emotions. An Essay in Aid of Moral Psychology*, New York: Oxford University Press, 2003; Frijda, Nico, *The Emotions*, Cambridge: Cambridge University Press, 1986.
14 Walton, Kendall, *Mimesis as Make-Believe*, Cambridge, MA and London: Harvard University Press, 1990, 251.
15 Ibid., 252.
16 Ibid.
17 Ibid., 252, 255.
18 Carroll, Noël, 'Reviewed Work: Mimesis as Make-Believe: On the Foundations of the Representational Arts. by Kendall L. Walton', *The Philosophical Quarterly*, 45(178), 1995, 93–9, 93.
19 Ibid., 94.
20 Walton, *Mimesis as Make-Believe*, 196.
21 Ibid., 2.
22 Ibid., 196.
23 Ibid., 198.
24 Ibid., 198–9.
25 Ibid., 200.
26 Ibid., 201.
27 Ibid., 202.
28 Ibid., 250–2, 268.
29 Ibid., 202.
30 Ibid.
31 Ibid.
32 Ibid., 196.
33 Ibid., 68, 69.
34 Ibid., 204.
35 Le Poidevin, Robin, *Arguing for Atheism*, London and New York: Routledge, 2003, 107–24.
36 For theorists in favour or that promote radical theology (otherwise known as the 'Death of God Movement'), see publications by Altizer, Thomas. J. J., *The Call*

to *Radical Theology*, Albany: State University of New York Press, 2012; Raschke, Carl, *Postmodernism and the Revolution in Religious Theory: Toward a Semiotics of the Event*, Charlottesville and London: University of Virginia Press, 2012; Taylor, Mark. C., *After God*, Chicago and London: The University of Chicago Press, 2007; Wyschogrod, Edith, 'Crucifixion and Alterity: Pathways to Glory in the Thought of Altizer and Levinas', in *Thinking Through the Death of God: A Critical Companion to Thomas J. J. Altizer*, ed. McCullough, Lissa and Brian Schroeder, Albany: State University of New York Press, 2004; Cupitt, Don, *After God: The Future of Religion*, London: Weidenfeld & Nicolson, 1997; Hamilton, William, and Thomas J. J. Altizer, *Radical Theology and the Death of God*, Harmondsworth: Penguin, 1968; and Van Buren, Paul. M., *Theological Explanations*, London: SCM Press, 1968.

37 Le Poidevin, *Arguing for Atheism*, 112.
38 Ibid., 113.
39 In *Mimesis as Make-Believe* Walton says that in areas in which metaphysical 'realism' is prominent, his theory of make-believe could be applied, including religion, saying: 'I suspect that make-believe may be crucially involved as in certain religious practices', 7.
40 Le Poidevin, *Arguing for Atheism*, 118–19.
41 Ibid., 116–17.
42 Ibid., 119.
43 Le Poidevin phrases this as 'a degenerate type of spiritual life', 120.
44 By 'fictional world' I do not necessarily mean an 'alternative world' like the world of 'Harry Potter', I also mean films that are set in realities that are very similar to our own, like *The Breakfast Club* or *Good Will Hunting*, for example.
45 Le Poidevin, *Arguing for Atheism*, 115.
  *Interesting that this notion of being duped or 'fooled' is brought up again.
46 For more on this, see Lear, Jonathan, *Freud*, New York and London: Routledge, 2005, 23–41.
47 Ibid., 115.
48 Ibid., 116.
49 Ibid.
50 Ibid.
51 Johnson, Samuel, *Preface to Shakespeare*, Frankfurt am Main: Outlook, Verlag GmbH, 2018, 14.
52 Murray, Nathan, 'A Possible Source for the Apocryphal Anecdote Concerning the Reception of Little Nell's Death', *Notes and Queries*, 65(3), 2018, 375–7, 376.
53 Ibid., 377.
54 For potential support for this, see Moran, Richard, 'The Expression of Feeling in Imagination', *The Philosophical Review* 103(1), 1994, 75–106 and Goldie, Peter, 'Getting Feelings into Emotional Experience in the Right Way', *Emotion Review*, 1(3), 2009, 232–9.

55 Stecker, 'Should We Still Care About the Paradox of Fiction?'.
56 Note that in Stecker's paper this proposition, 'to be moved: we must believe that fictional entities exist', is written as follows: '(2) To pity someone, one must believe that they exist and are suffering' (295).
57 Ibid., 295.
58 However, one might not find this unconvincing if one holds the view that perhaps such emotions do require realism about past and future. Therefore, one might criticize Stecker here because it is not true that we treat people or imagine persons to exist in a fictional realm just because they have passed or are yet to be born. That is to say, that we do not imagine those that we have lost to now exist in fiction. To further this point, one could draw our attention to the notion that we might have moral duties towards the/a future generation, but we do not have a 'duty' towards fictional characters, for instance.
59 Ibid., 295. Moran, says Stecker, first pointed this out in his paper, 'The Expression of Feeling in Imagination' (1994). Imaginative resistance deals with contemplating morally alien or repugnant outlooks, which might not be an issue when engaging with religious discourse. However, Moran's theory might offer two interesting outlooks on the state of 'imagining' for this investigation. The first might be that imagining is dependent on the will (contra to 'belief' which might exist *in*dependent of will). The second is that one resists to imagine that which one does not wish to transfer to their day-to-day life or endorse as authentically one's own. Moran's Humean approach (which is also developed by Walton) suggests that the primary source of imaginative resistance is our *inability* to imagine morally deviant situations. In contrast, Gendler has since suggested that it is not that we are unable to imagine, but it is, rather, our *unwillingness* that is the primary source (Gendler, Tamar Szabó, 'The Puzzle of Imaginative Resistance', *The Journal of Philosophy*, 97(2), 2000, 55–81).
60 Tullman, Katherine, 'HOT Emotions: Dissolving the Paradox of Fiction', *Contemporary Aesthetics*, 10, 2012, 1932–8478.
61 LeDoux, Joseph, *The Emotional Brain*, New York: Simon & Schuster, 1996, 163–5.
62 Tullman, 'HOT Emotions'.
63 Ibid.
64 Ibid.
65 The objection here would be if one claims to be emotional about one's thought about a character, and not the thought itself.
66 Ibid.
67 Ibid.
68 Ibid.
69 Lear's assessment of Freud can help to defend, I think, Tullman's Hot theory, namely the idea that beliefs are not easily or necessarily associated with one's puzzling emotional reaction or behavioural response to otherwise perplexing

situations. For the 'assignment of belief' is a somewhat reflective impulse to assign rationality to one's responses, which arguably aligns with Tullman's suggestion that we look elsewhere, as it were (to aliefs specifically) for what might cause our reactions rather than to insist upon belief as a necessary component.

70 Gendler, Tamar Szabó, 'Alief and Belief', in Gendler's *Intuition, Imagination, and Philosophical Methodology*, Oxford: Oxford University Press, 2010. Oxford Scholarship Online, 2011. doi:10.1093/acprof:oso/9780199589760.003.0014, 257.
71 Rozin, Paul, Linda Millman, and Carol Nemeroff, 'Operation of the Laws of Systematic Magic in Disgust and Other Domains', *Journal of Personality and Social Psychology*, l(4), 1986, 703–12.
72 Ibid., 257.
73 Ibid., 255.
74 Walton, Kendall, 'Fearing Fictions', *The Journal of Philosophy*, 75(1), 1978, 5–27, 6. Earlier I quoted the passage from Walton's *Mimesis as Make-Believe*, 196.
75 Gendler, 'Alief and Belief', 258.
76 It is unclear as to whether the concept of 'alief' could also explain more complex emotions such as 'pity' and 'jealousy' because Gendler tends to focus on behaviour and basic emotions, specifically physiological responses.
77 Ibid., 259.
78 Ibid., 262.
79 See Nussbaum, Martha, 'Emotions as Judgments of Value and Importance', in *Thinking About Feeling*, ed. Solomon, Robert C., New York: Oxford University Press, 2004, 183–99; Walton's *Mimesis as Make-believe* and 'Fearing Fictions'; James, William, 'What Is an Emotion?', *Mind*, 9(34), 1884, 188–205; Prinz, Jesse, 'Embodied Emotions', in *Thinking About Feeling*, ed. Robert C. Solomon, New York: Oxford University Press, 2004, 44–58; Ledoux, *The Emotional Brain*, 163–5; Carroll, Noël, *The Philosophy of Horror*, New York: Routledge, Chapman and Hall, Inc., 1990; Solomon, Robert, 'Emotions, Thoughts and Feelings', in *Thinking About Feeling*, ed. Robert C. Solomon, New York: Oxford University Press, 2004, 76–90.
80 A phrase used by Gendler.
81 Gendler, 'Alief and Belief', 281.
82 Ibid., 262.
83 Ibid., 264.
84 Ibid.
85 Ibid., 651.
86 Ibid., 641.
87 Ibid.
88 Ibid., 262.
89 Ibid., 263.
90 Radford, 'How Can We Be Moved by the Fate of Anna Karenina?', 80.
91 Ibid., 92.

92 Ibid., 85.
93 Ibid., 81.
94 Ibid., 68.
95 Ibid., 83.
96 Ibid., 83, 84. This also seems to disregard Radford's fourth solution: that our emotional response to fiction is not too dissimilar to our emotional response to non-fictional contexts, such as hypothetical scenarios or when caught in a web of 'what ifs'.
97 Ibid., 84.
98 Ibid., 85.
99 Ibid., 86.
100 Ibid., 86. Also an argument against Radford's fifth solution: the emotion we feel towards a fictional entity is really an emotional response to a real person.
101 Ibid., 88.
102 Ibid., 89, 90.
103 Ibid., 78.
104 Ibid., 90.
105 Ibid., 91, 92.
106 Ibid., 92.
107 Ibid., 93. Originally from Winch, Peter, 'Understanding a Primitive Society', *American Philosophical Quarterly*, 1(4), 1964, 307–24, 322.
108 Radford, 'How Can We Be Moved by the Fate of Anna Karenina?', 92.
109 Ibid., 93.
110 Ibid., 60.
111 Ibid.
112 Le Poidevin, *Arguing for Atheism*, 119.
113 Eshleman, Andrew S., 'Can an Atheist Believe in God?', *Religious Studies*, 41, 2005, 183–99, 188.
114 Weston, 'II – Michael Weston', 92.

Chapter 5

1 The phrase 'humane' that I am using here is from John Cottingham in his *Philosophy of Religion*, Cambridge: Cambridge University Press, 2014, 11. It is not in reference to humanism: the philosophical, non-religious view that seeks to find meaning in the natural world, the purpose of human life and universal moral law by appealing to reason rather than revelation.
2 It goes without saying that rigorous argumentation and precise thinking are not only useful but vital when it comes to philosophical investigation. What is being

suggested is that the philosopher resists using models of philosophy that essentially reduce all cognition to a single rigid template, and, instead, try to develop a comprehensive and more 'humane' model of philosophy.

3 Wittgenstein, Ludwig, *Tractatus Logico-Philosophicus*, 1921, trans. Pears, D. F. and B. F. McGuinness, London: Routledge, 1961, 6.41 and McDowell, John, *Mind and World*, Cambridge and London: Harvard University Press, 1996, 85.
4 That is not to say that it cannot be, it is certainly plausible to imagine an individual questioning the creation of the universe, for example, and coming to a conclusion through analytical reasoning that there must have been a 'first cause' or an 'unmoved mover'.
5 For more on this, see McGilchrist, Iain, *The Master and His Emissary*, New Haven: Yale University Press, 2009.
6 Cottingham, *Philosophy of Religion*, 2.
7 Ibid., 65.
8 Stump, Eleonore, *Wandering in Darkness*, Oxford: Oxford University Press, 2012, 24.
9 Ibid.
10 Ibid.
11 Ibid.
12 Ibid.
13 Ibid., 25.
14 Ibid.
15 Ibid.
16 Ibid., 24.
17 Ibid., 24–5.
18 Ibid., 24.
19 Ibid., viii.
20 Cottingham, John, 'What Is Humane Philosophy and Why Is It at Risk?', *Royal Institute of Philosophy Supplement*, 65, 2009, 233–55, 237.
21 Ibid., 237.
22 Cottingham, *Philosophy of Religion*, 171.
23 Cottingham, John, 'Detachment, Rationality and Evidence: Towards a More Humane Religious Epistemology', *Royal Institute of Philosophy Supplement*, 81, 2017, 87–100, 97.
24 Ibid., 87.
25 Ibid., 92.
26 Ibid., 93.
27 Ibid.
28 Cottingham, *Philosophy of Religion*, 169.
29 Cottingham, John, *Why Believe?* London and New York: Continuum, 2009, 99–100.
30 Ibid., 101.

31 Ibid., 103.
32 Cottingham, *Philosophy of Religion*, 171.
33 My own use of italics (Ibid., 3).
34 Ibid., 3.
35 Ibid., 3.
36 Ibid., 176.
37 Ibid., 7 (Cottingham, *Philosophy of Religion*)
38 Cottingham, 'Detachment, Rationality and Evidence', 92.
39 Cottingham, *Philosophy of Religion*, 2.
40 Cottingham, John, *Philosophy and the Good Life: Reason and the Passions in Greek, Cartesian and Psychoanalytic Ethics*, Cambridge: Cambridge University Press, 2010, 4.
41 In C. S. Lewis's *The Screwtape Letters*, London: Collins, 2012, Screwtape refers to humans as 'amphibians': 'half spirit and half animal'. For more on the hybrid nature of human beings, see Pope, Alexander, *An Essay on Man and Other Poems*, Mineola, New York: Dover publications, INC, 1994; Epistle II, 3-4, 7-8,13-1; Pascal, Blaise, *Pensees*, c. 1660, ed. Lafuma, Louis, Paris: Editions du Seuil, 1962, no. 678 and Augustine, *De civitate Dei* (1973) (413–26), ix, 13.
42 Cottingham, *Philosophy and the Good Life*, 4. This might remind us of Winch's passage quoted by Weston, that we are not like beasts because we do not merely live, but we have a conception of life (Winch, Peter, 'Understanding a Primitive Society', *American Philosophical Quarterly*, 1(4), 1964, 322).
43 Cottingham, 'Detachment, Rationality and Evidence', 94.
44 Ibid.
45 Ibid., 96.
46 Ibid., 7 (Cottingham, Philosophy of Religion).
47 Ibid., 99.
48 Ibid.
49 Ibid., 100.
50 Ibid., 99.
51 Ibid., 91.
52 Ibid., 96.
53 Ibid.
54 Ibid., 99.
55 It is worth noting that this left-hand column, the associated epistemic virtues with the left hemisphere, ought not to be drawn into the realism/non-realism debate and the 'religious seriousness' impasse. In other words, it is not being suggested here that fictionalism (when used as a vehicle by the non-realist) is the 'more serious' position of the two. Rather, it is a comment on the epistemic virtues or 'skill sets' that might be associated with a particular 'part' of the brain, in conjunction with McGilchrist's findings and used by Cottingham and Stump to advocate the humane turn.

56 Le Poidevin, Robin, 'Playing the God Game: The Perils of Religious Fictionalism', in *Alternative Concepts of God: Essays on the Metaphysics of the Divine*, ed. Andrei Buckareff and Yujin Nagasawa, Oxford: Oxford University Press, 2016, 10.
57 Le Poidevin, Robin, *Religious Fictionalism*, Cambridge: Cambridge University Press 2019, 35.
58 Ibid., 39.
59 Ibid.
60 Ibid., 40.
61 It might be of interest to note here that a similar discussion may also be taking place among theologians, namely the nature and desirability of an analytic approach to theology. For more on this, see Oliver, Simon, 'Analytic Theology', *International Journal of Systematic Theology*, 12, 2010, 464–75 and *Analytic Theology: New Essays in the Philosophy of Theology*, ed. Oliver D. Crisp and Michael C. Rea, Oxford: Oxford University Press, 2009.
62 Le Poidevin, 'Playing the God game', 1.
63 Le Poidevin, Robin, *Arguing for Atheism*, London and New York: Routledge, 2003, xx–xxi.
64 Ibid., xx.
65 Ibid., xxi.
66 Cottingham, *Philosophy of Religion*, 22.
67 Part of a lecture given by McGilchrist titled 'The Divided Brain & The Making of the Western World', for the Royal Society of Arts, Manufactures and Commerce in 2010.
68 Cottingham, 'Detachment, Rationality and Evidence', 100.
69 Cottingham, John, 'Transcending Science: Humane Models of Religious Understanding', in *New Models of Religious Understanding*, ed. Fiona Ellis, Oxford: Oxford University Press, 2018, 29.
70 Ibid., 31.
71 Cottingham, John, 'Philosophy and Self-improvement: Continuity and Change in Philosophy's Self-conception from the Classical to the Early-Modern Era', in *Philosophy as a Way of Life: Ancients and Moderns*, ed. Michael Chase, Stephen Clark, and Michael McGhee, Oxford: Blackwell, 2013, 148–66, 148.
72 Cottingham, *Philosophy of Religion*, 151.
73 Cottingham, 'Detachment, Rationality and Evidence', 91.
74 Ibid.
75 Ibid., 92 (Cottingham, "Detachment, Rationality and Evidence").
76 Ibid., 92.
77 Ibid.
78 Ibid., found in Seamus Heaney, 'Joy or Night', in *Finders Keepers: Selected Prose 1971–2001*, London: Faber, 2002.
79 Ibid., 92.
80 Ibid.

81 Ibid.
82 Ibid., 93.
83 Ibid.
84 Ibid.
85 Ibid.
86 Ibid.
87 Ibid., my own use of italics.
88 Cottingham, 'Transcending Science', 41.
89 Ibid., 26.
90 Ibid., 27, 23.
91 Ibid., 33. However, Cottingham does say that he believes that the 'humane' model 'has the advantage of taking us closer to traditional religious thought and practice' (ibid., 33).
92 Ibid., 27.
93 Ibid., 27, 31.
94 Ibid., 31.
95 Ibid., 40.
96 Lipton, Peter, 'Science and Religion: The Immersion Solution', in *Realism and Religion: Philosophical and Theological Perspectives*, ed. Michael Scott and Andrew Moore, Aldershot: Ashgate, 2007, 43 and Le Poidevin, *Religious Fictionalism*, 32.
97 Le Poidevin, *Religious Fictionalism*, 32. For more on Lipton's approach, see 'Science and Religion'. For more on Braithwaite's approach, see Le Poidevin's *Religious Fictionalism* and Braithwaite, Richard, 'An Empiricist's View of the Nature of Religious Belief' (1955), Ninth Arthur Stanley Eddington Lecture, reprinted in *The Philosophy of Religion*, ed. Mitchell, Basil, Oxford: Oxford University Press, 1971, 72-91.
98 Peter Lipton, 'Science and Religion', 32.
99 Le Poidevin, Robin, *Agnosticism: A Very Short Introduction*, New York: Oxford University Press, 2010, 118.
100 Cottingham, John, *In Search of the Soul: A Philosophical Essay*, Princeton and Oxford: Princeton University Press, 2020, 131.
101 Ibid., 132, found in Nagel, Thomas, *Mind and Cosmos*, Oxford and New York: Oxford University Press, 2012, 85.
102 Nagel, *Mind and Cosmos*, 85.
103 Ibid., 132. See also Cottingham, John, 'Human Nature and the Transcendent', *Royal Institute of Philosophy Supplement*, 70, 2012, 233-54, 233-5.

Chapter 6

1 Throughout this chapter I will use the terms 'theology'/'theological' and 'religion'/'religious' interchangeably. This is because Victoria Harrison in her work

('Mathematical objects and the Object of Theology', *Religious Studies*, 2017, 53, 479–96) uses the term 'theology' (and 'theological realism'), whereas this book has used the term 'religious' (and 'religious realism') but we are talking about the same topic, that is, how realism is construed in philosophy of religion.

2 Four types of philosophical approaches to apprehending the reality of mathematical objects that I will later argue correspond with the four types of philosophical approaches to apprehending the reality of *the* theological object that I plotted on the second axis (a spectrum of commitment). That is, two types of realism, one more ontologically robust than the other, fictionalism and (standard) non-realism. Four positions that I argue can be found in both discourses.

3 I will be using the philosophical view of 'mathematical platonism' in conjunction with Øystein Linnebo's construal (2018). According to Linnebo, platonism with a small case 'p' includes the following three characteristics: (1) existence, (2) abstractness and (3) independence. It might also include (4) necessity (although this final claim has traditionally been made by most platonists, some philosophers who are generally regarded as platonists, for instance Quine and some adherents of the aforementioned indispensability argument, reject this additional modal claim). It might help to compare 'platonism' to two different views, the first being Platonism with a capital 'P'. Linnebo says the following on the distinction. 'Platonism must be distinguished from the view of the historical Plato. Few parties to the contemporary debate about platonism make strong exegetical claims about Plato's view, much less defend it. Although the view which we are calling "platonism" is inspired by Plato's famous theory of abstract and eternal Forms (see the entry on Plato's metaphysics and epistemology), platonism is now defined and debated independently of its original historical inspiration.' Therefore, I will be referring to platonism with a lowercase 'p'. The second view is object realism. The object realist will agree with (1) existence and (2) abstractness but not (3) independence and (4) necessity. I will suggest that the branch of mathematical realism that Harrison gestures towards is closer to mathematical platonism, but I will argue that the best way to formulate the analogy might require realism as construed by the object realist instead. That is, the less rigorous ontological position (Linnebo, Øystein, 'Platonism in the Philosophy of Mathematics', *The Stanford Encyclopedia of Philosophy* (Spring 2018 Edition), Edward N. Zalta (ed.), https://plato.stanford.edu/archives/spr2018/entries/platonism-mathematics/).

4 Harrison makes this distinction in 'Mathematical Objects and the Object of Theology'.

5 Ibid., 484. See Shapiro, Stewart, *Thinking About Mathematics*, Oxford: Oxford University Press, 2011.

6 Harrison, 'Mathematical Objects and the Object of Theology', 484. For more on Hale's concern, see Hale, Bob, *Abstract Objects*, Oxford: Basil Blackwell, 1987. An example of someone who is prepared to doubt this is Penelope Maddy in her

Realism in Mathematics, Oxford: Clarendon, 1990 (she thinks that we perceive sets of objects).

7 Øystein Linnebo explains that although these characteristics are challenged, '[t]he claim that mathematical objects are abstract has been less controversial. It is not hard to see why. If possible, our philosophical account of mathematics should avoid claims that would render our ordinary mathematical practice misguided or inadequate. But if mathematical objects had spatiotemporal location, then our ordinary mathematical practice would be misguided and inadequate. We would then expect mathematicians to take a professional interest in the location of their objects, just as zoologists are interested in the location of animals. By taking mathematical objects to be abstract, our actual practice becomes far more appropriate' (Linnebo, Øystein, *Philosophy of Mathematics*, Princeton and Oxford: Princeton University Press, 2017, 10).
8 Linnebo, *Philosophy of Mathematics*, 31.
9 Linnebo, 'Platonism in the Philosophy of Mathematics'.
10 Colyvan, *Introduction to The Philosophy of Mathematics*, Cambridge: Cambridge University Press, 2012, 36. Might it also be the case that someone believes in mathematical ontology but not thinking that mathematical truths are true in virtue of that ontology? Consider the following position: the (knowable) truths of arithmetic are true in virtue of our calculating activity and that calculating activity gives rise to the existence of numbers. Some object realists might agree with this, while others will disagree because they 'take the mathematical realism to be the book that some mathematical statements are objectively true and that they are made true by the existence of mathematical objects', and will argue that if the statement 'there is an even prime' is taken to be objectively true, 'how could it be unless there is an even prime'? (ibid., 37).
11 Ernst, Bruno, *The Magic Mirror of M. C. Escher*, Cologne: Taschen, 1978, 3. Quoted in Colyvan, Mark, *An Introduction to the Philosophy of Mathematics*, Cambridge: Cambridge University Press, 2012, 36.
12 Linnebo, 'Platonism in the Philosophy of Mathematics'.
13 Ibid.
14 Ibid.
15 To clarify, platonists think that '4 + 4 = 8' would be true even if there had been no language-users, and so no numerals.
16 Linnebo, *Philosophy of Mathematics*, 11.
17 Wigner, Eugene, 'The Unreasonable Effectiveness of Mathematics in the Natural Sciences', *Communications on Pure and Applied Mathematics*, 1960, 13, 1–14; Hersh, Reuben, *What Is Mathematics, Really?* Oxford: Oxford University Press, 1997; Azzouni, J., *Deflating Existential Consequence: A Case for Nominalism*, Oxford: Oxford University Press, 2004 and Yablo, Stephen, 'Does Ontology Rest on a Mistake?', *Aristotelian Society*, Supplementary Volume, 1998, 72, 229–61.

18 Colyvan, *Introduction to the Philosophy of Mathematics*, 55.
19 Ibid., 56.
20 Ibid.
21 Ibid., 55.
22 Shapiro, *Thinking about Mathematics*, 226.
23 Ibid.
24 Colyvan, *Introduction to the Philosophy of Mathematics*, 37. See Hilary, *Philosophy of Logic*, New York: Harper (1971), reprinted in *Mathematics, Matter and Method: Philosophical Papers*, vol. 1, Second edition, Cambridge University Press, 1979, 323–57.
25 Colyvan, *Introduction to the Philosophy of Mathematics*, 37 (my own italics).
26 Ibid.
27 Ibid.
28 Ibid., Maddy, *Realism in Mathematics*.
29 Ibid., 43.
30 Linnebo, *Philosophy of Mathematics*, 11.
31 Ibid., 7.
32 Ibid.
33 Ibid., 4. As I mentioned before, although the claim that all truths of pure mathematics are necessary has traditionally been made by most platonists, some philosophers who are generally regarded as platonists (for instance, Quine and some adherents of the indispensability argument) reject this additional modal claim (Linnebo, 'Platonism in the Philosophy of Mathematics'). Quine, Willard van Orman, 'Existence and Quantification', in *Ontological Relativity and Other Essays*, New York: Columbia University Press, 1969, 91–113.
34 Linnebo, *Philosophy of Mathematics*, 8.
35 Ibid.
36 Ibid.
37 'Frege held that the numbers exist, of necessity, independent of the mathematician' (Shapiro, *Thinking about Mathematics*, 125). Gödel's mathematical realism concerns an 'ideal realism of objects which exist independently of us', and that this 'mathematical world is timeless and eternal' (ibid., 211). 'On traditional views', mathematical objects 'exist of necessity', whereas (in Quinean terms) the non-realists 'trade ontology for "ideology"' (ibid., 246). That is to say, the 'platonist might attribute some sort of ontological independence to the individual natural numbers', insofar as they do not rely on the existence of anything external to them, including other numbers (ibid., 258).
38 Ibid., 27 (own use of italics).
39 Ibid.
40 This issue is of course linked to the epistemology problem of how we can know or gain access to this kind of reality, with a theory sometimes called 'mathematical

intuition' often at the forefront of the discussion, but this is not of our concern here in this chapter.

41 Shapiro, *Thinking About Mathematics*, 99. Mill's account of apparent necessity 'is similar to Hume's book about causality and "necessary connection". Hume suggested that our belief that one thing causes another is based on constant experience of the two things together, to point to that when we see one of them we expect the other' (ibid., 99).
42 Harrison, 'Mathematical Objects and the Object of Theology', 494.
43 Ibid., 46. To clarify, Harrison's suggestion that God is 'acausal' is meant to coincide with the classical idea that God was not 'caused' by something greater than God, which is to say that nothing came before God (Aquinas's idea of God as 'first' or 'prime mover').
44 When it comes to Harrison's epistemological claims, she does so on the basis of drawing our attention to the notion of mathematical intuition. Through mathematical intuition, Harrison explains, 'we form a mental representation of objective abstract entities and this allows us to know necessary mathematical truths'. So if we adapt this idea to the theological case, she suggests that 'we might venture to claim that through theological intuition we form a mental representation of the object of theology and what we come to know about this entity is a necessary truth' (according to the work on Jerrold Katz expanding on Gödel's view) (ibid., 494).
45 However, I should also mention that Harrison states that 'this idea is by no means limited to Christian theology', although, as I said, she does use this phrase, 'the central object of Western theological traditions – God' and makes reference only to the Christian tradition (ibid., 479, 490).
46 Ibid., 490.
47 Ibid.
48 Ibid.
49 Ibid. We might want to consider, then, that the theist might deny that all causal relations are physical causal relations for precisely this reason.
50 Ibid., 490.
51 Ibid., 492.
52 Ibid., 493.
53 Ibid., 494.
54 Ibid.
55 Ibid.
56 Ibid.
57 Ibid.
58 Ibid., 492.
59 Ibid., 493.
60 Blackburn, Simon, *Essays in Quasi-Realism*, New York and Oxford: Oxford University Press, 1993.
61 Harrison mentions the fact that even if the God of CPT 'was an object located within space-time, and possessing the capability to enter into physical causal

relations facilitated by that' that the traditional realist 'would seem to face a particularly challenging form of the problem of evil' (ibid., 494).
62 Ibid., 490.
63 Ibid., 481.
64 Ibid.
65 Linnebo, Øystein, 'Platonism in the Philosophy of Mathematics'.
66 For more on the concept of supervenience, see Kim, Jaegwon ('Concepts of Supervenience', *Philosophy and Phenomenology Research*, 45(2), 1984, 153–76; '"Strong" and "Global" Supervenience Revisited', *Philosophy and Phenomenology Research*, 48(2), 1987, 315–26; 'Supervenience as a Philosophical Concept', *Metaphilosophy*, 21(1/2), 1990, 1–27; *Supervenience and Mind: Selected Philosophical Essays*, Cambridge: Cambridge University Press, 1993); Petrie, Bradford, 'Global Supervenience and Reduction', *Philosophy and Phenomenology Research*, 48(1), 1987, 119–30; Paull, R. Cranston and Sider R. Theodore, 'In Defence of Global Supervenience', *Philosophy and Phenomenology Research*, 52(4), 1992, 933–54 and Moyer, Mark, 'Weak and Global Supervenience Are Strong', *Philosophical Studies: An International Journal for Philosophy in the Analytic Tradition*, 138(1), 2008, 125–50.
67 Kim, 'Concepts of Supervenience', 153–76, 154.
68 Kim, 'Supervenience as a Philosophical Concept', 1–27, 6.
69 Ibid., 8.
70 Ibid.
71 Kim, '"Strong" and "Global" Supervenience Revisited', 315–26. Here times are omitted, but of course objects may be A-indiscernible at one time, but not at another.
72 The possible worlds quantified over might include all metaphysically possible worlds, or only nomologically possible worlds (etc.), depending upon what degree of modal force is intended.
73 Kim, '"Strong" and "Global" Supervenience Revisited', 317.
74 Kim, 'Concepts of Supervenience', 160.
75 Ibid.
76 Ibid.
77 Ibid., 161.
78 Ibid., 162, 171.
79 Ibid., 174.
80 Nagel, Thomas, *Mind and Cosmos*, New York: Oxford University Press, 2012.
81 Otherwise known as Aristotelian essentialism.
82 Horgan, Terence, 'Supervenience and Microphysics', *Pacific Philosophical Quarterly*, 63, 1982, 29–43, 37 and Horgan, Terence, 'From Supervenience to Superdupervenience: Meeting the Demands of a Material World', *Mind*, 102, 555–86, 571.
83 Hoffmann, Vera and Albert Newen, 'Supervenience of Extrinsic Properties', *Erkenntnis*, 67, 2007, 305–19, 311.
84 Kim, 'Supervenience as a Philosophical Concept', 22.

85 Ibid.
86 The following three examples are from the following articles: Currie, Gregory, 'Individualism and Global Supervenience', *The British Journal for the Philosophy of Science*, 35(4), 1984, 345–58, 349; Walton, Kendall, 'Categories of Art', *Philosophical Review*, 79(3), 1970, 334–67 and Putnam, Hilary, 'The Meaning of "Meaning"', *Philosophical Review*, 7, 1975, 131–93.
87 Some naturalists insist that the limits of nature are to be circumscribed by science, and express a similar antipathy towards anything and everything supernatural, which includes any metaphysical stance about phenomena such as 'value'. One way around this has been to expand the limits of science to accommodate modes of enquiry which seem better placed to accommodate such phenomena. However, other philosophers such as David Wiggins and John McDowell fear that this response still encompasses a residual commitment to scientism. Instead, they defend a conception of nature and naturalism which go beyond such parameters, while giving due respect to the findings of modern science. Having said that, they do agree that nature, thus conceived, must be shorn of any reference to gods or God. Fiona Ellis, on the other hand, argues that such an expansion can provide a form of theistic naturalism which can accommodate the distinction – and indeed, the relation – between God and nature. For more, see Ellis (*God, Value and Nature*, Oxford: Oxford University Press, 2014; 'Nature, Enchantment, and God', in *The Philosophy of Re-enchantment*, ed. M. Meijer and H. de Vries, Routledge, 2020 and *Liberal Naturalism and God*, Routledge, (Routledge handbooks), 2021 and its bibliography for more on Wiggins and Dowell).
88 Harrison, 'Mathematical Objects and the Object of Theology', 494.
89 Ibid., 490.
90 Ibid., 490. The others include 'eternality' and 'indestructibility', which, again, I suggest are more reflective of a platonistic/traditional realist viewpoint and not an object realist/post-traditional viewpoint.
91 For more on 'coextension' and 'necessary coextension', see Kim, Jaegwon, 'Supervenience and Supervenient Causation', *Southern Journal of Philosophy*, 22(1), 1984, 45–56 and Bacon, John, 'Supervenience, Necessary Coextension, and Reducibility', *Philosophical Studies: An International Journal for Philosophy in the Analytic Tradition*, 49 (2), 1986, 163–76.
92 Kim, 'Concepts of Supervenience', 176.

Conclusion

1 Fox, Matthew, *Meister Eckhart: A Mystic-Warrior for Our Times*, California: New World Library, 2014, 15.

Bibliography

Abrams, Nancy Ellen, *A God that Could Be Real: Spirituality, Science, and the Future of Our Planet*, Masschetus: Beacon Press, 2015.

Adorno, Theodor, *Minima Moralia*, London: Verso, 2005.

Alonso, F. M., 'What Is Reliance?', *Canadian Journal of Philosophy*, 44(2), 2014, 163–83.

Alston, William, 'Swinburne on Faith and Belief', in *Reason and the Christian Religion: Essays in Honour of Richard Swinburne*, ed. Alan Padgett, Oxford: Clarendon, 1994, 201–26.

Alston, William P., 'Dispositions and Occurrences', *Canadian Journal of Philosophy*, 1(2), 1971, 125–54.

Altizer, Thomas J. J., *The Call to Radical Theology*, Albany: State University of New York Press, 2012.

Armstrong, D. M., *Belief, Truth and Knowledge*, Cambridge: Cambridge University Press, 1973.

Azzouni, J., *Deflating Existential Consequence: A Case for Nominalism*, Oxford: Oxford University Press, 2004.

Bacon, John, 'Supervenience, Necessary Coextension, and Reducibility', *Philosophical Studies: An International Journal for Philosophy in the Analytic Tradition*, 49(2), 1986, 163–76.

Baker, Derek and Jack Woods, 'How Expressivists Can and Should Explain Inconsistency', *Ethics*, 125(2), 2015, 391–424.

Barry, *Stroud, Hume*, London: Routledge, 1977.

Biernot, Daniel and Christoffel Lombaard, 'The Prayers, Tears and Joys of Don Cupitt: Non Realist, Post-Christian Spirituality Under Scrutiny', *HTS Teologiese Studies/ Theological Studies*, 74(3), 2018, 1–12.

Blackburn, Simon, *Essays in Quasi-Realism*, New York and Oxford: Oxford University Press, 1993.

Blackburn, Simon, 'Quasi-realism no Fictionalism', in *Fictionalism in Metaphysics*, ed. M. Kalderon, Oxford: Clarendon Press, 2005, 322–50.

Blackburn, Simon, 'Religion and Ontology', in *Realism and Religion, Philosophical and Theological Perspectives*, ed. Andrew Moore and Michael Scott, Aldershot: Ashgate, 2007, 47–60.

Blackburn, Simon, *The Oxford Dictionary of Philosophy*, Oxford: Oxford University Press, 2005.

Braithwaite, Richard, 'An Empiricist's View of the Nature of Religious Belief', in *The Philosophy of Religion*, ed., Basil Mitchell, Oxford: Oxford University Press, 1971.

Braithwaite, Richard, 'An Empiricist's View of the Nature of Religious Belief' (1955), Ninth Arthur Stanley Eddington Lecture, reprinted in *The Philosophy of Religion*, ed. Mitchell, Basil, Oxford: Oxford University Press, 1971, 72–91.

Bratman, Michael, *Faces of Intention: Selected Essays on Intention and Agency*, Cambridge: Cambridge University Press, 1999.

Buchak, Lara, 'Can It Rational to Faith?', in *Probability in the Philosophy of Religion*, ed. Jake Chandler and Victoria S. Harrison, Oxford: Oxford University Press, 2012, 225–48.

Buchak, Lara, 'Faith and Steadfastness in the Face of Counter-Evidence', *International Journal for Philosophy of Religion*, 81, 2017, 113–33.

Buchak, Lara, 'When Is Faith Rational?', in *Norton Introduction to Philosophy*, Second edition, ed. Byrne, Alex, Josh Cohen, Liz Harman, and Gideon Rosen, New York and London: W. W. Norton and Company, 2018, 115–32.

Bultmann, Rudolf, 'What Sense Is There to Speak of God?', *The Christian Scholar*, 43(3), 1960, 213–22.

Burley, Mikel, 'Phillips and Realists on Religious Beliefs and the Fruits', *International Journal for Philosophy of Religion*, 64(3), 2008, 141–53.

Carroll, Noël, 'Reviewed Work: Mimesis as Make-Believe: On the Foundations of the Representational Arts. by Kendall L. Walton', *The Philosophical Quarterly*, 45(178), 1995, 93–9.

Carroll, Noël, *The Philosophy of Horror*, New York: Routledge, Chapman and Hall, Inc., 1990.

Clifford, William K., 'The Ethics of Belief', in *The Ethics of Belief and Other Essays*, ed. T. Madigan, Amherst, MA: Prometheus, 1999, 70–96, (originally published in 1877).

Cohen, L. Jonathan, *An Essay on Belief and Acceptance*, Oxford: Clarendon Press, 1992.

Colyvan, Mark, *An Introduction to the Philosophy of Mathematics*, Cambridge: Cambridge University Press, 2012.

Cottingham, John, 'Detachment, Rationality and Evidence: Towards a More Humane Religious Epistemology', *Royal Institute of Philosophy Supplement*, 81, 2017, 87–100.

Cottingham, John, 'Human Nature and the Transcendent', *Royal Institute of Philosophy Supplement*, 70, 2012, 233–54.

Cottingham, John, 'Philosophy and Self-improvement: Continuity and Change in Philosophy's Self-conception from the Classical to the Early-Modern Era', in *Philosophy as a Way of Life: Ancients and Moderns*, ed. Michael Chase, Stephen Clark, and Michael McGhee, Oxford: Blackwell, 2013, 148–66.

Cottingham, John, 'Transcending Science: Humane Models of Religious Understanding', in *New Models of Religious Understanding*, ed. Ellis, Fiona, Oxford: Oxford University Press, 2018, 23–41.

Cottingham, John, 'What Difference Does It Make? The Nature and Significance of Theistic Belief', *Ratio*, 19(4), 2006, 401–20.

Cottingham, John, 'What Is Humane Philosophy and Why Is It at Risk?', *Royal Institute of Philosophy Supplement*, 65, 2009, 233–55.
Cottingham, John, *In Search of the Soul: A Philosophical Essay*, Princeton and Oxford: Princeton University Press, 2020.
Cottingham, John, *Philosophy and the Good Life: Reason and the Passions in Greek, Cartesian and Psychoanalytic Ethics*, Cambridge: Cambridge University Press, 2010.
Cottingham, John, *Philosophy of Religion: Towards A More Humane Approach*, Cambridge: Cambridge University Press, 2014.
Cottingham, John, *The Spiritual Dimension: Religion, Philosophy and Human Value*, Cambridge: Cambridge University Press, 2005.
Cottingham, John, *Why Believe?* London and New York: Continuum, 2009.
Craig, Edward, 'Hume on Thought and Belief', *Royal Institute of Philosophy Lecture Series*, 20, 1986, 93–110.
Crisp, Oliver D. and Michael C. Rea, *Analytic Theology: New Essays in the Philosophy of Theology*, Oxford: Oxford University Press, 2009.
Cupitt, Don, 'A Secular Christian', *Sofia*, 110 Christmas 2013.
Cupitt, Don, 'Face to Faith: Learning to Live with One Foot in the Grave', *Sofia Website*, https://sofia.org.nz/cupgrave.html (this article first appeared in the Guardian's 'Face to Faith' column in December 1993).
Cupitt, Don. 'Non-realist Faith', (1987) in *Is Nothing Sacred? The Non-Realist Philosophy of Religion*, New York: Fordham University Press, 2002, 33–45.
Cupitt, Don, *Above Us Only Sky*, Santa Rosa, CA: Polebridge Press, 2008.
Cupitt, Don, *After All: Religion Without Alienation*, London: SCM Press, 1994.
Cupitt, Don, *After God: The Future of Religion*, London: Weidenfeld & Nicolson, 1997.
Cupitt, Don, *Creation out of Nothing*, London: SCM Press; Philadelphia: Trinity Press International, 1990.
Cupitt, Don, *Emptiness and Brightness*, Santa Rosa, CA: Polebridge Press, 2001.
Cupitt, Don, *Kingdom Come in Everyday Speech*, London: SCM Press, 2000.
Cupitt, Don, *Life, Life*, Santa Rosa, CA: Polebridge Press, 2003.
Cupitt, Don, *Long-Legged Fly: A Theology of Language and Desire*, London: SCM Press, 1987.
Cupitt, Don, *Taking Leave of God*, London: SCM Press, 1980.
Cupitt, Don, *The Leap of Reason*, London: Sheldon Press, 1976 (Second edition 1985, US edition 1976).
Cupitt, Don, *The Meaning of It All in Everyday Speech*, London: SCM Press, 1999.
Cupitt, Don, *The Meaning of the West: An Apologia for Secular Christianity*, London: SCM Press, 2008
Cupitt, Don, *The New Religion of Life in Everyday Speech*, London: SCM Press, 1999.
Cupitt, Don, *The Religion of Being and the Revelation of Being*, London: SCM Press, 1998.
Cupitt, Don, *The Revelation of Being*, London: SCM Press, 1998.

Cupitt, Don, *The Sea of Faith*, London: SCM Press Ltd, 1994 (paperback edition 1985, US edition 1988, Chinese 2015, Second edition, revised, 1994, 'Classics' reprint 2003).

Cupitt, Don, *The Time Being*, London: SCM Press, 1992.

Cupitt, Don, *Turns of Phrase: Radical Theology from A to Z*, London: SCM Press, 2011.

Cupitt, Don, *What Is a Story?* London: SCM Press, 1991 ('Xpress' reprint 1995).

Cupitt's Official Website. University of Chester and Gladstone's Library. https://doncupitt.chi.ac.uk/don-cupitt/.

Currie, Gregory, 'Individualism and Global Supervenience', *The British Journal for the Philosophy of Science*, 35(4), 1984, 345–58.

Davis, Brian, *Thomas Aquinas's Summa Theologiae: A Guide and Commentary*, Oxford: Oxford University Press, 2018.

de Sousa, Ronald, *The Rationality of Emotion*, Cambridge, MA and London: The MIT Press, 1987.

De Vries, Hent and Geoffrey Hale, *Minimal Theologies: Critiques of Secular Reason in Adorno and Levinas*, Baltimore, MD: Johns Hopkins University Press, 2019.

Deng, Natalja, 'Religion for Naturalists', *International Journal for Philosophy of Religion*, 78(2), 2015, 195–214.

Dorsch, Fabian, 'Hume', in *Routledge Handbook of Philosophy of Imagination*, ed. Amy Kind, New York: Routledge, 2016, 40–54.

Eastwood, Jessica. 'Theistic Expansive Naturalism: Which God?', *Religious Studies*, 2023, 1–15. doi:10.1017/S0034412523000112.

Edmonds, David and Nigel Warburton, *Philosophy Bites*, Oxford: Oxford University Press, 2012.

Ellis, Fiona, 'Between Orthodox Theism and Materialist Atheism', in *Current Controversies in Philosophy of Religion*, ed. Draper, Paul, New York and Abingdon, Oxon: Routledge, 2019, 146–59.

Ellis, Fiona, 'Nature, Enchantment, and God', in *The Philosophy of Re-enchantment*, ed. M. Meijer and H. de Vries, New York: Routledge, 2020, 178–94.

Ellis, Fiona, *God, Value and Nature*, Oxford: Oxford University Press, 2014.

Ellis, Fiona, *Liberal Naturalism and God*. Routledge, (Routledge handbooks), 2021.

Ernst, Bruno, *The Magic Mirror of M. C. Escher*, Cologne: Taschen, 1978.

Eshleman, Andrew S., 'Can an Atheist Believe in God?', *Religious Studies*, 41, 2005, 183–99.

Field, Hartry, *Science Without Numbers*, Princeton: Princeton University Press, 1980.

Fox, Matthew, *Meister Eckhart: A Mystic-Warrior for Our Times*, California: New World Library, 2014.

Frijda, Nico, *The Emotions*, Cambridge: Cambridge University Press, 1986.

Gendler, Tamar Szabó, 'Alief and Belief', in *Gendler's Intuition, Imagination, and Philosophical Methodology*, Oxford: Oxford University Press, 2010. Oxford Scholarship Online, 2011. doi:10.1093/acprof:oso/9780199589760.003.0014.

Gendler, Tamar Szabó, 'The Puzzle of Imaginative Resistance', *The Journal of Philosophy*, 97(2), 2000, 55–81.

Gerrig, Richard J., *Experiencing Narrative Worlds: On the Psychological Activities of Reading*, New Haven: Yale University Press, 1993.

Goldie, Peter, 'Getting Feelings into Emotional Experience in the Right Way', *Emotion Review*, 1(3), 2009, 232–9.

Goodman, Nelson, *Fact, Fiction, and Forecast*, Cambridge, MA: Harvard University Press, 1955.

Gorman, Michael M., 'Hume's Theory of Belief', *Hume Studies*, 19(1), 1993, 89–101.

Grant, Rihannon, 'Doctrine and Fanon', in *The Sacred in Fantastic Fandom: Essays on the Intersection of Religion and Pop Culture*, ed. Carole M. Cusack, John W. Morehead, and Venetia Laura Delano Robertson, Jefferson: McFarland & Company Publishers, 2019, 33–48.

Hale, Bob, *Abstract Objects*, Oxford: Basil Blackwell, 1987.

Hamilton, William and Thomas J. J. Altizer, *Radical Theology and the Death of God*, Harmondsworth: Penguin, 1968.

Harris, Paul L., *The Work of the Imagination*, Oxford: Blackwell, 2000.

Harrison, Victoria S., 'Mathematical Objects and the Object of Theology', *Religious Studies*, 2017, 53, 479–96.

Heaney, Seamus, 'Joy or Night: Last Things in the Poetry of W. B. Yeats and Philip Larkin', in *The Redness of Poetry: Oxford Lectures*, London: Faber, 1995, 159.

Hebblewaite, Brain, 'A Critique of Don Cupitt's Christian Buddhism', in *Is God Real?* ed. Joseph Runzo, London: Palgrave Macmillan, 1993, 135–48.

Hersh, Reuben, *What Is Mathematics, Really?* Oxford: Oxford University Press, 1997.

High, Dallas M., 'On Thinking More Crazily than Philosophers: Wittgenstein, Knowledge and Religious Beliefs', *International Journal for Philosophy of Religion*, 19(3), 1986, 161–75.

Hilario, Gerald, 'The Notions of God by Emmanuel Levinas', October 10, 2019. https://ssrn.com/abstract=3467746 or http://dx.doi.org/10.2139/ssrn.3467746.

Hoffmann, Vera and Albert Newen, 'Supervenience of Extrinsic Properties', *Erkenntnis*, 67, 2007, 305–19, 311.

Hölderlin, Friedrich, 'Was Is Gott?', from *Hymische Entwüfe* (Sketches for Hymns), 1800–1905, in *Selected Poems*, London: Penguin, 1998.

Hookway, Christopher, 'James's Epistemology and the Will to Believe', *European Journal of Pragmatism and American Philosophy*, 3(1), 2011, 3–38.

Horgan, Terence, 'From Supervenience to Superdupervenience: Meeting the Demands of a Material World', *Mind*, 102, 1993, 555–86, 571.

Horgan, Terence, 'Supervenience and Microphysics', *Pacific Philosophical Quarterly*, 63, 1982, 29–43, 37.

Howard-Snyder, Daniel, 'Can Fictionalists Have Faith? It All Depends', *Religious Studies*, 55(4), 2019, 447–68.

Howard-Synder, Daniel, 'Does Faith Entail Belief?', *Faith and Philosophy: Journal of the Society of Christian Philosophers*, 33(2), 2016, 142–62.

Howard-Synder, Daniel, 'Faith', in *The Cambridge Dictionary of Philosophy*, Third edition, ed. Audi, Robert, New York: Cambridge University Press, 2015, referenced in Open-mindedness in Philosophy of Religion (2019), p. 126 without page numbers.

Howard-Synder, Daniel, 'Propositional Faith: What It Is and What It Is Not', *American Philosophical Quarterly*, 50(4), 2013, 357–72.

Howard-Snyder, Daniel, 'The Skeptical Christian', in *Oxford Studies in Philosophy of Religion*, ed. Kvanvig, Jonathan, Oxford: Oxford University Press, 2017, 142–67.

Howard-Snyder, Daniel and Daniel J. McKaughan, 'Faith', in *The Encyclopedia of Philosophy of Religion*, ed. Goetz, Stewart and Charles Taliaferro, New York: Wiley-Blackwell, 2021. https://doi.org/10.1002/9781119009924.

Howard-Synder, Daniel and Daniel J. McKaughan, 'Theorizing about Faith with Lara Buckak', *Religious Studies*, 58, 2022, 297–326.

Hume, David, 'Of the Standard Taste' (1757), reprinted in his *Essays: Moral, Political and Literary*, Indianapolis: Liberty Fund, 1985, 226–49.

Hume, David, *A Treatise of Human Nature*, Selby-Bigge, Oxford: University Press, 1941.

Hume, David, *An Enquiry Concerning Human Understanding*, New York: Library of Liberal Arts, 1955.

Hyman, Gavin, 'Don Cupitt', in *The Palgrave Handbook of Radical Theology*, ed. Christopher D. Rodkey and Jordan E. Miller, London: Palgrave Macmillan, 2018, 135–54.

Hyman, Gavin, *New Directions in Philosophical Theology: Essays in Honour of Don Cupitt*, Aldershot, Hants: Ashgate Publishing Company, 2004.

Insole, Christopher 'A Trace on the Wind', *The Times Literary Supplement*, 30, 2006. The Times Literary Supplement Historical Archive, 1902–2013, https://link.gale.com/apps/doc/EX1200542248/TLSH?u=duruni&sid= TLSH&xid=b790f12c.

Insole, ChristopherJ., 'Realism and Anti-realism', in *The Oxford Handbook of the Epistemology of Theology*, ed. Abraham, William James and Frederick D. Aquino, Oxford: Oxford University Press, 2017.

Insole, Christopher J., *The Intolerable God*, Michigan and Cambridge: Wm. B. Eerdmans Publishing Co, 2016.

Jackson, Elizabeth, 'Belief and Credence: Why the Attitude-Type Matters', *Philosophical Studies*, 176(9), 2019, 2477–96.

Jackson, Elizabeth, 'Belief, Credence, and Faith', *Religious Studies*, 55(2), 2019, 153–68.

Jackson, Elizabeth, 'How Belief-Credence Dualism Explains Away Pragmatic Encroachment', *The Philosophical Quarterly*. 69(276), 2019, 511–33.

Jackson, Elizabeth, 'The Relationship Between Belief and Credence', *Philosophy Compass*, 15(6), 2020, 1–13.

Jackson, Elizabeth, 'Wagering Against Divine Hiddenness', *The European Journal for Philosophy of Religion*. 8(4), 2016, 85–105.

Jackson, Elizabeth and Andrew Rogers, 'Salvaging Pascal's Wager', *Philosophia Christi*, 21(1), 2019, 59–84.

James, William, 'What Is an Emotion?', *Mind*, 9(34), 1884, 188–205.

Jay, Christopher, 'Testimony, Belief, and Non-doxastic Faith: The Humean Argument for Religious Fictionalism', *Religious Studies*, 52(2), 2016, 247–61.

Jenkins, C., 'Lewis and Blackburn on Quasi-realism and Fictionalism', *Analysis*, 66, 2006, 315–19.

Johnson, Samuel, *Preface to Shakespeare*, Frankfurt am Main: Outlook, Verlag GmbH, 2018.

Jose, Paul and William Brewer, 'Development of Story-Liking: Character Identification, Suspense, and Outcome Resolution', *Developmental Psychology*, 20, 1984, 911–24.

Joyce, Richard, 'Moral Fictionalism', in *Fictionalism in Metaphysics*, ed. Kalderon, Mark Eli, Oxford: Oxford University Press, 2005, 287–313.

Joyce, Richard, *The Myth of Morality*, Cambridge: Cambridge University Press, 2001.

Jütten, Timo, 'Adorno on Hope', *Philosophy & Social Criticism*, 45(3), 2019, 284–306.

Kappel, Klemens and Emil F. L. Moeller, 'Epistemic Expressivism and the Argument from Motivation', *Synthese*, 191(7), 2014, 1–19.

Kilby, Karen, *Karl Rahner: Theology and Philosophy*, London and New York: Routledge, 2004.

Kim, Jaegwon, 'Concepts of Supervenience', *Philosophy and Phenomenology Research*, 45(2), 1984, 153–76.

Kim, Jaegwon, 'Supervenience and Supervenient Causation', *Southern Journal of Philosophy*, 22(1), 1984, 45–56

Kim, Jaegwon, 'Supervenience as a Philosophical Concept', *Metaphilosophy*, 21(1/2), 1990, 1–27.

Kim, Jaegwon, '"Strong" and "Global" Supervenience Revisited', *Philosophy and Phenomenology Research*, 48(2), 1987, 315–26.

Kim, Jaegwon, *Supervenience and Mind: Selected Philosophical Essays*, Cambridge: Cambridge University Press, 1993.

Kolodiejchuk, Brian, *Mother Teresa: Come Be My Light: The Private Writings of the Saint of Calcutta*, New York: Doubleday, 2007.

Le Poidevin, Robin, 'Playing the God Game: The Perils of Religious Fictionalism', in *Alternative Concepts of God: Essays on the Metaphysics of the Divine*, ed. Buckareff, Andrei and Yujin Nagasawa, Oxford: Oxford University Press, 2016, 178–92.

Le Poidevin, Robin, 'World Within Worlds: The Paradoxes of Embedded Fiction?', *British Journal of Aesthetics*, 35(3), 1995, 227–38.

Le Poidevin, Robin, *Agnosticism: A Very Short Introduction*, New York: Oxford University Press, 2010, Online publication, 2013. doi:10.1093/actrade/9780199575268.001.0001.

Le Poidevin, Robin, *Arguing for Atheism*, London and New York: Routledge, 2003.

Le Poidevin, Robin, *Religious Fictionalism*, Cambridge: Cambridge University Press 2019.

Lear, Jonathan, *Freud*, New York and London: Routledge, 2005.

LeDoux, Joseph, 'Rethinking the Emotional Brain', *Neuron*, 73(4), 2012, 653–76.

LeDoux, Joseph, *The Emotional Brain*, New York: Simon & Schuster, 1996.

Levinas, Emmanuel, *Difficult Freedom: Essays on Judaism*, Baltimore, MD: The John Hopkins University Press, 1990.

Lewis, C. S., *The Screwtape Letters*, London: Collins, 2012.

Lewis, D. K., 'Quasi-realism is Fictionalism', in *Fictionalism in Metaphysics*, ed. M. Kalderon, Oxford: Clarendon Press, 2005, 314–21.

Linnebo, Øystein, 'Platonism in the Philosophy of Mathematics', *The Stanford Encyclopedia of Philosophy* (Spring 2018 edition), Edward N. Zalta (ed.). https://plato.stanford.edu/archives/spr2018/entries/platonism-mathematics.

Linnebo, Øystein, *Philosophy of Mathematics*, Princeton and Oxford: Princeton University Press, 2017.

Lipton, Peter, 'Science and Religion: The Immersion Solution', in *Realism and Religion: Philosophical and Theological Perspectives*, ed. Michael Scott and Andrew Moore, Aldershot: Ashgate, 2007, 31–46.

Mabrito, Robert, 'Are Expressivists Guilty of Wishful Thinking?', *Philosophical Studies*, 165, 2013, 1069–81.

MacNabb, D. G. C., *David Hume: His Theory of Knowledge and Morality*, Oxford: Basil Blackwell, 1951.

Maddy, Penelope, *Realism in Mathematics*, Oxford: Clarendon, 1990.

Malcolm, Finlay, 'Can Fictionalists have Faith?', *Religious Studies*, 54(2), 2018, 215–32.

Malcolm, Finlay and Michael Scott, 'Faith, Belief and Fictionalism', *Pacific Philosophical Quarterly*, 98, 2017, 257–74.

Marušić, Jennifer Smalligan, 'Does Hume Hold a Dispositional Account of Belief?', *Canadian Journal of Philosophy*, 40(2), 2010, 155–83.

Mathews, Shailer, *The Growth of the Idea of God*, New York: Macmillan Co., 1930.

McDowell, John, *Mind and World*, Cambridge, MA and London: Harvard University Press, 1996.

McGilchrist, Iain, 'The Divided Brain & The Making of the Western World', for the Royal Society of Arts, Manufactures and Commerce in 2010.

McGilchrist, Iain, *The Master and His Emissary*, New Haven, CT: Yale University Press, 2009.

McGrath, David, 'Defeating Pragmatic Encroachment?', *Synbook*, 195(7), 2018, 3051–64.

Meland, Bernard, *Realities of Faith*, Oxford: Oxford University Press, 1962.

Moran, Richard, 'Art, Imagination and Resistance', a talk given before the *American Society for Aesthetics*, 1992.

Moran, Richard, 'The Expression of Feeling in Imagination', *The Philosophical Review* 103(1), 1994, 75–106.

Moyal-Sharrock, Danièle, 'Certainty as Trust: Belief as a Nonpropositional Attitude', in *Understanding Wittgenstein's on Certainty*, Houndmills, Basingstoke, Hampshire and Londonk: Palgrave MacMillan, 2004, 181–201.

Moyer, Mark, 'Weak and Global Supervenience Are Strong', *Philosophical Studies: An International Journal for Philosophy in the Analytic Tradition*, 138(1), 2008, 125–50.

Murray, Nathan, 'A Possible Source for the Apocryphal Anecdote Concerning the Reception of Little Nell's Death', *Notes and Queries*, 65(3), 2018, 375–7.
Nagasawa, Yujin, 'A New Defence of Perfect Being Theism', *Philosophical Quarterly*, 58, 577–96, 2008.
Nagasawa, Yujin, 'Anselmian Theism', *Philosophy Compass*, 6, 2011, 564–71.
Nagasawa, Yujin, *Maximal God: A New Defence of Perfect Being Theism*, Oxford: Oxford University Press, 2017.
Nagel, Thomas, *Mind and Cosmos*, Oxford and New York: Oxford University Press, 2012.
Nielsen, Kai, 'Wittgenstein and Wittgensteinians on Religion', in *Wittgenstein and the Philosophy of Religion*, ed. Robert L. Arrington and Mark Addis, London: Routledge, 2001, 137–66.
Nolan, Daniel, Greg Restall, and Caroline West, 'Moral Fictionalism Versus the Rest', *Australasian Journal of Philosophy*, 83(3), 2005, 307–30.
Nussbaum, Martha, 'Emotions as Judgments of Value and Importance', in *Thinking About Feeling*, ed. Solomon, Robert C., New York: Oxford University Press, 2004.
Pace, Michael, 'The Epistemic Power of Morally Positive Thinking: Justification, Moral Encroachment, and James' "The Will to Believe"', *Noûs*, 45(2), 2011, 239–68.
Palmqvist, Carl-Johan, 'Desiderata for Rational, Non-doxastic Faith', *SOPHIA*, 61, 2022, 499–519. https://doi.org/10.1007/s11841-021-00862-4.
Palmqvist, Carl-Johan, 'Forms of Belief-less Religion: Why Non-doxasticism Makes Fictionalism Redundant for the Pro-religious Agnostic', *Religious Studies*, 57(1), 2021, 49–65.
Parfit, Derek, *On What Matters, 3*, Oxford: Oxford University Press, 2017.
Pascal, Blaise, *Pensées, c. 1660*, ed. Louis Lafuma, Paris: Editions du Seuil, 1962.
Paull, R. Cranston and Sider R. Theodore, 'In Defence of Global Supervenience', *Philosophy and Phenomenology Research*, 52(4), 1992, 933–54.
Peels, Rik, 'The Ethics of Belief and Christian Faith as Commitment to Assumptions', *Religious Studies*, 46(1), 2010, 97–107.
Pendlebury, Michael, 'How to Be a Normative Expressivist', *Philosophy and Phenomenology Research*, 80, 2010, 182–207.
Pepe, Alexander, *An Essay on Man and Other Poems*, Mineola, New York: Dover publications, INC, 1994.
Petrie, Bradford, 'Global Supervenience and Reduction', *Philosophy and Phenomenology Research*, 48(1), 1987, 119–30.
Philips, D. Z., 'On Really Believing', in *Is God Real?* ed. J. Runzo, Basingstoke: Macmillan, 1993, 85–108.
Phillips, D. Z., 'Philosophy, Theology and the Reality of God', in *Wittgenstein and Religion*, ed. D. Z. Phillips, New York: St Martin's Press, 1993, 1–9.
Philips, D. Z., *Wittgenstein and Religion*, New York: St Martin's Press, 1993.
Plantinga, Alvin, 'Reason and Belief in God', in *Faith and Rationality*, ed. Alvin Plantinga and Nicholas Wolterstorff, Notre Dame: University of Notre Dame Press, 1983, 16–93.

Plantinga, Alvin, *God and Other Minds*, Ithaca and London: Cornell University Press, 1990.
Plantinga, Alivin, *Knowledge and Christian Belief*, Cambridge: Wm. B. Eerdmans, 2015.
Price, H. H., *Belief*, New York: Humanities Press, London: George Allen & Unwin, 1969.
Price, H. H., *Thinking and Experience*, Cambridge, MA: Harvard University Press, 2013.
Prinz, Jesse, 'Embodied Emotions', in *Thinking About Feeling*, ed. Robert C. Solomon, New York: Oxford University Press, 2004, 44–58.
Putnam, Hilary, 'The Meaning of 'Meaning'', *Philosophical Review*, 7, 1975, 131–93.
Putnam, Hilary, *Philosophy of Logic*, New York: Harper (1971), reprinted in *Mathematics, Matter and Method: Philosophical Papers*, vol. 1, Second edition, Cambridge University Press, 1979, 323–57.
Quine, Willard van Orman, 'Existence and Quantification', in *Ontological Relativity and Other Essays*, ed. Quine, Willard van Orman, New York: Columbia University Press, 1969, 91–113.
Radford, Colin, 'How Can We Be Moved by the Fate of Anna Karenina?', *Proceedings of the Aristotelian Society*, Supplementary Volumes, 49, 1975, 67–93.
Raschke, Carl, *Postmodernism and the Revolution in Religious Theory: Toward a Semiotics of the Event*, Charlottesville and London: University of Virginia Press, 2012.
Rath, Beth, 'Christ's Faith, Doubt, and the Cry of Dereliction', *Approaches to Faith*, 81, 2017, 161–9.
Roberts, Robert C., *Emotions. An Essay in Aid of Moral Psychology*, New York: Oxford University Press, 2003.
Robinson, Jenefer, *Deeper Than Reason*, Oxford: Oxford University Press, 2005. Oxford Scholarship Online, 2006. doi:10.1093/0199263655.001.0001.
Rosen, Gideon, 'Modal Fictionalism', *Mind*, 99, 1990, 327–54.
Rozin, Paul, Linda Millman, and Carol Nemeroff, 'Operation of the Laws of Systematic Magic in Disgust and Other Domains', *Journal of Personality and Social Psychology*, 1(4), 1986, 703–12.
Ryle, Gilbert, *The Concept of the Mind*, Watford, Hurts: William Brendon and Son, 1949.
Sachs, Carl, 'The Acknowledgement of Transcendence: Anti-theodicy in Adorno and Levinas', *Philosophy and Social Criticism*, 37(3), 2011, 273–94.
Schärtl, Thomas, 'Constructing a Religious Worldview: Why Religious Antirealism Is Still Interesting', *European Journal for Philosophy of Religion*, 6(1), 2014, 133–60.
Scott, Michael, 'Realism and Anti-realism', in *The Routledge Handbook of Contemporary Philosophy of Religion*, ed. Graham Oppy, London and New York: Routledge, 2015, 205–18.
Scott, Michael, *Religious Language*, New York: Palgrave Macmillan, 2013.
Scott, Michael and Finlay Malcolm, 'Religious Fictionalism', *Philosophy Compass*, 13(3), 2018. 1–11.
Shapiro, Stewart, *Thinking About Mathematics*, Oxford: Oxford University Press, 2011.

Silk, Alex, 'How to Be an Ethical Expressivist', *Philosophy and Phenomenological Research*, 91, 2015, 195–222.
Singer, Peter, 'Dialogue 9: Hegel and Marx', in *The Great Philosophers: An Introduction to Western Philosophy*, ed. Bryan Magee, Oxford and New York: Oxford University Press, 1987, 188–209, reprinted 2009.
Solomon, Robert, 'Emotions, Thoughts and Feelings', in *Thinking About Feeling*, ed. Robert C. Solomon, New York: Oxford University Press, 2004, 76–90.
Spearritt, Gregory, 'Don Cupitt: Christian Buddhist?', *Religious Studies*, 31(3), 1995, 359–73.
Stecker, Robert, 'Should We Still Care About the Paradox of Fiction?', *The British Journal of Aesthetics*, 51(3), 2011, 295–308.
Stone, Jerome, *The Minimalist Vision of Transcendence: A Naturalist Philosophy of Religion*, Albany: State University of New York Press, 1992.
Stump, Eleonore, *Wandering in Darkness*, Oxford: Oxford University Press, 2012.
Swinburne, Richard, 'Science and Religion: Exploring the Spectrum', *Life Story Interviews*, Interviewed by Paul Merchant, The British Library, Ref. no. C1672/15, 2015–2016.
Swinburne, Richard, *Epistemic Justification*, Oxford: Oxford University Press, 2001. Oxford Scholarship Online, 2003. doi:10.1093/0199243794.001.0001.
Swinburne, Richard, *Faith and Reason*, Second edition, Oxford: Oxford University Press, 2005. Oxford Scholarship Online, 2007. doi:10.1093/acprof:oso/9780199283927.001.0001. Scholarship Online, 2007, 20. doi:10.1093/acprof:oso/9780198235446.001.0001.
Swinburne, Richard, *The Coherence of Theism*, Oxford: Oxford University, 2016.
Swinburne, Richard, *The Existence of God*, Oxford: Clarendon Press, 2004.
Tanner, Michael, 'Morals in Fiction and Fictional Morality/II', *Proceedings of the Aristotelian Society*, Supplementary Volume, 68, 1994, 51–66.
Taylor, Mark C., *After God*, Chicago and London: The University of Chicago Press, 2007.
Tejedor, Chon, 'The Early Wittgenstein on Ethical Religiousness as a Dispositional Attitude', in *Wittgenstein, Religion and Ethics: New Perspectives from Philosophy and Theology*, ed. Mikel Burley, New York: Bloomsbury Publishing, 2018, 13–32.
Tillich, Paul, *The Courage to Be*, Second edition, New Haven and London: Yale University Press, 2000.
Townsend, Dabney, *Hume's Aesthetic Theory: Taste and Sentiment*, London and New York: Routledge, 2001.
Tullman, Katherine, 'HOT Emotions: Dissolving the Paradox of Fiction', *Contemporary Aesthetics*, 10, 2012, 1932–8478.
Van Buren, Paul M., *Theological Explanations*, London: SCM Press, 1968.
Van Fraassen, Bas, *The Scientific Image*, Oxford: Clarendon Press, 1980.
Van Roojen, Mark, 'Expressivism', in *Routledge Encyclopedia of Philosophy*, Taylor and Francis, 2015.

Van Roojen, Mark, 'Moral Cognitivism vs. Non-Cognitivism', *The Stanford Encyclopedia of Philosophy* (Fall 2018 Edition), Edward N. Zalta (ed.). https://plato.stanford.edu/archives/fall2018/entries/moral-cognitivism/.

Vrana, S. R., B. N. Cuthbert, and P. J. Lang, 'Processing Fearful and Neutral Sentences: Memory and Heart Rate Change', *Cognition and Emotion*, 3, 1989, 179–95.

Walton, Kendall, 'Categories of Art', *Philosophical Review*, 79(3), 1970, 334–67.

Walton, Kendall, 'Fearing Fictions', *The Journal of Philosophy*, 75(1), 1978, 5–27.

Walton, Kendall, 'Morals in Fiction and Fictional Morality/I', *Proceedings of the Aristotelian Society*, Supplementary Volume, 68, 1994, 27–50.

Walton, Kendall, *Mimesis as Make-Believe*, Cambridge, MA and London: Harvard University Press 1990.

Wigner, Eugene, 'The Unreasonable Effectiveness of Mathematics in the Natural Sciences', *Communications on Pure and Applied Mathematics*, 1960, 13: 1–14.

Williams, Christopher, 'False Delicacy', in *Feminist Interpretations of David Hume*, ed. Anne Jaap Jacobson, State College: Penn State University Press, 2000, 239–62.

Winch, Peter, 'Understanding a Primitive Society', *American Philosophical Quarterly*, 1(4), 1964, 307–24.

Wittgenstein, Ludwig, *Culture and Value*, ed. G. H. Von Wright, trans. Peter Winch, Oxford: Basil Blackwell Oxford, 1980.

Wittgenstein, Ludwig, *Philosophical Investigations*, Third edition, ed. G. E. M. Anscombe, R. Rhees, and G. H. von Wright, Oxford: Blackwell, 1968.

Wittgenstein, Ludwig, *Tractatus Logico-Philosophicus*, 1921, trans. Pears, D. F. and B. F. McGuinness, London: Routledge, 1961.

Wyschogrod, Edith, 'Crucifixion and Alterity: Pathways to Glory in the Thought of Altizer and Levinas', in *Thinking Through the Death of God: A Critical Companion to Thomas J. J. Altizer*, ed. Lissa McCullough and Brian Schroeder, Albany: State University of New York Press, 2004, 89–104.

Yablo, Stephen, 'Does Ontology Rest on a Mistake?', *Aristotelian Society*, Supplementary Volume, 72: 229–61, 1998.

Zamulinski, Brain, 'Christianity and the Ethics of Belief', *Religious Studies*, 44(3), 2008, 333–46.

Zamulinski, Brian, 'Reconciling Reason and Religion: A Response to Peels', *Religious Studies*, 46(1), 2010, 109–13.

Index

Abrams, Nancy Ellen 79
abstractness 169, 182, 232 n.3 (Ch 6)
acquiescing 91–3
Adorno, Theodor 6–7. *See also* minimalism
agnosticism 27, 53, 83–4, 90–1, 142, 158, 162, 185, 196–7, 208–9 n.1 (Ch 1)
alief 127–32
Alston, William 35, 210–11 n.23 (Ch 1)
Anna Karenina 108, 110, 113, 131–2, 134
Anselm 8–9, 176, 201, 207 n.32 (Intro)
Aquinas, Thomas 45–7
Aristotle 186
assuming 20, 29, 78–85, 203
atheism 13, 73, 84, 94, 208–9 n.1 (Ch 1), 220 n.66 (Ch 3)

belief. *See also* Aquinas; Braithwaite; Bultmann; Hume; Plantinga; Ryle; Swinburne; Wittgenstein
  discordant behaviour 127–32
  dispositional 34–41
  ethics of 84–7
  involuntary belief-that and voluntary belief-in 26, 30–45
  involuntary belief-that without voluntary belief-in 27, 45–9
  make- 113–19, 137
  non-religious, dispositional 38–40
  non-religious, propositional 31–4
  occurrent 31–4
  religious, dispositional 40–1
  religious, propositional 34–8
  voluntary belief-in without involuntary belief-that 27, 53–7, 59–81, 84–103
  voluntary belief-that and voluntary belief-in 27, 50–3
Blackburn, Simon 100
brain 125, 132, 141–54, 164, 186, 203

Braithwaite, Richard 54–7, 59
Buchak, Lara 91–3
Bultmann, Rudolf 54–5, 59–60

Christianity
  Braithwaite 56
  Bultmann 55
  Cottingham 146, 153, 157–8
  Cupitt 62, 68, 70–3
  Descartes 70–2
  Ellis 8
  faith 2, 4, 36, 47–8
  fictionalism 4, 153–4
  Howard-Synder 80–3
  McKaughan 80–3
  non-realism 14
  Pascal 70–2, 86
  Plantinga 38
  Wittgenstein 102
  Zamulinski 84–7
Classical philosophical theism (CPT)
  Cupitt 59–67, 72–3, 75–6
  Descartes 72
  Ellis 8
  faith 1
  fictionalism 9, 18, 27, 53, 90, 94–6, 153, 209 n.1 (Ch 1)
  God 2–6, 12, 16–17, 26–7, 78
  involuntary belief-that without involuntary belief-in 30, 45
  mathematical analogy 174, 177–83, 190, 194–5
  Pascal 37
  Plantinga 37
  standard non-realist 53
  traditional realism 41, 53
  unconditionally necessary 41–2, 52, 103–4
  voluntary belief-that and voluntary belief-in 50–2
  wholly independent 41–2, 52, 103–4
Clifford, William 51–2, 84–6, 93,

conditionally necessary 17–18, 27, 30, 41–3, 52, 57, 78–9, 104–5, 166, 180, 191–9
consciousness 126, 163, 184, 186–7, 192
cosmos 100, 196–7
Cottingham, John 145–50, 155–64
credence 87–90. *See also* Jackson
Cupitt, Don. *See also* non-realism ('standard' religious)
   God is life 65–7
   God of language 63–5
   God (of CPT) in the programme 62–3
   immanence 73–4
   nihilism 74
   non-realism 60–1, 67–76

Deng, Natalja 96–7
Derrida 63–4
Descartes, Rene 70–2
desire 87–90, 128
doubting realist 77–80, 85–6, 89–90, 93–8, 103–6
doxasticsm 10, 81–2, 86, 92–4, 112

Eckhart, Meister 204
Ellis, Fiona 7–8. *See also* minimalism
emotion
   alief 127–32
   cognitive approach 110–11
   HOT 125–7
   non-cognitive approach 111, 124–38
   paradox of 107–14
   quasi- 113–19
emotionally coherent 19–21, 107, 119, 135–6, 139, 141
epistemic humility 23, 183, 185, 187–9, 192
epistemic virtues 151–5, 162, 164, 203, 229 n.55 (Ch 5)
existence
   fictionalist 15, 96
   mathematical 17–18, 169–72, 190, 194
   ontological 15
   paradox of fiction 122
   post-traditional 17–18, 41–4, 52, 78–9, 179, 182, 190, 196–9
   realism/non-realism distinction 15
   semantic 15

traditional realist 25, 50–2, 103–4
unconditionally necessary 17–18, 41–4, 52, 78–9, 105, 183, 190, 192–3, 196–9
wholly independent 17–18, 41–4, 52, 78–9, 104, 183, 190, 199

faith
   as acquiescing 91–3
   with belief-in 30–40, 50–7
   as beliefless assuming 79–84
   with belief-that 30–53
   as 'Cliffordian' assuming 84–7
   devil's 27, 29, 45–9
   fictionalist 27
   non-realist 27
   post-traditional 27–8
   as rational steadfastness 87–91
   traditional 26–7, 30
   without belief-in 45–9
   without belief-that 53–106
fictionalism (religious)
   arguments for 95–9
   belief 27, 93–9
   conception of God 4, 9, 15, 98, 152–3
   faith 27, 97–9
   humane turn 150–64
   ontology 15, 97–8, 152–3
   practice 93, 96–8
   semantics 15
Fiona the fictionalist 7, 49, 98, 101–3, 107, 151–2
Foucault 63–4

Gendler, Tamar 127–32, 137
God
   classical philosophical theism (CPT) 2–6, 12, 16–17, 26–7, 78
   of CPT in the programme 62–3
   is life 65–7
   of language 63–5
   minimalist 3, 6–10, 12–13, 16–18, 21–2, 25, 27, 41, 48, 52, 57, 60–1, 65–9, 75, 78, 104, 165–7, 173, 176–91, 194, 197–8, 201–4, 206–7 n.24, 207 n.32 (Intro)
   post-traditional 12, 17–18, 23, 25, 29, 41, 44, 49, 98–9, 163–4, 168, 177–80, 183–6, 190–7, 201

that-than-which-a-greater-cannot-be-conceived 8–9, 12, 17–18, 22, 41, 45, 48, 66–9, 75, 103–6, 176–9, 196–8, 201, 207 n.32 (Intro)

Harrison, Victoria 173–8, 181–3, 190–1, 194–8, 231–2 nn.1, 3 (Ch 6), 235 nn.42–5, 61 (Ch 6)
Hegel, G. W. Friedrich 22
Horgan, Terence 187
Howard-Snyder, Daniel 79–84
Humane Turn 141–50, 154–5
Hume, David 31–4

imagination 33, 137, 152, 156, 160, 225 n.59 (Ch 4)
independence 182, 232 n.3 (Ch 6)
Insole, Chris 10–15, 22, 76
intellectually coherent 19–20, 98–9, 104–5, 139, 201, 203

Jackson, Elizabeth 87–91
Jaegwon, Kim 185, 187
James, William 50–2

Kant 22, 74, 141

language
    Blackburn 100
    Braithwaite 59
    Bultmann 59
    Cupitt 63–6, 73–4
    fictionalism 4, 15, 101–2, 117, 154
    God of- 63–6
    Le Poidevin 117
    non-realism 1
    post-traditional 41
    realism/non-realism distinction 12
    traditional, religious 4, 9, 41, 44
    Wittgenstein 40, 100–2
Le Poidevin, Robin
    emotion 117–24
    fictionalism 98–9, 101
Ledoux, Joseph 125–6, 129
Leftlow, Brian 43
Levinson, Emmanuel 6–7. See also minimalism
Lily the laxed realist 29, 45, 47–9
Lipton, Peter 99–100

Malcolm, Finlay 92, 94
mathematics
    fictionalism 170
    God of CPT analogy 174–98
    Harrison 168, 173–8, 181–3, 190–1, 194–8, 231–2 n.1 (Ch 6), 235 nn.44–5, 61 (Ch 6)
    non-realism 170
    objects of mathematics 168–9
    object realism 168–9, 171–3
    object of theology 173–4
    platonism 168–73, 183, 232 n.3 (Ch 6)
    post-traditional God analogy 173, 176–98
    post-traditionalism realism analogy 180–3
    traditional realism analogy 180, 191–5
McGilchrist, Iain 143
McKaughan, Daniel 79–84
McLaughlin, Brian 185
    Cupitt 64, 68, 70
    -dependent (mathematical) 170
    -dependent (religious) 11, 15, 22
    Derrida 64
    Descartes 70
    Einstein 155
    Harrison 181–3, 190–1, 195
    Hegel 22
    Hume 31–3
    -independent (mathematical) 181–3, 190–1, 195
    -independent (religious) 11, 12, 17, 45, 48, 101–2, 153, 161–4, 172, 181, 190–1, 201–2
    McGilchrist 143
    Pascal 70
    possible worlds 42–3, 179
    post-traditional 1, 42–4, 60, 104, 179
    Ryle 39–40
    Singer 22
    supervenience 186
mind
    -body problem 166
    Cottingham 146, 161–4
minimalism (theological). See also Adorno; Ellis; Levinson
    Cupitt's conception of God 65–7, 75

de Vries, Hent 6–7, 13
distinct conception of God 8–9, 12, 66–7
ontology 9
theological landscape 6–7
morality
  alief 137, 225 n.59 (Ch 4)
  assertion 56, 59
  commitment 5
  fictionalism 15, 96, 152–4, 158–9
  God as moral judge 4, 8, 18
  humane turn 21, 141, 150, 156, 158, 227 n.1 (Ch 5)
  immorality 51
  non-naturalist account 43, 183–4
  statement 5
Nagel, Thomas 163, 186

naturalism 7–8, 13, 23, 159, 189, 192, 237 n.87 (Ch 6)
nihilism 6–7, 69, 73–5
non-doxastism 81, 86, 92–4
  Buchak 91–2
  Howard-Synder 79–84
  Jackson 87–91
  McKaughan 79–84
  Zamulinski 84–7
non-realism ('standard' religious). *See also* Cupitt
  cognitivism 11
  Cupitt's conception of God 5, 61–7
  epistemology 11
  faith 27
  ontology 11–12, 14, 190
  semantics 14

objectivity 67, 72, 74, 89, 171
Øystein, Linnebo 232 n.3 (Ch 6), 233 n.7 (Ch 6)

paradox of fiction 107–39
Pascal, Blaise 70–2
Philips, D. Z. 40, 60
Plantinga, Alvin 37–8
Platonism
  mathematical 18, 166, 168–73, 180, 182–3, 190–8, 232–3 nn.3, 15 (Ch 6), 234 nn.33, 37 (Ch 6)

post- 64, 74–5
  reality 17
  religious 17
Polly the post-traditionalist 45, 48–9
possible worlds 42–3, 176, 185–9.
  See also post-traditional realism; supervenience; truth
  post-traditional realism 179, 186–9, 192
  supervenience 179, 184–9, 192, 236 n.72 (Ch 6)
  truth 42–3
post-traditional believer 12, 98–9, 178
post-traditional realism (religious).
  See also possible worlds; supervenience
  belief 41–5, 48–9, 103–5
  conception of God 8–9, 12, 17–18, 22, 52, 103–5, 201
  faith 27–8, 57, 103–5
  mathematical analogy 17–18, 42–3, 165, 176–83, 189, 193–9
  ontology 13, 15–17, 22, 41–5, 52, 103–5, 176, 180, 189–90, 192–9, 201
problem of evil
  argument 12–13, 95
  fictionalism 95–6
Putnam, Hillary 188

Radford, Colin 107–10, 113
Rahner, Karl 22
rational steadfastness 87–91
realism ('standard' religious). *See also* post-traditional realism
  cognitivism 11
  conception of God (CPT) 9, 12, 18
  epistemology 11
  faith 26–7, 30
  mathematical analogy 17–18, 42–3, 173–6, 182, 193–9
  ontology 11–12, 14, 16–17, 41–5, 190, 193–9
  semantics 14
  traditional 12–13, 17, 25–7
Reginald the realist 49, 98, 101–3
Rozen, David 127, 138
Ryle, Gilbert 38–40

science
    fictionalism   103
    of God   7
    naturalism   237 n.87 (Ch 6)
    of nature   70, 72
    neuro-   125–7
    or God   8, 99–100
    transcending   159–64
Scott, Michael   92, 94
semi-independent   27, 41–5, 52, 57, 104, 118, 166, 179–80, 183–92, 199
Singer, Peter   22
soul   31, 69, 163
spiritual
    Cupitt   67, 70
    fictionalism   96, 137, 154
    humane turn   21, 141, 150, 159, 163
    post-traditional realism   22, 178
spiritually coherent   19, 141
steadfastness   87–91
Stecker, Robert   124
Stump, Eleonore   144–5
sui generis reality   2, 13, 16–18, 22, 42, 44, 53, 104, 189
supervenience   166, 183–4. *See also* mathematical analogy; possible worlds; post-traditional realism (religious); realism ('standard' religious)
    Aristotle   186
    epistemic humility   183, 185, 187–9, 192
    global   187–9, 192
    Horgan   187, 236 n.82 (Ch 6)
    Kim   184–5, 187
    Leftow   43
    mathematical analogy   189–90
    McLaughlin   185
    Nagel   186
    non-reductive   184, 189, 192
    possible worlds   179, 184–9, 192, 236 n.72 (Ch 6)
    post-traditional realism   166, 183–9, 192–3
    Putnam   188
    reductive   184

regional   187
    strong   184–6, 193
    traditional realism   193–4
    weak   184–6, 189, 192
Swinburne, Richard
    belief   34–7
    conception of God   4

that-than-which-a-greater-cannot-be-conceived   8–9, 12, 17–18, 22, 41, 45, 48, 66–9, 75, 103–6, 176–9, 196–8, 201, 207 n.32 (Intro)
theological realism or religious seriousness impasse   1–2, 5, 8, 13, 22, 61, 69–70, 202
theology
    the abstract object   173–8, 198, 204
    minimalist   6–8, 129, 206–7 n.24 (Intro)
    ontology   189–94, 198, 204
    philosophical   2, 22, 129
    radical   117
Tillich, Paul   22
transcendence   6–8, 59, 62, 74–5, 163
transcendent   6, 7, 59, 62–3, 69, 101, 163, 202, 206 n.24 (Intro)
truth
    bald   146, 158
    Braithwaite   55–6
    cognitivist non-realist   11
    cognitivist realist   11
    contingent   42
    Cottingham   155–8
    Cupitt   63
    epistemological non-realist   11
    epistemological realist   11
    fictionalist   5, 15–16, 93, 160
    Heidegger   157–8
    Howard Synder   93
    James, William   52
    mathematical   170, 172, 233 n.10 (Ch 6), 234 n.33 (Ch 6), 235 n.44 (Ch 6)
    McKaughan   93
    nature of general   122–4
    nature of religious   146–9, 157–8
    possible worlds   42–3
    semantic non-realist   14
    semantic realist   14

supervenience 188
unconditionally necessary 42
Wittgenstein 100, 103
Tullmann, Katherine 125–7

Unconditionally necessary 17–18, 30, 41–3, 52, 57, 78, 104–5, 191–9

Walton, Kendall 113–17
Western, Michael 132–7
wholly independent 18, 78, 105, 169, 183, 190
Wittgenstein, Ludwig 40, 100–2

Zamulinski, Brian 84–7

www.ingramcontent.com/pod-product-compliance
Lightning Source LLC
Chambersburg PA
CBHW071820300426
44116CB00009B/1384